"Col. Smith has a great grasp of what the forthcoming debate will require. The Congress must reduce the spending at the very time our enemies are overtaking our capabilities. The debate needs to be engaged now. This book comes on the scene at just the right time."

DENNY SMITH, FORMER US CONGRESSMAN
AND AIR FORCE F-4 PILOT

"Organizational responsiveness to rapidly changing external threats will require an adaptive structure and leadership committed to synergistic employment of all US and coalition forces. This book is 'out of the box' thinking and is very timely given the recent and evolving Air Force roles and missions."

BRIGADIER GENERAL AL RACHEL, USAF (RET.)

"With the Air Force bracing itself for a future of tight budgets, rapid technological change, and strategic uncertainty, its leaders at all levels must begin to ask themselves and each other some tough questions about the direction in which their service is headed. Those airmen willing to actively engage such discussions would do well to turn to Smith's book as the basic point of departure for debates concerning the intricate relationship between the Air Force's past, present, and future."

Strategic Studies Quarterly

TOMORROW'S AIR FORCE

TRACING THE PAST, SHAPING THE FUTURE

JEFFREY J. SMITH

INDIANA UNIVERSITY PRESS   *Bloomington & Indianapolis*

This book is a publication of

INDIANA UNIVERSITY PRESS
Office of Scholarly Publishing
Herman B Wells Library 350
1320 East 10th Street
Bloomington, Indiana 47405 USA

iupress.indiana.edu

Telephone orders 800-842-6796
Fax orders 812-855-7931

∞ The paper used in this publication
meets the minimum requirements of
the American National Standard for
Information Sciences–Permanence of
Paper for Printed Library Materials,
ANSI Z39.48–1992.

Manufactured in the
United States of America

Cataloging information is available
from the Library of Congress.

ISBN 978-0-253-01078-0 (cloth)
ISBN 978-0-253-01092-6 (ebook)

1 2 3 4 5   19 18 17 16 15 14

FOR MY DAD

No one has had a greater influence on me . . .

As the Air Force is compelled in the near future to reduce its force structure under the pressure of budget reductions, there will be a strong tendency to preserve those forces which have dominated the mission spectrum in the past rather than those which might dominate in the future. To be explicit, there will be a natural tendency to preserve the fighter and bomber forces at the expense of the supporting forces . . . this tension between institutional proclivities and perceptions of the future illustrates the importance of the latter to the evolution of air power theory . . .

. . . If the Air Force mission is effectively redefined so as to be rationalized with history and future trends, less chauvinistic in its claims and demands, and embracing rather than discriminating among its contributors and practitioners, then the Air Force leadership has a fair chance of creating a vibrant, committed military institution.

CARL BUILDER, *The Icarus Syndrome*

CONTENTS

PREFACE

THIS BOOK IS THE RESULT OF A NUMBER OF CONVERGING events in my life. The first came in 1986 when I was accepted into the United States Air Force as an officer candidate with a follow-on opportunity to attend pilot training. Prior to entering the USAF, I was trained as a junior high and high school mathematics teacher. However, with the responsibility of raising a growing family together with my desire to continue my education, the USAF appeared to be a great opportunity to meet both needs. When I entered the USAF, I really did not understand what "service" meant. At that time in my life, the USAF was simply a job that provided for my family and offered an intriguing opportunity to fly airplanes. Now, twenty-seven years later, I have a very different perspective of what that decision back in 1986 really meant and how that decision changed my entire life.

The second major event occurred in 1998, when I was diagnosed with a brain tumor and underwent two extensive brain surgeries. Having survived what I can only describe as the most challenging event I could have ever imagined, I made some personal decisions in the months following the ordeal. The first was that I would not waste a single day of my life. It was that decision that started a drive to learn more, take on more projects, and experience everything life could offer. For me, as an Air Force officer, that naturally meant I would take on every opportunity the Air Force could provide. Within that context, I was given the opportunity to attend the School of Advanced Airpower Studies (SAAS), as it was called then. My year as an SAAS student literally changed the way I looked at the world – changed the way I asked questions – changed the way I solved problems. In line with my desire to get everything out of every day, S A A S took my thinking to a new level. What I learned about myself and, importantly, what I learned about airpower at the strategic level provided me with an important insight for my service and for the future of the U S A F.

The third major event was the opportunity to attend a doctoral program at Washington State University. Although it was a grueling challenge to complete the entire PhD program in three years (an Air Force requirement), what I learned about research, writing, and methodology cannot be understated. Scholarship at the doctoral level provided me an environment of inquiry that connected with something internal within my brain, something I did not even know existed. It propelled my thinking, logic, and desire to investigate the world around me to a new level.

Apart from these three major events, over my career I discovered several things about my service. The first was that as airmen, we have a long and distinguished history – a history of men and women and their flying machines that brought together their love for flight with their passion to serve in the defense of our great nation. This history is what helps to define us as airmen. This same history tells the story of how a fledgling group of aviators started what would become the world's most powerful and respected airpower service. I quickly discovered that the historical icons of the U S A F were all visionaries who transformed their ideas into a world-class capability. No airmen in the U S A F can read about these great leaders of our past and their influence without absorbing a level of shared pride and commitment – as airmen, we all share a common heritage.

Additionally, I have learned that our service is a resilient and forward-looking enterprise made up of men and women who take pride in doing the mission every day without complaint. Although every organization has its nay-sayers, I can say without reservation that the U S A F is dominated by professional enlisted and officer personnel that take the core values of *Integrity First, Service Before Self, and Excellence in All We Do* as hallmarks of who they are – not just what they do. Being an "airman" is about more than just a job – it is about an identity. I am aware of few professions that so infuse its members with such an internal sense of worth, dignity, and professionalism as does the service of which I have proudly been a part these many years. When I entered the U S A F back in 1986, I was not an airman; today, the term defines who I am from the inside out.

I also learned over the years that "service" is not something reserved only for those that wear the blue Air Force uniform. In my case, as is the common case of so many, service is a family affair. Lisa, my spouse of thirty years, has endured seventeen different addresses, spent many nights alone while I deployed to various contingencies, and accepted the challenges associated with not being able to have her own career due to the inability to stay in one location long enough. My two sons, Zach and Caleb, also had to "serve" within my capacity as an airman. Both had to endure moving in and out of different schools every two to three years. Both had to leave friends, girlfriends, sport teams, and church youth groups. The social dynamic for my sons was challenging, and as I look back on my years of service, I see that it was and still remains indeed a family affair.

I share these personal insights in order to impress upon the reader the sheer weight of personal responsibility I felt in writing about my service's future. I did not take lightly the investigation of our history, nor did I gloss over the areas where I felt we missed the mark. As an organization, although we have a valued past, we also have made some mistakes; my goal in writing this is to help shape a future Air Force that has learned from some of those mistakes. Not everyone who reads this book will agree with my assessment. In fact, when I sent this work out to a number of active and retired Air Force officers asking for their input, I received some negative comments. One retired general officer refused to provide me any comments more than to say that he completely disagreed with my findings and that he could not endorse the work. Fortunately, I did not need his endorsement, and the vast majority of those who reviewed the manuscript saw the important debate that this book attempts to start. And that is really the point – this work is intended to encourage the community of airmen and interested partners into thinking about the future. What can the USAF as a service do better in support of our national interests? What organizational changes need to be considered going forward? How might changing external responsibilities in the global community affect USAF future operations? These are just a few of the questions this book attempts to frame within both the historical and the current context of the USAF. I am hopeful that this effort to stir debate will prove successful.

DISCLAIMER CLAUSE

The views expressed in this book are those of the author and do not reflect the official policy or position of the United States Air Force, the Department of Defense, or the U.S. government.

ACKNOWLEDGMENTS

THIS BOOK WOULD NOT HAVE BEEN POSSIBLE WITHOUT THE help of so many friends and family. My mother, Fern Smith, was the original editor who checked all of the draft pages and made hundreds of corrections. She was the first person to read the entire work as it was being written. My wife, Lisa, endured many hours alone as I worked late into the night researching, writing, and organizing the manuscript – thank you for your patience and support. Tom Preston provided important insight into the research and helped me to stay on track. I also want to recognize John Kepko, my best friend and confidant. John helped me create most of the original illustrations and endured many hours and late nights listening to and debating my ideas. His direction and insight as a retired Air Force officer was the single most important element of this work. Finally, I want to thank the United States Air Force for providing me the time to research and write this book. My time serving in the Air Force has been incredible from the very first day. All my experiences, from flying low-levels over the Sierra Nevadas as a second lieutenant instructor pilot to combat missions in Iraq and Afghanistan, have shaped my world view and developed my "airman's" perspective. This book is a result of those accumulated experiences.

TOMORROW'S AIR FORCE

Every phase of evolution commences by being in a state of unstable force and proceeds through organization to equilibrium.

KABBALAH

INTRODUCTION

THE TWENTY-FIRST CENTURY BROUGHT SIGNIFICANT challenges to the United States and the Department of Defense in terms of national security. Combined with increasing fiscal concerns, every military service is undergoing important self-assessment alongside internal budgetary review. In the USAF specifically, questions regarding priorities, future capabilities, and procurement of systems are at the center of debate at the highest leadership levels. Unfortunately, many of the questions regarding the shape, direction, and capabilities of the USAF require that decisions be made today with results of those decisions not being fully measurable for ten to twenty years into the future. Based on the need for out-in-front logistics, forward planning requirements, and contract decisions requiring years of lead time, USAF leadership needs to be well informed regarding how their service should be shaped in the years ahead. In fact, it is my contention that the USAF will need to adapt to numerous current and forthcoming changes both in and out of the Air Force if they intend to remain a relevant and valued service. In short, the USAF must adapt to the looming changes that confront it or risk decaying into irrelevance.

My intention in writing this book was to provide important insight for United States Air Force leaders as well as those airpower advocates trying to answer the hard questions regarding future airpower requirements. As I will highlight throughout this work, the USAF as an institution carries many of the same characteristics that most large organizations have – each is required to meet specific responsibilities within the "market-place." In order to remain relevant and profitable, institutions within the traditional business economy must constantly evaluate the degree to which their product or service is meeting external market requirements. For the U.S. military, and the USAF specifically, the "marketplace" is the security requirements, external threats, and organizational capacities directed by U.S. elected governmental policy makers. Equally, in the USAF, the external requirements in terms of threats, security challenges, and obligations become the "market" against which capability and preparedness must be measured.

To provide senior leaders with objective recommendations, quantitative assessment, and bias-free analysis from which they can make important developmental decisions for the USAF, in this work I use recognized organizational modeling as the basis to explain USAF historical change and to anticipate current and future change.[1] A thorough examination of the organizational modeling literature suggests three major drivers for examining and explaining organizational change within large bureaucratic institutions: *external exigencies, internal culture,* and *transitional leadership.*[2] Examining how these three drivers change over time helps trace, explain, and even anticipate the needed changes an organization must undergo if it is to remain relevant. As Reitz and Heffron point out in their work on organizational change modeling, "any factors outside the organization that modify or threaten the organization's ability to produce or market its goods or services serve as external forces for change." Organizations "constantly receive inputs from their environment and must respond to changes in those inputs."[3] Institutions that fail to recognize the changing requirements in the marketplace, that remain wedded to an internal culture out of step with advancing opportunities, or that are held back by dogmatic leadership often fail to succeed. The media distribution company Blockbuster failed to recognize the streaming video capability of digital media and instead remained overly wedded to the DVD distribution system. Their inability to effectively transition their internal perspective, elevate visionary leadership, and meet emerging external demands ultimately resulted in their demise. On the other hand, companies like Apple continually seek to remain out in front of external requirements for new products, ensure an internal culture that remains flexible to new ideas, and encourage leadership to think strategically. These same indicators and practices of effective organizational change apply to the USAF.

Throughout this work the continued reference to organizational change models offers validated explanation for why the USAF changed through the years. There is a simple yet important relationship that exists within the organizational change models: a triad of leadership, culture, and external pressures in regard to organizational change. Applying a systematic analysis to how these three variables change over time reveals important insight with respect not only to how and why the USAF changed throughout its history, but to how it may well change in the coming years. In each case study offered in this work, the three indicators (independent variables) of external requirements, internal culture, and leadership are central to explaining the noted changes and form the basis for much of the future analysis.

Furthermore, work drawn from group psychology, outlining the importance of institutional identity and "in-group" versus "out-group" dynamics, serves to support much of the change noted throughout the history of the USAF. As group psychology literature suggests, when the in-group is challenged by external pressures, the in-group is likely to resist and will be slow to recognize the need for change.[4] Furthermore, as Schein and others involved in organizational change research point out, the dominant group within an organization is often reluctant to recognize the need for change, due in part to the possible decrease in power, status, or influence that the change may bring upon the group.[5] These factors play a significant role in explaining organizational change and apply equally in the analysis of the USAF. The organizational change models together with the insights drawn from group psychology form a modeling framework that effectively explains historical USAF change and then aids with the predictions regarding future USAF change.

The evolution of ideas that encouraged this work derived from the following questions:

- Is today's USAF appropriately organized to meet current and future external challenges?
- How does the USAF effectively change its organization to meet emerging responsibilities?

- How might analysis of previous USAF organizational change inform an understanding of current and future change?
- Do general organizational change models offer useful explanatory capability that can guide analysis within the specific context of the USAF?
- Is it possible to develop an objective, systematic, and valid prediction for how the USAF might undergo future organizational change?

Answers to these questions are important to USAF senior leadership and strategic planners responsible for making decisions today that will have ramifications fifteen to twenty years into the future. Considering the length of time required for research and development of specific technologies designed to meet external responsibilities, anticipating what the organizational structure of the USAF should be in the future is required – today. Unfortunately, much of the work that informs airpower decisions is based on speculation, individual bias regarding what "systems" are important, and political considerations outside of the USAF. In this time of fiscal austerity, it is extremely problematic that Congress insists on making large budget cuts, and that when DoD offers areas for those cuts based on operational and national security needs analysis, Congress then denies and/or modifies the DoD proposals because they affect members' political districts or states. What is needed is a systematic, rigorous, and objective analysis that examines why and how the USAF has organizationally changed in the past in order to have a template or guiding directive for determining and predicting how and why the USAF may organizationally change in the future. Armed with such analysis, USAF planners can better determine procurement decisions, institute appropriate long-term policy, and better organize, train, and equip its force for the future. Furthermore, armed with an objective plan going forward, DoD leadership can better work with Congress to possibly initiate cuts where operationally appropriate. If this book is able to provide, even to a small degree, insight as to what might be expected (anticipated), USAF leadership will be better equipped to make the necessary decisions today that will shape the USAF of the future.

This book is presented using three periods of analysis: Period One, 1907–1947; Period Two, 1947–1992; and Period Three, 1992–2030. For the first two periods, the timeframes were selected based on when major organizational change took place. The first two periods are used exclusively to test the explanatory power of the organizational models to ensure they effectively explain historically known organizational change within the context of the USAF. These first two major historical periods are important to fully understand how and why the USAF underwent organizational change. Explaining the historical elements that frame past USAF organizational change provides the insight required when considering how and why the USAF will need to change in the future. These first two major historical sections of the book prepare for the important and relevant discussion offered in the third section regarding current and future USAF organizational change. It cannot be overstated how important understanding of the first two sections of analysis is to understanding the third and final section of analysis. In the final section of this book, offered as Period Three (1992–2030), considerations are given to the changes that USAF leadership should be aware of and anticipate in order to appropriately prepare their service for future contingencies.

Beginning in 1907 and using the guidance from organizational change modeling, Period One examines the major *external events,* analyzes the *internal culture,* and quantifies the USAF *leadership characteristics* through the year 1947. As offered in the analysis, when airpower first was introduced by the U.S. Army into military service, the overarching and dominant perspective centered on a ground-operations perspective. However, through the unfolding of Period One, the external exigencies, internal cultural shifts, and emerging leadership within the Army air service began to develop disequilibrium between the dominant ground-operations perspective and the emerging bomber-operations perspective. Culminating during and directly after the events of World War II, the Army air capability eventually won its independence and became its own military service on September 18, 1947. It is this date in 1947 that is identified as the first major organizational change experienced within the new airpower service.

Period Two begins in 1947 and is characterized by the implications of change observed at the end of Period One. Period Two analysis considers

those external events, internal cultural shifts, and organizational leadership as they evolved from 1947 to 1992. The end of Period Two analysis
comes in 1992 when the culmination of the bomber-operations perspective under the organizational structure of Strategic Air Command is
replaced by the emerging and dominating fighter-operations perspective
and the new Air Combat Command.

The next major section presents analysis of Period Three (1992 to
2030), broken down into two parts. In part one of Period Three analysis, organizational change modeling is used as a guide to explain the
observed external events, internal culture, and organizational leadership from 1992 to 2011. During analysis of this timeframe within Period
Three, important and current trends are identified that form the basis
from which future USAF change will be required. Part two of Period
Three analysis covers the time from 2012 to 2030, with the work existing
entirely within a predictive context. However, based on the emerging
external exigencies highlighted in the part one of Period Three, as well
as internal cultural imbalances and transitional leadership perspectives,
the predictions are grounded in logical, unbiased analysis. The final
chapter in this book offers a concise summary and recommendations to
senior USAF leadership.

The most important requirement of this work is for readers and senior USAF planners to remain objective, draw their responses based
on data and sound logic, and ensure they themselves are not projecting
their own bias in terms of their willingness (or not) to accept needed
organizational change. Addressing the reality that some leaders struggle
with changing the structure they are most comfortable with, Gen Mike
Worden (retired) offers important insights:

> This organizational condition leans towards myopia and monistic thinking,
> often manifested in a consuming focus on a purpose or mission that favors the
> dominant culture. When these organizations face inevitable environmental or
> contextual change that challenges the existing paradigm, they fail to recognize
> the need for change because of their uniformity of perspective. This perspective
> also limits alternatives and adaptability to the change.... Broad education and
> experience and a diversity of views at the senior executive level are necessary to
> cultivate visionary leaders. These leaders must appreciate obvious immediate
> concerns and manage and anticipate change with a view towards a greater,
> more holistic, enduring contribution to the future. These concerns include an

understanding of how both internal and external forces influence the institution. For the military, battlefield victory embraces only one dimension of its professional requirements . . . military leaders must develop political and social insights to function successfully in today's security environment. In today's time of geostrategic change, as reflected by the end of the cold war, institutions that maintain broad, pluralistic, and pragmatic perspectives can better recognize and adjust to the new paradigm or realities.[6]

Worden makes clear the need for leaders to remain objective and to consider a broad perspective on how things really are and how USAF operations might need to adapt.

Overall, military planners, defense decision makers, and interested airpower advocates should find this work helpful in advancing sound analysis and providing for those in the position of USAF leadership an objective assessment for how and why the USAF must usher in significant changes. The predictions offered will only be validated with time; however, the decisions that the USAF must make now in order to prepare for an uncertain future must be based on every resource available today. To that end, this work is committed.

PERIOD ONE: 1907–1947

PERIOD ONE ANALYSIS PRESENTS AN IMPORTANT HISTORICAL narrative for how and why airpower became a formidable force within the U.S. military. The original dynamic that ushered in this new opportunity in warfare was not necessarily focused on the domain of air so much as the enterprise of a new technology. As the period unfolds, however, the theoretical idea of airpower and the domain of "air" as a new and unique perspective began to develop in both the hearts and the minds of emerging airmen. The narrative this period provides is vital to understanding how the USAF developed both its initial footing and its changing organizational construct. From the early years dominated by a ground-centric perspective, where airpower was seen by military leadership as merely an ancillary extension of the ground war, to the culminating point over Japan, where airpower delivered a decisive attack to help end World War II, Period One, from 1907 to 1947, helps to explain both the evolution of airpower and the early dynamics of USAF organizational change.

With us air people, the future of our nation is indissolubly bound up in the development of air power.

WILLIAM "BILLY" MITCHELL

1

THE BIRTH OF MILITARY AIRPOWER

WITH THE ADVENT OF AIRPOWER INTO MILITARY OPERATIONS in the early twentieth century, a new era of war-fighting strategy slowly emerged. The traditional operations by Army and Navy forces that enjoyed centuries of tradition, lessons learned, and accepted strategies would be confronted and challenged by airpower's primary new characteristic – control of the sky. Although lighter-than-air systems had been used for many years to rise above the battle space in an attempt to spot and track enemy movement, balloon aircraft were unable to provide the maneuverability and attack opportunity the new emerging aircraft enjoyed. Operations ranging from traditional spotting of enemy positions and movement and signaling ground forces to delivering time-sensitive communications to rear or forward leadership and eventually providing an air-to-ground attack option all characterize early airpower operations. These capabilities altered how wars were planned and forced military strategists to consider the extent to which traditional military operations might change. From its earliest inception in military operations, airpower advocates and the leaders responsible for its application struggled with a continual and common challenge – how best to *organize* this new weapon of war.

The advent of airpower in U.S. military operations begins in 1907. Encouraged by the technological breakthroughs of the Wright brothers, early U.S. Army personnel believed that the new airpower capability could be used to the Army's advantage. However, from 1907 through the end of World War II, airpower pioneers, driven by their belief in the efficacy of airpower, were confronted by both encouragement and conflict. Throughout this early period, heated debate regarding the appropriate role, leadership, resources, and buildup of airpower prevailed, in the environment of a single underlying challenge – airpower's organizational structure. However, in September of 1947 a major organizational development instituted and established the new United States Air Force as a separate and independent arm of the U.S. military. The objective of Period One analysis is to examine and trace the events that affected airpower's organizational construct in an attempt to better understand the major organizational change that occurred in 1947.

BIRTH OF MILITARY AIRPOWER: 1907–1911

Following the advent of heavier-than-air powered winged flight by the Wright brothers in 1903, it did not take long before the airplane was considered for military application. Army officers involved in the Army's Signal Corps immediately began developing plans for how the new technology might be ushered into Army service.[1] Following several demonstration flights and considerable convincing by emerging airpower advocates, the Army developed the first organizational element for fixed-wing flight operations. On August 1, 1907, the newly formed Aeronautical Division was given responsibility for "all matters pertaining to military ballooning, air machines, and all kindred subjects."[2] Thus, the beginning of a formally recognized and organized military aviation arm was born into the U.S. Army.

As would be expected within the Army, the new technology of airpower was seen from a ground-centric and ground support perspective.[3] Furthermore, aviation in general was clearly subservient to the greater and more demanding concerns of ground combat.[4] Because traditional Army culture was characterized by the perspective and belief that territorial offensive operations, direct engagement of enemy ground forces, and strategic ground maneuvers were all primary and central in war, the initial influence for how airpower would be used and organized in support of this perspective dominated earlier Army aviation.[5] Drawing personnel solely from the existing ranks of the Army, the new Aeronautical Division was developed and perceived by Army leadership as just another tool for supporting its ground operations missions.

The first official Army pilot, Lt Thomas E. Selfridge, learned to fly through the instruction of Orville Wright but unfortunately died in an aircraft accident on September 17, 1908.[6] Despite the death of Selfridge, the Army pressed ahead with the procurement of aircraft and increased the size and responsibility of its Aeronautical Division. In August of 1909 the Army accepted delivery of its first two aircraft into military service.[7]

Although airpower continued to inspire and draw new pioneers and interest to the military aviation field, the first ten years were "plagued by miserly funding, an indifferent Army, contentious manufacturers, and *no serious threat to national security to spur development*."[8] In 1911, the inadequacy of funds allotted to Army aviation within the Aeronautical Division made organization and development nearly unsustainable. Although James Mann, a congressman from Illinois, requested approval in the Army appropriations bill for $250,000 for aviation funding, Congress instead cut the proposed amount in half – "an indication of both the lowly status of military aviation and the weakness of the aviation lobby."[9] However, despite these challenges in the early years, airpower continued to advance in terms of technology and of personnel intrigued by and fixated on what possibilities aircraft might offer future warfare.

INITIAL ORGANIZATIONAL CHALLENGE: 1911–1915

The initial few years following the emergence of airpower into military operations are important to analyze, for it is in those years that the first sign of an internal airpower perspective begins to develop. The term "airmen" is used to identify those within the Army air service who fly or support flying operations. This new unique title reflects the development of an in-group, with certain actions, perspectives, and beliefs beginning to separate certain individuals from others who do not share the same allegiances or responsibilities. Furthermore, within the years 1911–1915, airpower attracted various Army leaders who crossed over to become airmen; these leaders began to formalize both the training and the maintenance of airpower operations.

One of the earliest "new-generation" officers, who entered into flying operations as a young aviator, was 2Lt Henry "Hap" Arnold. After learning to fly at the Wright brothers' factory, Arnold was sent to College Park, the new advanced Army flying school that offered pilots the operational training required for incorporating airpower into Army operations. After advancing to instructor pilot, Arnold began to organize and formalize operations at College Park in order to account for the shortfalls he perceived in training:

> By the fall of 1912, the Signal Corps began to send pilot trainees to factory schools to qualify for the basic license and then to College Park for the additional instruction needed to meet War Department standards. Besides introducing the pilot to the techniques of flight, the factory schools afforded better instruction in the maintenance and repair of engines and airframes than was available at College Park. As pilot instruction became systematized, so too did maintenance procedures. In 1911, while training at Dayton, Arnold prepared the first set of detailed instructions on how to care for the airplane. In addition, while training at the Wright factory, he and Milling photographed all the components of the Wright airplane, labeling each one to simplify the instruction of mechanics and the stocking and orders of the parts.[10]

These steps began the process of formally organizing and preparing airpower operations as a unique and specified arm of the U.S. Army.

However, as group psychology suggests, as individuals became part of the new group of airmen, the group began to take on its own identity and began perceiving out-group decisions with respect to how those decisions affected their own in-group desires. Hurley offers that "the airmen stationed at College Park believed that the airplane could do more than serve as a vehicle for aerial reconnaissance."[11] This is an early sign that the airmen were not only forming their own school, operational perspectives, and military tactics, but that they were also developing their own beliefs and identities – identities that differed from the Army's status quo.

Despite the development of a new airmen class that perceived and envisioned a greater role for airpower, the Army retained all control over procurement, fiscal expenditures, and technology. In this way, conflict began to enter into the organizational process whenever there was disagreement between what the traditional Army wanted and did, and what the new group of airmen wanted. When Riley Scott, a former Army officer, offered the Army his new invention, which he called the Bomb-Sight, that could drop an eighteen-pound bomb "accurately from an altitude of 400 feet," the Army chose not to buy the new technology. Scott then im-

proved the Bomb-Sight and sold it to the French.[12] Furthermore, when
a new machine gun that could be adapted to an airplane was offered for
procurement to the Army, "the Army Ordnance Department decided
against large-scale procurement because it already had a standard machine gun."[13] The dynamic between the emerging new group of airmen
and the traditional Army culture that focused on ground operations
set the stage for increasing conflict between those with the authority to
purchase (Army leaders) and those with the desire to develop the aviation arm (new airmen).

As suggested by organizational change models, internal culture is
often developed through perceptions, artifacts, and shared beliefs that
over time become norms. One of the earliest shared perspectives among
all airmen during this time period was the simple fact that flying airplanes was dangerous. The death toll on new pilots was high in the early
years, and recognition of this fact was understood at the highest Army
levels.[14]

> The hazards and uncertainties of aviation made it imperative that the Army
> compensate for the risks taken by airmen, and to encourage more volunteers
> Congress considered giving fliers extra pay and accelerated promotion.
> Although the Army had routinely granted extra pay for overseas service or as
> a result of temporary promotion for special assignments, flight pay did not be-
> come a reality until 1913. That same year Congress tied promotion to proficiency
> in the air by authorizing qualified aviators to advance to the next higher grade.
> Flight pay, along with various forms of temporary promotion, would remain a
> source of controversy until well after World War II.[15]

These organizational directives, although warranted, further reified the
separation of airmen from the traditional Army population. As the in-
group of airmen became more divergent (responsibilities, promotion
system, pay), they further developed their own culture, identified themselves as part of a larger movement, and began developing strongly held
values and beliefs. These attributes of an emerging culture are predicted
by organizational modeling and reinforce the possibility that organizational change will follow. It is important here to understand that the
emerging culture within the airmen's group was slowly departing from
the traditional Army culture that characterized the previous years. The
conflict that arose from this demarcation between old and new cultures

was not contained or realized solely within the Army; the U.S. Congress also had its airpower voices.

One of the earliest critiques levied by airmen was what they perceived to be a "lack of clearly defined status and function for aviation within the service."[16] Several airmen began voicing the need for air operations to be organized separately from the traditional Signal Corps in order to establish and develop their unique military contribution. Inspired by airpower and the call for greater autonomy, Representative Hay offered a bill in Congress calling for aviation to be removed from the Signal Corps and given its own branch within the Army.[17] Although Congress failed to pass the bill into law, the exposure aviation received, the debate among congressmen, and the lines drawn within the Army leadership regarding their different perspectives, all forced airpower organizational considerations into the public arena; the debate regarding the organizational elements of airpower was now a current and open reality.

Internally within the Army, a continued discourse took place as to who should lead this new military arm. According to airpower scholars, "many pilots in military aeronautics were growing impatient with the nonpilots commanding them."[18] The struggle concerned having Army officers leading air operations, many of whom were not even pilots, making training, manning, and procurement decisions without the flying experience needed to appropriately command such responsibilities. Members of the emerging airpower culture believed that airpower leadership should comprise qualified and experienced pilots in order to understand the greater needs of aviation operations, and those leaders who were not pilots were seen as outsiders. Any dynamic involving an internal struggle over leadership is not conducive to good order and discipline within military ranks. Non-flyers began to see flyers as mavericks, spending their days playing with their flying machines, while flyers, on the other hand, began to see non-flyers (especially those in senior leadership positions) as myopic detractors – keeping airpower from realizing its full potential.[19] However, without an external event capable of testing airpower's emerging claim to being more than a mere signaling platform, airmen were left to struggle against a traditional Army system that showed little in the way of promoting airpower.

Within these years of emerging and developing airpower operations, a clear division erupted between the new airmen and the traditional Army. Fortunately, there were important senior ranking officers who saw the importance of aviation to future Army battles. Gen Pershing, for one, is reported to have said that "an army without aviation would be defeated by an army that possessed it."[20] Various members of Congress also saw the potential of aviation in war and continued to offer bills that would advance its development. Although much of this congressional support was also tied to defense contracts from which their individual states might benefit, the resulting debate for advancing airpower was ensured a place well outside of internal Army boundaries alone. However, by the end of 1915, "the nation that invented the airplane had adapted it to military uses but had allowed it to remain an appendix to the Army."[21]

The day has passed when armies on the ground or navies on the sea can be the arbiter of a nation's destiny in war. The main power of defense and the power of initiative against an enemy has passed to the air.

WILLIAM "BILLY" MITCHELL, NOVEMBER 1918

2

WORLD WAR I AND THE
INTERWAR YEARS

THE TWO TIMEFRAMES PRESENTED IN THE FOREGOING HIS-
torical overview both share a missing ingredient in terms of forces that
drive institutional change: they lack any significant external event. Although the time frame from 1911 to 1915 did show some change from
limited external events, the first major external event for airpower in this
period is World War I. As this chapter will show, the cultural and leadership changes emerging from the newly formed airpower group within
the Army would now be confronted by the measurable and empirical
realities of war.

Although the Army failed to procure technology that would have
enabled aircraft to drop bombs more accurately, airmen continued to
argue for airpower operations to expand beyond just reconnaissance.[1]
During the years from 1915 to 1917, a number of advances and experi-
ments took place that showed airpower's ability to strafe troops (attack
enemy ground troops from the air) and drop bombs. However, airpower
supporters continued to call for more autonomous authority, greater
flexibility to use airpower in new ways, and expanded operations outside
of traditional ground strategies.[2] One of the more enlightened debates
emerging among airpower supporters was the idea that aircraft could
over-fly enemy positions and bomb industry and war-making factories.
Rather than being directly and continuously tied to a ground assault,
airmen began to see the potential of airpower to target important enemy
positions that the traditional Army would not normally be capable of
targeting. Unfortunately, the airpower supporters "had trouble making
converts among officers never exposed to [such] enthusiasm." Further-

more, "the high command of the U.S. Army continued to believe that aviation should gain control of the air over the battlefield and assist the ground forces...."[3] Unfortunately, the dominant Army perspective still maintained and guaranteed that pilots and airpower would be subservient to ground operations. In fact, on reconnaissance sorties where the pilot was accompanied by another "observer" officer, the observer held the position of supervisor for the mission and the pilot was seen as the observer's "aerial chauffeur."[4]

Perhaps the most influential airman within this period regarding the organizational development of airpower was then-Col William "Billy" Mitchell. Although later in the period his outspoken tactics would cause him tremendous trouble, during the early stages of airpower's development, Mitchell rose to the top. However, it did not take long before Mitchell, in characteristic style, began to openly question the Army's traditional ground-operations perspective, and further challenge Army leadership directly. When confronted in 1917 with the possibility of a senior officer (Brig Gen Foulois) being brought in to take over command of Signal Corps, Mitchell wasted no time in offering his opinion. Mitchell made it clear that although new arrivals to Signal Corps "meant well and had some experience in aviation," he considered them "an incompetent lot." He further suggested an analogy between the new arrivals and a cavalry with "200 men who had never seen a horse, 200 horses who had never seen a man, and 25 officers who had never seen either."[5] Mitchell's borderline insubordination was the first real open challenge to the traditional Army leadership that controlled aviation's organizational path. Although these brief pre-war encounters would be heightened during and especially after the war, the Army continued to maintain authority and dominance over airpower.

The trend and building conflict between traditional Army culture that perceived the best use of airpower as support for its ground maneuvers and the emerging and increasingly more vocal airmen (e.g., Mitchell), who believed airpower could operate outside of Army ground operations, continued right up until the U.S. entrance into World War I on April 6, 1917. Unfortunately, as Mortensen points out, "Until the United States became a belligerent [in World War I], its Army had contributed nothing to the wartime development of military aircraft and aerial tactics."[6] As was the case in the prior years of this period, the organizational changes taking place came more in the form of debate, dissent, and a growing discontent among airmen opposed to the traditional Army leadership that dominated the decision process.

When the United States entered World War I, the Army Signal Corps was not adequately prepared for the challenge it would soon face. Although the years since the introduction of the airplane into military service (1907) were marked by considerable breakthroughs in both technology and perspective, the state of Army airpower in the early months of 1917 was not nearly appropriate for the requirements demanded in war. Fortunately, Army aviation had attracted a number of dedicated and diligent officers who had continually worked to advance airpower's roles and missions (in many cases at odds with the traditional Army status quo). With the requirements and challenges of World War I, Army aviation had both the responsibility and the opportunity to prove its capability.

As was the case with all nations involved in the war, the United States was forced to develop a rapid and productive buildup of required force structure. With the requirement of war now a reality, "the Army's air arm, in a scant eight months, reoriented, equipped, and trained hundreds of thousands of men; procured thousands of aircraft; *organized and reorganized itself;* and undertook some of the largest air operations of the war."[7] The hostilities confronted in the war forced the Army to recognize the need to give airpower more attention, and through this realization, airpower tactics, capability, and technology improved tremendously.[8] The importance of airpower was realized almost immediately by Army leadership. The capability to fly beyond the enemy's front lines and into the rear quadrants afforded not only important intelligence gathering, but also allowed specific targeting of important enemy logistical nodes. "The previous concerns airmen had regarding being viewed as an 'aerial chauffeur' for observer officers quickly reversed; by 1918 the pilot was in command of his airplane, with the observer doubling as aerial gunner."[9]

Other countries, specifically the United Kingdom, also realized the importance of airpower in the war. Organizationally, the UK acknowledged early that airpower's unique contribution would require formal independence. On April 1, 1918, the Royal Air Force was established as a separate and independent arm of the British military. Although the

U.S. Army fell short of following the UK's lead, the new organizational autonomy did not go unnoticed. The Wilson administration ordered that procurement decisions and organizational directives regarding Army aviation be moved out of the traditional Signal Corps process and instead report directly to the Secretary of War.[10] The recognition at the highest level of government that airpower required increased attention beyond traditional Army perspectives set the stage for the new airmen leadership to move forward with their ideas of expansion.

In terms of technology, unlike most other weapon systems, the airplane could be used for multiple purposes: visual and photographic reconnaissance, artillery adjustment, infantry liaison, counter air operations, bombing and strafing in close support of ground forces, and interdiction of enemy lines of communication.[11] The need to develop an organizational system to manage effectively the rapidly growing requirements of airpower personnel, technology, and processes soon became apparent. From this, airpower advocates came to believe that airpower required a unique "airman's perspective" in order to ensure its proper use; in World War I, the air Battle of St. Mihiel provided evidence and operational experience that further supported this assertion.[12]

The Battle of St. Mihiel was the largest use of coordinated airpower ever committed in World War I, providing clear lessons on the employment of military airpower. With over 1,500 U.S. and Allied aircraft, Col Mitchell set out to develop the battlefield plan for the employment of airpower.[13] Mitchell implemented several new organizational elements for the command and control of airpower. First, he took control of all the planning and subsequent operations of aircraft at St. Mihiel, allowing ground commanders to have one point of contact in planning and developing how they would use airpower. It also allowed him to organize and plan how best to meet the ground commander's requirements without having to compete with other airpower commanders for control.[14] Second, airpower had the latitude to accomplish strike missions that did not directly support ground operations but had strategic level objectives "far from the battlefield."[15] Third, airpower operations were pre-planned and fully coordinated in the greatest of detail to include daily instructions, organization and chain of command, liaison procedures, artillery communication operations; pursuit, bombardment, and reconnaissance procedures; methods for assigning missions, intelligence gathering/disseminating procedures, and prescribed duties for various aviation commanders. History records that the "US offensive [at St. Mihiel] gained all its objectives quickly and with relatively few casualties."[16] Furthermore, the personnel (Mitchell), technology (numerous mission capabilities of aircraft), and processes (overall campaign plan and organization for battle) of airpower played a major role in the overall success at St. Mihiel. In a congratulatory letter to First Army Air Service (the air arm at St. Mihiel), the commanding officer, Gen Pershing, praised the airmen for the "successful and very important part" they had played in the battle.[17]

The Battle of St. Mihiel, and World War I in general, taught airmen several enduring lessons. Robin Highman's chapter "Airpower in World War I, 1914–1918" draws the following conclusion: "The Great War in the air exhibited traits and trends that would be evident in the subsequent evolution of this highly technical, consuming, new military arm. It did then, and continues today to require very skilled professional management to make it efficient."[18]

By the end of the war on November 11, 1918, "the Army air arm increased from a mere 1,200 officers and men to a force of almost 200,000, with 25 percent serving overseas. During the early months of the American participation in the conflict, some 38,000 volunteers sought to become flyers. . . ."[19] Furthermore, throughout the war the American public romanticized the "men and their flying machines,"[20] while from the perspective of the airmen who flew, "dangerous though it was, aviation seemed a nobler, more individualistic, and cleaner form of service than warfare in the trenches."[21]

With the combination of successful operational necessity in battle, together with an increasingly dominant perspective by both airmen and outside observers as to the efficacy of airpower, World War I can be seen as a significant external event that influenced airpower organizational structure more than any other event up to that time. The effects of airpower were felt at the highest level of government and throughout the Army. Furthermore, the internal culture governing the operation of airpower during this time was shaped by real-world experiences – both success and failure. Airpower leadership transitioned, in part, to those who held a common perception of the advantage afforded by air operations.

The group of airmen expanded and developed shared experiences that became norms. Artifacts, values, and beliefs were written into airpower doctrine and operational procedures. All of this had tremendous influence on culture, leadership, and overall airpower organization.

INTERWAR YEARS: 1920–1933

Coming out of what most airmen believed was the vindication of airpower, leaders such as Billy Mitchell and Hap Arnold believed that airpower would finally be elevated to its rightful place. However, although the operations in World War I pushed airpower to the forefront in many regards, the traditional ground-operations nature and perspective of the U.S. Army would not be easily overrun. The post-war environment found an Army that was recovering from a dreadful ground engagement, limited resources, and significant requirements to downsize.

Mitchell, upon his return from France, believed that he was the rightful leader to take over the Army Air Service. However, upon his return he discovered that Maj Gen Charles Menoher, a decorated artillery officer with no aviation experience, was given the position instead. The concern regarding non-flyers supervising airpower operations was not new. Mitchell, in a letter dated April 1, 1918, offered the following criticism (among many others) to Gen Foulois, Chief of the Air Service: "As to the non-flying officers of superior rank in the Air Service, these in fact have and are exercising direct command over the training and practical use of tactical air units. This is well known to be wrong. . . ."[22] Now, following what Mitchell and others believed was a highly successful war in terms of proving the capability of airpower and airmen, Mitchell found that he was to work under the leadership of a non-flyer. To make matters worse, Mitchell was to be his assistant. As John Shiner describes it,

> that Mitchell became Menoher's principal assistant served only to underscore
> the belief on the part of the Army's leadership that aviation was subordinate to
> operations on the ground, a view that Mitchell and others were beginning to
> challenge. On the basis of his experience in France, Mitchell had concluded that
> neither land nor sea campaigns could succeed without control of the air.[23]

Although several senior Army generals acknowledged the importance of airpower to modern warfare, nearly all continued to believe that airpower was not decisive and therefore should not be elevated to an independent or separate status from the Army. Gen Pershing, a long-time advocate of airpower, suggested that airpower, although important, should remain an auxiliary to ground operations.[24] However, because of the experiences in World War I and the increased and vocal leadership of Mitchell and other airpower advocates (both in and out of the Army), the Army's traditional authority and oversight of airpower would be deeply challenged.

Internally, airmen had gained a level of prestige that propped up their in-group identity, fostered an in-group allegiance that began circumventing their Army allegiance, and created an environment of us-versus-them. Airmen believed that only a flyer with wartime experience could fully understand and lead air operations. The Army, however, continued to believe that senior ranking ground officers would be the best choice for managing the Air Service. Nowhere was this more evident than in the Army's promotion system. After the end of the war, the Army returned to a seniority-based promotion system where those who were in their grade (rank) the longest received the first opportunity for promotion. Because many of the airmen were young officers, this meant that the senior-level positions in the Army Air Service would have to be filled by non-flyers from outside the Air Service. Furthermore, because there was no mandatory retirement, the young and highly experienced aviators did not see a path to the leadership positions that would afford them the opportunity to direct the development and course they perceived airpower needed to take.[25]

During these years, Mitchell pushed hard against the Army's organizational restraints and lobbied Congress to make airpower its own independent air force equal and separate from both the Army and the Navy. However, the strong Army lobby in Washington diverted Mitchell's call for independence and instead worked for the creation of the National Defense Act of 1920. Although Mitchell and his supporters were clearly derailed, the Act did make important organizational changes that improved the Air Service. For one, the Air Service was recognized as a separate combat arm and provided for an increase in the senior rank of the Air Service commander. Furthermore, and more importantly, the Act acknowledged the long-held complaint regarding non-flyers filling leadership officer positions in the Air Service. According to the Act, no more than 10 percent of the officers serving in the Air Service could be non-flyers and only flyers could command flying units.[26] These and several other elements of the Act organizationally changed the structure, operational authority, and legitimacy of airpower within the Army. Although Mitchell continued to call for a completely independent air force, the National Defense Act of 1920 did provide significant improvement and moved the Air Service closer to the autonomy it desired.

Although the organizational changes that resulted from congressional involvement enhanced and supported airpower's position within the Army, most airmen felt as a general rule that the Army leadership (non-flyers) did not appreciate their contributions and began blaming Army leadership for the problems within the Air Service.[27] This decrease in Army loyalty and increased commitment to airpower further reified the lines developing between traditional Army perspectives and those of the new airmen.[28] Within this challenging environment, Mitchell took on the full weight of the fight and began to systematically, and single-handedly, develop an argument for independence. Mitchell knew that the Army's primary argument against an independent air force was the lack of credible evidence that airpower could be decisive in war. In other words, the Army's position was that because airpower could not win a war on its own, it should remain subservient to the service that could win – the U.S. Army. For Mitchell, and others, the target was clear – develop airpower to prove that it did not need the Army or the Navy to win a war.

Likely due to the influence of the Italian strategist Giulio Douhet, Mitchell began to assert that airpower was in fact decisive. Douhet, writing in his work *Command of the Air*, posited that airpower alone could over-fly enemy strongholds and target the heart of the enemy's infrastructure and morale. Douhet suggested that a bomber aircraft capable of defending itself from hostile enemy aircraft and loaded with bombs (explosive and incendiary) could so demoralize the enemy population that there would be no need for any type of Army or Navy engagement. He further suggested that the will of an enemy to wage war resides in the morale of the people to continue supporting the war. He reasoned that airpower could target civilian populations at will and could therefore affect their morale to the point of near-immediate surrender.[29] Although the targeting of civilians was downplayed considerably, the argument put forward by Douhet regarding the efficacy and decisiveness of the bomber strategy became the hallmark of Mitchell's campaign for independence. If Mitchell could show that airpower was a decisive weapon capable of operating at a strategic level not accessible to either the Army or the Navy, then the Army could no longer argue against independence. This argument, however, required Mitchell to take on the mantle of a *bomber perspective*. His position depended on the ability of airpower to deliver large amounts of ordnance well into the heart of the enemy's center – a strategy that could only be accomplished by bomber-type aircraft.[30] The verbal, operational, and political battle between the airmen and the Army had begun. The lines were drawn between the traditional ground-operations culture of the Army and the new bomber-operations culture of the airmen.

Unfortunately, Mitchell was more vocal and less politically savvy than he should have been. In 1925, frustrated by what he believed was a continued myopia and abuse of power by Army leadership, Mitchell publicly accused Army senior officers of lying about the capabilities of airpower. As the confrontation escalated, Mitchell found himself the target of a court-martial. Although Mitchell's court-martial trial gave him a venue for proclaiming his vision for an independent air force, the lack of discipline and accusatory style of his tactics did more to alienate him than to provide him with influence.[31] However, the public display and the heated confrontation clearly made an impression, not only on the Army, but also on members of Congress, who held the keys to airpower independence.

In 1926, Congress began hearings on the future and organizational direction that airpower should take within the Army. Furthermore, President Coolidge asked Dwight Morrow, a respected businessman, to head an inquiry regarding the future of aviation. During one of the Morrow board hearings, "General Patrick proposed an Air Corps that [would] enjoy the same autonomy within the Army that the Marine Corps did in the Navy Department." Lt Col Benjamin Foulois testified, "I am convinced that aviation will never reach its proper place in the scheme of national defense so long as it remains under the control of the War Department General Staff [U.S. Army]."[32] The Morrow board, accompanied by a number of additional inquires, resulted in Congress passing the Air Corps Act of 1926. Shiner describes the Act's outcome:

> As soon as the Morrow Board's recommendations had become law, the Air Corps drew up the necessary plans covering acquisition, construction, and *internal reorganization* for each successful increment [toward] a five year plan. Once the expansion was completed, the Air Corps would have one air wing on the East Coast, another on the West Coast, one in the southern United States, and one each in Panama and Hawaii.[33]

Although at first the Act was viewed as an organizational breakthrough for the airmen striving for greater autonomy, the Air Corps remained under the strong rule of the Army, resulting in a continued struggle for resources, personnel, and authority.[34]

During the five years that followed, the resources allotted to the Air Corps were continually less than they requested; however, the Army was suffering from across the board financial cuts, and the Air Corps would have to share in the tightening of budgets. The airmen, possibly blinded by their own perspectives and their developing bias against the traditional ground-operations Army, "tended to blame the leadership of the Army for the cuts in funding and considered this yet another example of the General Staff's lack of interest in military aviation."[35] This of course is a good example of how an in-group perspective can perceive reality in light of their needs without consideration of the entire context. Shiner points out that the aviators were "apparently ignoring the fact that by the end of June 1932, the air arm received more than 20 percent of the Army's budget, an increase of more than eight percent since fiscal year 1926."[36]

As an important development of this timeframe, the Air Corps Tactical School (ACTS) was opened and eventually found its permanent home at Maxwell Field, Alabama. The importance of the ACTS was that its objective was to focus on the strategic, operational, and tactical attributes of airpower. ACTS further provided a mechanism for airmen to develop formal and standard operating procedures and airpower doctrine, and also the opportunity to quantify airpower requirements in number and type of aircraft as well as personnel and training. However, it did not take long before the primary and dominant message coming out of the "think-tank" of ACTS called for a bomber aircraft that could

over-fly enemy positions and strike strategic targets within the enemy's
heartland:

> Inspired initially by Mitchell and probably at least aware of Douhet, a cadre of
> students and faculty members developed a theory of aerial warfare that empha-
> sized the long-range bomber almost to the exclusion of other types of aircraft.
> The Tactical School eventually went beyond Mitchell, who had believed in bal-
> anced forces, strong in bombers, but capable also of air defense and the support
> of land armies. A doctrine emerged from the Tactical School that the bombers of
> the next war would be able to fight their way to the industrial and administrative
> centers of the enemy and destroy the very means of making war, avoiding a long
> and bloody land campaign aimed at defeating the hostile army. In effect, a few
> airmen were describing a new way to fight a war, a substitute for the traditional
> strategy of bringing the enemy's army to bay and destroying it, as American
> generals had done with varying success in the Civil War and World War I.[37]

Further, with respect to the important impact that ACTS was making,
Michael Sherry summarizes the thinking and subsequent doctrine that
came out of the ACTS:

> The Air Corps Tactical School had established a body of literature and a tradi-
> tion of theorizing about aviation. . . . The new doctrine of precision bombing was
> the product of their efforts and the vehicle of their ambitions. Briefly, airmen,
> especially at the tactical school, argued that strategic airpower could contribute
> to victory or secure it by attacks on the enemy state, especially its economic
> institutions. These attacks need not be indiscriminate, indeed should be targeted
> at only a few key components whose destruction would disrupt the functioning
> of the entire state. The enemy's will or capacity to fight would then collapse.[38]

However, despite the ACTS position on the efficacy of long-range
bombardment, the traditional War Department doctrine did not change
their perspective on how wars should be fought. The Army stood by
their belief that "Army aviation, regardless of its means of employment,
always supported ground forces . . . and continued to define victory in
terms of the destruction of the hostile army and the occupation of enemy
territory. . . ."[39] Notwithstanding, ACTS continued to offer its airpower
perspective, to bring new recruits into their way of thinking, and to take
every opportunity to showcase and fortify their airman's perspective.
In one sense, ACTS was the formal Air Corps voice of Billy Mitchell;
however, the difference was that ACTS provided a cognitive and practical argument within the boundaries of accepted Army protocol. Importantly, for the first time airpower had a legitimate and organized voice

in which to formulate and propagate its vision for airpower operations through the formal writing and publishing of airpower doctrine. Over the next decade, leading up to World War II, ACTS would continue to be an influential and guiding center for developing the airmen perspective.

Although the initial interwar years from 1920 to 1933 did not end with the development of an independent air force, there was a clear path of organizational change both from external pressures and from a developing and evolving internal culture. Mitchell, who played a significant role in the process, failed to effectively bring about the major organizational change he so desperately desired. He did, however, force the debate into the public arena, which resulted in yet additional external pressures to address the future of military aviation. Although significant external pressure from the congressional ACTS of 1920 and 1926 edged the organizational structure of airpower closer to the autonomy it desired, the continued strength of the traditional Army perspective remained influential. What does appear to be reflected in the historical record is a significant transition in the cultural dominance of the airmen and eventually the development and acceptance of a "bomber culture." In part, due to the need to develop an argument capable of repudiating the Army's assertion that airpower was not decisive, the bomber perspective became the default position and resonated throughout the Air Corps. Not only did the emerging airmen culture continue to grow, as it had since the beginning of the period, but the added and shared belief that bombers would be the hallmark of future airpower operations became the centerpiece of nearly all airpower debates. The effect this decisive bomber option had on the culture of airmen cannot be understated. Simply put, airmen believed and valued the fact that their identity, autonomy, and future independence would be determined by their ability to prove the efficacy and decisiveness of the *strategic bomber.*

INTERWAR YEARS: 1934–1939

In the years leading up to World War II, the airmen in the Army Air Corps, and especially those in the ACTS at Maxwell Field, continued to develop their airpower perspectives. With each passing year, the technological breakthroughs within both civilian and military aviation offered new opportunity and increased possibility for expanded operations. Aircraft were being built that could fly faster and at higher altitudes, carry greater payloads, and operate with high levels of reliability. As was the case in the years immediately following World War I, there continued to be small, incremental changes to the organizational structure of air-power. Perhaps the most important organizational change came in the form of the development of the General Headquarters Air Force (GHQ Air Force).

As was the early case of the Morrow Board that examined the di-rection and changes needed within the broader aviation organizational structure, the new Drum Board (named for its director Maj Gen Hugh Drum of the U.S. Army) was appointed by Gen MacArthur to examine an Air Corps proposal for coastal defense operations and subsequent expansion of Air Corps resources. According to Shiner,

> the Drum Board, which included . . . four ground-oriented generals, rejected the Air Corps plan – because it cost far too much and bore no relation to any probable threat to the United States and the insistence on independent action because it clashed with the view of the General Staff on the proper role of mili-tary aviation. The board's final report, released in October 1933, played down the aerial threat to the United States and emphasized that actions of the Air Corps in coastal defense would be part of a broader Army counter invasion plan.[40]

However, the board did endorse the creation of a GHQ Air Force and the development of long-range reconnaissance and attack capability that could interdict approaching coastal threats before they were in range of the U.S. homeland. Furthermore, "the board recognized the need for a consolidated aerial striking force that would train in peacetime for massed operations in time of war."[41] The endorsement of a GHQ Air Force was a significant organizational step in that airpower would be given equal recognition with the GHQ Army (even if in name only). However, because the Army retained the budgetary decision authority, airpower would continue to be subservient to the perspectives held by senior Army leadership. This is not to say that the GHQ Air Force did not expand; in fact, although they did not receive the funding for the 4,500 aircraft that they had asked for in the initial request, they did receive funding for just over 2,300 aircraft – an increase of nearly 50 percent.[42]

Throughout much of 1934, the Air Corps and the newly formed GHQ Air Force continued to struggle with a divergent and often con-flictual relationship between Army airmen and Army ground leadership.

Another board – the standard attempt to resolve what was becoming a growing and vocal separation within the Army (air versus ground perspectives) – was created to examine and consider possible organizational change. President Roosevelt formed the Howell Commission to "investigate all facets of American aviation."[43] The final report of the board, although very similar to previous reports, offered additional support for advancing military aviation. The commission's January 1935 report stated that "aircraft have now passed beyond their former position as useful auxiliaries, and must in the future be considered and utilized as an important means of exerting directly the will of the Commander in Chief."[44] It further offered that in the future, airpower might best be organized under its own independent service, equal and separate from the U.S. Army. Although it stopped short of endorsing immediate independence for airpower, the report's inclusion of independence as a future consideration clearly opened up the possibility.

Events of the years from 1933 to 1935 are significant for the analysis of airpower organizational change within the period. The establishment of the GHQ Air Force, the continued interest by outside senior governmental leaders, and the growing capabilities of aircraft all combined to strengthen the airmen's coalition. The GHQ Air Force was a good compromise between the airmen, who were demanding greater autonomy and operational flexibility to prepare for and develop an air arm that could accomplish strategic strikes separate from any ground plans, and the Army ground-operations officers, who wanted airpower to directly support their ground and territorial maneuvers. Creation of the GHQ Air Force addressed and resourced both missions, which brought, for a time, some stability and calm within the often contentious airpower organizational debate. However, by 1937, a clash between two senior airpower leaders reopened the debate and once again brought to the forefront the real divisions, both ideological and operational, between the Army perspective and the airmen perspective.

In 1937, airpower fell under the organizational structure of both the GHQ Air Force and the Air Corps. GHQ commander Maj Gen Andrews and Air Corps commander Maj Gen Westover were forced to try to determine who had authority for the increasingly complex require-

ments demanded by the expanding air arm. Andrews's position supported the all-out development of a bombardment strategy that would
be the backbone of the Air Corps. Westover, a disciplined Army officer, refused to endorse any plan that did not support the current Army
doctrine. Although Westover agreed with Andrews on the subject of
bomber dominance, Westover was unwilling to forward any organizational changes that did not line up with current Army structure. In support of Westover's position, those in the traditional Army responsible
for public relations were critical of the airmen's bomber claims and their
self-promoting call for greater legitimacy. In a letter to a senior flyer (Brig
Gen Johnson) dated May 26, 1938, Lt Col A. D. Surles, chief of public
relations on the General Army Staff, openly challenged and questioned
airpower claims. The divide between the traditional Army perspective
and the increasingly separate airmen perspective was widening. Mean-
while, Andrews became ever more convinced that airpower must be a
separate and independent force.[45] Central to this resurrected debate was
the now common and widely believed axiom among airmen that the
strategic, long-range bomber was the future of warfare.

Throughout the Air Corps and the GHQ Air Force, nearly all airmen believed that strategic bombing would and could be decisive in war.
Although Andrews and Westover disagreed as to the best way to accomplish the organizational requirements for building a strategic bombardment force, they did agree on the end-state:

> Indeed, it was becoming convincingly clear that the GHQ Air Force would be
> built around the bomber. New types of these aircraft were beginning to appear,
> and the emerging leaders of the Air Corps were believers in strategic bombard-
> ment.... During the remainder of the 1930s, a consensus would arise among
> the Army's senior airmen that the next war would be fought in Europe, that
> airpower would provide the key to victory, and that the bomber would provide
> the means of obtaining independence from the Army.[46]

The new bomber culture was now fully seated within all levels of the airpower organizational structure. From the academic schools at Maxwell
Field to the highest level of leadership within the GHQ Air Force and
Air Corps, strategic bombardment and the notion that a well-organized
bomber force could have significant and even determinant results in war

was a near undisputed belief and value. New recruits to the Air Corps were quickly saturated by the doctrine of strategic bombardment, and all but a very few voices were in common agreement.

The new and public doctrine of strategic bombing was eagerly accepted by the American public as well as within the Air Corps. Following the horrific trench warfare witnessed in World War I, Americans were enthusiastic about the possibility of victory from the air. The public support in this regard afforded the Air Corps good relations with Congress, which directly correlated to increased procurement and development expenditures – especially in the form of new bomber aircraft.[47] The growing support for the strategic bombardment strategy even encouraged leaders such as Westover to comment publicly that, "high speed and otherwise high performing bombardment aircraft, together with observation aircraft of superior speed and range and communication characteristics, will suffice for the adequate air defense of this country." He further asserted that "the ability of bombardment aircraft to fly in close formation and thus to ensure greater defense against air attack . . . warrant the belief that no known agency can frustrate the accomplishment of the bombardment mission."[48] By the end of 1937, top airpower leaders such as Arnold, Andrews, and Walker "shared the conviction that the long-range bomber solved virtually all problems of aerial warfare."[49] This overwhelming support and complete faith in the efficacy and sufficiency of bombers led to procurement decisions that discounted the need for fighter and pursuit aircraft and instead myopically focused on the drive for bigger, faster, and greater numbers of bomber aircraft.[50]

This wave of support and expansion of airpower under the banner of strategic bombardment did not necessarily persuade Army ground-operations leaders to relinquish their control on much of the Air Corps budget. The need for a bomber fleet capable of long-range, high-payload, self-defending strategic operations had little to no direct correlation with traditional ground operations. Furthermore, in order to meet the operational capabilities called for by strategic bombardment, a four-engine bomber was proposed and requested in large numbers. However, Gen Malin Craig, Chief of Staff, "was reluctant to spend large sums on four engine bombers" and believed that "allowing the Air Corps to acquire large numbers of four engine bombers would merely encourage its fascination with strategic bombardment. . . ."[51] Craig, offering Congress his opposition for spending too much money on the new four-engine B-17 bomber, suggested that the inflated cost of the bombers would decrease the numbers of other aircraft required, would divert the Air Corps from supporting the ground operations, and would jeopardize other important Army requirements.[52] Fortunately, Congress sided with the Air Corps and provided close to what it requested in terms of B-17 bomber procurement. Nevertheless, the rift between the ground culture and the bomber culture within the Army was reaching a clear breaking point. The one pressure that had the power to divert attention away from the central debate was the looming prospect of war against Germany. On November 14, 1938, the president ordered an expansion of air capability as a move to deter Hitler. This was the only support and guidance the Air Corps needed to press forward with their strategic bombardment plans.[53]

The period from 1920 to 1939 comprising the interwar years offered a significant amount of external pressures, internal cultural changes, and leadership influences. The approval for the GHQ Air Force, the congressional and presidential mandates for increased funding, and the widespread support by the American population (nine of ten Americans in a 1939 survey wanted an increase in military aviation) all combined to change the organizational characteristics and structure of airpower.[54] Moreover, toward the end of this period, the possibility of war in Europe was an ever-increasing reality that further forced national leadership to expand the capabilities of the military air arm. The bomber culture that had emerged and solidified itself in the years following World War I believed in its sufficiency and ability to be decisive. Although there was a continued and consistent theme regarding strategic bombardment, the airmen failed to accomplish their ultimate objective – independence. However, as was noted with the major external event of World War I, one might anticipate, as organizational modeling suggests, that the U.S. involvement in World War II would offer additional opportunity for organizational change.

The idea of strategic airpower dominated the thinking of Army Air Corps leaders. Although airmen continued to debate and develop several airpower functions, strategic bombardment took center stage as the United States entered World War II.[55] Moreover, the doctrine of strategic bombardment required that specific bomber technology be further developed and funded. In the years between World War I and World War II, leaders realized that airpower organization required new thinking and action.

3

WORLD WAR II

THE INTERWAR YEARS LEADING UP TO AMERICA'S INVOLVE-
ment in World War II brought tremendous change to the development
and the importance of airpower in war. Airpower advocates' outspoken appeal for the efficacy and advancement of airpower, equal to other
military arms, stimulated the establishment of the Army Air Corps;
"Mitchell was of course the leading visionary."[1] In 1935, the Army Air
Corps (promoted from the Army Air Service in 1926) won the development of the General Headquarters Air Force, organizing all operational
units under one command.[2] Although the formal establishment of the
Army Air Corps and the General Headquarters Air Force fell short of a
separate Air Force, it afforded airpower leaders greater autonomy to operate, plan, and develop airpower processes. The establishment of the Air
Corps Tactical School enabled airmen to further codify their ideas into
doctrine and begin formally educating personnel. Of over 1,091 students
who graduated from ACTS from 1920 to 1939, nearly 25 percent became
general officers in World War II (including eleven of the thirteen three-
star generals and all three of the four-star generals).[3]

In the months leading up to 1940, the Air Corps solidified bomber
doctrine, formalized strategic bombardment perspectives, and established itself as a unique and specific military capability within the U.S.
Department of War. Although the Army continued to try to control the
growth and direction the new bomber-operations culture demanded,
the external pressures from senior national leaders, public support, and
a cohesive, single voice Air Corps had the advantage – and within this
context, World War II broke out in Europe. Although America did not

37

immediately join the allies in fighting against Germany, the U.S. leadership under President Roosevelt began to plan for possible hostilities. Within the calculus of planning for what was clearly a major developing conflict, the Air Corps was central.

By mid-1940, the entire country saw the possibility of U.S. involvement in the war. On May 16, 1940, Roosevelt ordered a massive expansion of military air capability, calling for the development of 50,000 aircraft, expansion to 54 Air Groups, and 200,000 air officers, cadets, and enlisted personnel.[4] "Given the degree of confidence in the strategic bomber, its accuracy, and its capacity for self-defense," the Air Corps quickly began drawing up plans for a significant bomber expansion.[5] In outlining this expansion, the president acknowledged the need to supply countries already engaged in war with a steady stream of aircraft. In March of 1941 Congress passed the Lend-Lease Act, which would eventually provide Great Britain with nearly 26,000 aircraft, the Soviet Union with 11,400 aircraft, and China with 1,400 aircraft. Moreover, nearly 4,000 additional aircraft were provided to various allied countries engaged in the war.[6] The consequence of the president's order and the Lend-Lease Act was the creation of an environment that the airmen could never have dreamed would exist. However, "Acquisition of large numbers of aircraft and trained men to fly and maintain them did not necessarily produce true air power. The critical issue was whether the role of military aviation would ultimately be defined by ground officers or airmen."[7] Fortunately, new Chief of Staff Gen George Marshall, a career ground officer, appreciated the strategic capabilities offered by airpower and granted the Air Corps leadership a great deal of autonomy. However, Marshall did not support separating the Air Corps from the Army into its own independent service. Marshall's position in this regard was not based on a disbelief in the efficacy or relevance of airpower; rather, "he hoped to avoid any disruptive *organizational changes.*"[8] During what appeared to be imminent near-certain U.S. involvement in the war, Marshall gave the Air Corps the autonomy its leaders desired but held fast the organizational stability needed during time of crisis. Marshall, however, realized that some level of organizational change was needed to transition from a peace-time posture to war-time operational status.

In June of 1941, under Marshall's leadership, the U.S. Army Air Forces was established. Marshall did not want this new internal organization to be harnessed by the existing organizational structure, which split authority between GHQ Air Force and the Air Corps. With the establishment of the U.S. Army Air Forces, airpower had one single commander responsible for all air operations. In this way, Marshall was able to coordinate airpower operations through a single point of contact – Gen Hap Arnold, commander of U.S. Army Air Forces.[9] This new internal organization further allowed the air leadership to develop their own air-operations war plans for defeating Germany. When the president asked the services for an estimate of what might be needed if the United States went to war against Germany, the Army Air Forces developed the Air War Plans Division, Plan Number 1 (AWPD/1). "Drafted by advocates of strategic bombing, the document went far beyond estimating production requirements, offering nothing less than a plan for defeating Germany by means of aerial bombardment."[10] At this point, the Army Air Forces had the resources for building massive numbers of bombers, an Army Chief of Staff that was supportive of the airmen's bombardment perspective, and a formal plan in the president's hands outlining the strategic bombardment that airmen claimed could win the war. The posture and context of airpower stood just short of a significant turning point in terms of its organization and responsibilities. The missing ingredient was some type of a direct and measurable threat against the United States that the Air Force could rally around, that would focus their military capability. The airmen did not have to wait long: using airpower, Japan attacked Pearl Harbor U. S. Navy Base on December 7, 1941.

Following the Japanese attack at Pearl Harbor, the United States declared war on Japan and, shortly afterward, on Germany (following Germany's declaration against the United States). The United States, and specifically the Army Air Forces, found themselves fighting a world war across both the Atlantic and Pacific oceans, against very different enemies. For all the debate, argument, and accusations over the past two decades regarding what airpower could and could not do in war, the time had come for the Army Air Force to put its strategic bombardment ideas into real-time action. Just over four months after the Japanese attack at Pearl Harbor, Lt Col James Doolittle planned and carried out what has been called the Doolittle Raid. After receiving orders from senior leadership for a significant response to Japan's attack, Doolittle gathered sixteen B-25Bs and trained crews to fly them off an aircraft carrier. Nalty describes the events of the raid:

> On the morning of April 18, 1942, Doolittle released the brakes and sent the first B-25 thundering down the flight deck into a 40-mile-per-hour gale. His bomber clawed its way upward and led the force to Japan, where 13 of the raiders bombed Tokyo, while the other three attacked Kobe and Nagoya.[11]

Although the raid cost the lives of eleven airmen due to forced bailouts and crash landings from lack of fuel after the raid, the mission served its purpose. The United States possessed the capability through airpower to target the enemy's homeland.

Although the war in the Pacific would continue to challenge American fighting forces, especially the U.S. Navy and the Marines, the war in Europe would be the true testing ground for the Army Air Force and its proclaimed bomber doctrine. Great Britain's Royal Air Force also had a tremendous amount of faith in its bomber doctrine and was prepared, alongside the Americans, to unleash its bomber forces on Germany. Great Britain, of course, began its aerial campaigns in 1939, while the United States did not begin until 1943. Under the leadership of Maj Gen Carl Spaatz, commander of Eighth Air Force, the United States began a strategic bombing campaign. However, the Americans quickly discovered that their "self-defended" bomber aircraft were much more vulnerable to defending German fighter aircraft than they had anticipated. Losses during daytime bomber raids were so high that the British decided to shift their bombing strategy to night operations. Although night operations did afford the British a certain advantage from the cover of darkness, this came at the cost of bombing accuracy. Nalty (1997) again offers an accurate and precise synopsis of the emerging bomber context:

> When German defenses first compelled the [British] Bomber Command to abandon daylight raids and seek the concealment of darkness, British airmen had tried to destroy oil refineries and other fairly compact targets, only to discover that the raiders seldom found their objectives. An examination of 600 photographs taken from individual bombers at the time they released their bombs revealed that only 10 percent dropped their loads within 5 miles

of the assigned target. Since the air crews could not find and attack a particular structure by night, Bomber Command had to find a different target for the heavy bombers. Navigators could find German cities and bombardiers aim precisely enough to damage an urban area; consequently, industrial cities, rather than specific factories, became the target of British night attacks. In addition, Air Marshal Harris believed that "city-busting," or area bombing, destroyed the urban infrastructure of houses, shops, and utilities that supported the German war effort, satisfying Churchill's demand for results and possibly making an invasion unnecessary. Indeed, nighttime area bombing yielded impressive results, as Harris tried to "de-house" German workers by incinerating the industrial cities where they lived.[12]

This bombardment strategy paralleled Douhet's original claim back in 1921 that an enemy's population under the attack of aerial bombardment would eventually be forced to surrender without having their ground army defeated on the battlefield.[13]

However, there was significant disagreement in both Great Britain and in the United States as to the moral and strategic appropriateness of indiscriminate area bombing that targeted the enemy's civilian population.[14] For the Americans, on the other hand, daylight bombing "was an article of faith," and their doctrine hinged on the ability of bombers to reach and accurately hit their targets.[15] In order for airpower to prove its claims of the past two decades, it was paramount that bombers be given the opportunity to strategically strike Germany's industrial nodes – despite the danger to aircrews. Under the leadership of Spaatz and Arnold, the U.S. strategic bombing campaign intended to fly in large formations and target with accuracy the war-making factories within Germany, while the British would fly area-bombing missions at night. Throughout the duration of the war, strategic bombardment remained the hallmark of the Air Force and, although the doctrine of strategic bombardment fell well short of expected and proselytized pre-war assertions, the lessons learned regarding the necessity for a having a highly capable Air Force in modern war became undeniable. However, while World War II lessons learned would further reinforce many of the previous airpower beliefs, new airpower experiences would develop organizational requirements that have endured to this day. An examination of the airpower operations in North Africa and the bombing raids conducted over Europe help to illustrate several important organizational considerations.

Despite the lessons of World War I and the gains made during the interwar years, flawed airpower organization characterized the initial use of airpower in North Africa.[16] The official Army doctrine (*Army Field Manual 1–5*) spelled out that an air arm be attached to every major ground formation and subsequently remain under the authority of the ground commander, "who had the more important mission."[17] Furthermore, "there was no centralized control of either the tactical or strategic air forces." This doctrine all but eliminated the priority to gain air superiority over the battle space. Unfortunately, the idea that airpower's first mission would be to provide cover to ground troops in combat proved a major mistake. German fighters massed their resources and overwhelmed Allied aircraft, making losses prohibitive.[18] It became apparent to both ground and air leaders that air superiority was required before air forces could effectively support ground forces.

The Casablanca Conference in January of 1943 officially reorganized airpower in the Mediterranean theater under one commander, Air Marshal Tedder. Under Tedder and his immediate vice-commanders (Gen Carl A. "Tooey" Spaatz and Air Vice Marshal Coningham), Allied air forces could be concentrated and prioritized based on theater-wide requirements – the highest of which was air superiority. Tedder refused to parcel out airpower; rather, he diligently organized a comprehensive air campaign that addressed both tactical and strategic objectives. According to Gen William Momyer (retired), "The unity of airpower [after Casablanca] was not only sound in theory, but the theory stood the test of battle and proved to be the most effective method for the command and control of airpower in a theater operation."[19] Centralized control and theater-wide campaign planning under an experienced airman proved to be enduring requirements for properly organizing airpower in war; however, the skies over Europe had additional lessons to teach.

The European bombing campaigns in World War II have had perhaps the most published attention of any airpower activity. The immortalized words of former British Prime Minister Stanley Baldwin characterized the thinking process of Allied airpower over Europe: *"The bomber will always get through."*[20] An argument that the bombers did indeed always get through is easily made – but at what cost? Some casualty figures approximate the absolute loss of bomber crewmen to be nearly 50,000

United States Army Air Force and 50,000 Royal Air Force.[21] These loss rates have prompted continuous debate (often heated) about how the bombing campaign over Europe might have been more effectively and efficiently accomplished. Of the most common topics discussed (and the most elusive to common answers) are ideas about escort, precision capabilities, and target selection.

Airpower advocates prior to World War II believed a bomber, properly built with defensive capabilities, would be able to sufficiently defend itself – without escort – on offensive bombing missions; the development of the B-17 Flying Fortress is evidence of this belief.[22] Unfortunately, bomber crewmen found themselves the easy targets of faster, more maneuverable German fighters. Based on the devastating losses experienced over Europe, most B-17 crewmembers did not believe they would live to accomplish the minimum thirty sorties. Why bombers failed to have fighter escort to and from targets has several possible answers. The most obvious is that the airpower leaders' belief in the "self-defending bomber" discouraged the development of fighter aircraft with the required range to accompany bomber formations effectively.[23] In this case, the decision to use current or improved fighter technology might well have made the difference for the nearly 100,000 bomber crewmen who lost their lives.

The ability of Allied bombers to strike their targets has been yet another point of considerable contention. The percentage of bombs dropped that actually hit their intended targets was a level of magnitude less than airpower advocates had asserted it would be.[24] Some suggest that the lack of precision capabilities forced the British into its doctrine of area bombing – a doctrine that potentially killed more noncombatants than combatants.[25] The ability to successfully strike desired targets is a fundamental requirement for the doctrine of strategic bombardment. Max Hastings has concluded that "for all the technology embodied in the bomber aircraft [by the end of the war], its load once released was an astonishingly crude and imprecise weapon."[26] Subsequently, the technology needed to support the desires of airpower visionaries became of first importance in the years that followed World War II.

Finally, the question that continued to elude consensus was what targets should be hit and when? A new degree of analysis began to emerge across the map of Germany and its occupied territories. Airmen, together with intelligence and industrial experts, sought to determine the strategic targets whose destruction would cripple Germany's ability to continue waging effective war. While the Americans attempted to destroy German industry by targeting its industrial web, the British began area bombing to disrupt the morale of the German people.[27] Organizationally, this strategy by both air forces was untested and developed on a day-to-day basis. Although analysis of the success of either strategy has produced diverging opinions, one lesson can be drawn with little disagreement: the operational requirements for a codified organizational structure that outlines the accepted and proper use of airpower in war is necessary.

Although the volumes of details regarding all aspects of airpower during World War II are beyond the scope of this work, it is important to point out that up to this point in military aviation history, no external event had a greater impact on the organizational structure and demands of the Air Force than did World War II. The experiences solidified airpower with an airmen's identity separate from all other services and an air-minded bomber culture that would guide the Air Force for years into the future. However, although the Army Air Force provided tremendous effort and was clearly a significant and necessary element of winning both the Pacific and European conflicts, the overall assessment of the Air Force's pre-war bombardment strategy did not reach pre-war anticipated expectations. German industry was much more creative and dispersed; the accuracy of daylight bombers was significantly less than airmen envisioned it would be; the belief that bomber formations could adequately defend themselves was tremendously flawed; and the lack of insight and pre-war planning regarding the need for pursuit and fighter aircraft that could protect bomber formations to and from their targets proved near-catastrophic.[28] Although airpower in World War II solidified itself as *necessary,* it did not solidify itself as *sufficient.*

VICTORY AND INDEPENDENCE

The buildup of aircraft and personnel during World War II was impressive. By the end of the war against Germany in May of 1945, the Army Air

Force had peaked with nearly 2,300,000 personnel and tens of thousands of aircraft (Army Air Force, Navy, and Lend-Lease).[29] The number of missions flown, tonnage of bombs dropped, and the general expansion of airpower could not have been anticipated in pre-war America. However, the decisive capability of airpower did not appear to have come to fruition as the airpower advocates had claimed it would. The Army Air Force leadership knew that any post-war assessment of airpower's role in the European campaign had the potential to either support or deny what advocates continued to desire – the need for complete airpower independence. Knowing the importance and possible stakes of what a post-war bombing survey might provide in terms of future independence, Spaatz and Arnold began formalizing how such a survey should be conducted:

> Should an unbiased panel conclude that aerial bombardment had proved decisive against the Third Reich, the Army's historic strategy of defeating the hostile armies on the battlefield would have to yield to a policy of destroying, through air power, an enemy's capacity to make war. Since the inquiry that Arnold sought would affect future relationships among the armed services, it could not remain solely an Army Air Forces project, but he wanted the Air Forces in control. He therefore proposed that the Joint Chiefs of Staff assign to the Army Air Forces overall responsibility for conducting the investigation, with the Navy, Army Ground Forces, and Army Service Forces "represented in such proportion as deemed advisable for their immediate needs and in order that impartiality be assured." The key to Arnold's plan was the proposal of proportionate representation; as far as the Combined Bomber Offensive was concerned, the Navy had not participated, and its main interest could only be the relationship of aerial bombardment to German submarine warfare. Since the future of his service [Navy] would not be jeopardized by an investigation of the air war against Germany, Admiral Ernest J. King, Chief of Naval Operations, readily agreed to Arnold's call for the study.[30]

It was clearly the intention of senior leadership within the Air Force that the bombing survey would "provide documentation to demonstrate the decisiveness of strategic bombing and thus justify an independent air force within the postwar armed forces, while at the same time yielding data helpful in planning the air war against Japan."[31] However, the survey, being an unbiased assessment, fell short of the support the airmen were seeking.

The analysts on the investigation team "tried to evaluate the contributions of air power within the context of a combined air, ground, and naval campaign, concluding that the Army Air forces had made an essential contribution to victory, even though it had not won the war itself."[32] The report further concluded that "Airpower . . . had not lived up to the expectations of prophets like Douhet and Mitchell, who expected a bolt from the blue that destroyed some vital industry and rendered the enemy powerless to resist, even though his army and navy remained intact."[33] In its final report, the Strategic Bombing Survey concluded that despite the autonomy that Marshal had given airpower's leadership to operate and plan their strategic air campaign, airpower "had indeed remained part of the larger Army, American, and Allied war machines."[34] Furthermore, and perhaps even more discouraging to the Air Force leadership, the final toll of U.S. aircrew killed in the European air war numbered over 50,000.[35] When comparing this horrific figure with the rhetoric of pre-war airpower, one can see that the bomber was not capable of acceptable self-defense and could not be counted on to always hit its targets, and the pre-war utopian strategic bombardment strategy was not effectively calibrated in the context of a thinking and capable enemy. Finally, due to the fact that the survey failed to support Arnold's and Spaatz's desire for proof of the decisiveness of airpower, it appeared once again that the Army would retain the credentials (with the Navy) to claim superiority and forestall any move the airmen might have toward independence.

Despite the disappointment of the post-war survey, the United States was still fighting the war against Japan. Airmen had little time to contemplate the consequential organizational changes that the experiences of World War II would most certainly force. Even if independence was not supported by the Strategic Bombing Survey, the organizational lessons of command and control, massing of forces, target selection process, coordination with allies, and bombing accuracy were but a few of the many elements of what most certainly would require a *reorganization* from top to bottom of the Army Air Force. In this sense, the bombing campaign in Europe during World War II provided such significant lessons learned and demanded such new and challenging external responsibilities for airpower that major organizational change following the war was near certain. However, missing from the calculus was the one element that continued to elude airmen: proof certain that their bomber culture and claims of sufficiency in war were true. The pre-war claims that airpower could provide an independent and decisive victory in war were simply not proven in the air operations over Europe.

END OF WAR WITH JAPAN: AUGUST 1945

Following the victory over Germany in May 1945, the United States contemplated how best to end the war in Japan. For much of the war against Japan, Army senior leadership assumed and planned for the eventual ground invasion of the Japanese mainland. Regardless of the fact that since 1943 the United States dominated the Japanese military across the Pacific, it appeared clear that the final blow and requirement for victory would be a bloody beach landing on Japan's main shores. The Air Force leadership, knowing that the fire-bombing of Tokyo in March of 1945 resulted in unmatched destruction and the death of nearly 100,000 Japanese, believed that the Japanese would surrender through a bombing campaign alone.[36] Army Air Forces, having near complete air superiority by 1945, believed they could plan and deliver the decisive blow through strategic bombardment of Japan's cities.

Continuing to base their strategy on a strategic bombing perspective (now fully an established airpower culture), the Army Air Force planned for its part in ending the war decisively.[37] Having delivered every conceivable type of strategic bombing strategy both day and night over Europe as well as significant fire-bombing raids on Tokyo and other key Japanese cities, finding that the Strategic Bombing Survey was less than supportive of their decisive assertions left Air Force leadership with little room left to advance their argument for independence. However,

> in the final days of the war against Japan ... a new aerial weapon would appear, the atomic bomb, a device so dreadful that it again raised the possibility that air power could not merely defeat an enemy in conjunction with ground and naval forces but could by itself utterly destroy the foundations of a hostile society.[38]

As the evidence was still coming in from the assessment in Europe, the Army Air Force was ordered by President Truman to deliver the first of two atomic bombs on Japan. On August 6, 1945, a B-29 dropped the atomic bomb Little Boy, and within seconds of detonation, thousands of Japanese in Hiroshima were killed. On August 9, just three days later, another B-29 delivered Fat Man on the Japanese city of Nagasaki, resulting once more in the instant annihilation of thousands of Japanese. Six days later, on August 15, 1945, the Japanese announced their surrender.[39]

Although the bombings resulted in the near-immediate and unconditional surrender of the Japanese, the aftermath and moral deliberations regarding the use of atomic weapons would continue for decades. However, one element of the bombings was beyond dispute – airpower alone delivered the decisive blow and negated any plans or reason for an Army invasion or territorial occupation. However horrifying, the Japanese-initiated war against the United States was over, and the Air Forces had the unquestionable proof they needed that airpower alone, given the new technology of bombers and atomic bombs, could bring an end to traditional ground wars. Within the context of victory in Europe, where the Air Force was not considered decisive but still unquestionably necessary for victory, and now with the decisive bombardment of Japan that ended the war, organizational change could no longer be avoided. Although it would take nearly two more years of planning, logistics, and congressional action, the Air Force and its airmen, through the influence of external exigencies, internal cultural changes, and continued transitional leadership throughout the period, finally had everything they needed to ensure independence. The combination of changes traced from 1907 through 1945 had finally reached the culminating point where the ground-centric organizational structure could no longer sustain the external requirements and meet the needs of the internal cultural and leadership parameters.

Following the final days of World War II, most military personnel were glad to be done with combat, looking forward to building their lives in a peacetime environment, and for some, retiring from the service. However, as most prepared for transition to peacetime operations, airpower leaders "began to work on the organizational structure of the postwar Army Air Forces, which was entering a period of transition that should, if all went well, result in independence."[40] Furthermore, new Army Chief of Staff Gen Dwight Eisenhower proclaimed publicly that "the Army does not belong in the air – it belongs on the ground."[41] Moreover, as early as December of 1945, less than four months since the end of hostilities, President Truman stated, "Air Power has been developed to a point where its responsibilities are equal to those of land and sea power." He further recommended Congress approve legislation to create an independent air force, an equal of the Army and Navy in a new department of defense.[42] The stage for independence was set and it was time to take action.

Within just a few weeks of the President of the United States and the Army Chief of Staff fully endorsing and encouraging the establishment of an independent air force, senior airpower leaders went to work:

> In mid-January 1946, based on his discussions with Eisenhower, Gen Carl Spaatz, who formally became commanding general early in February, decided to reorganize the Army Air Forces but only by creating components that could be absorbed by an independent air force. In this fashion he hoped to avoid a postwar reorganization as part of the Army followed by a second restructuring once independence had been gained.[43]

Furthermore, the atomic technology that gave airpower its autonomy would require a substantial and highly formalized organizational structure to support its operational capability. Spaatz would "lean forward" and begin the process of major organizational development with the intention of transitioning his work into a newly formed independent air force.

Finally, after considerable debate and compromise regarding changing lines of authority and responsibilities, the Congress passed legislation authorizing a complete reorganization of the military establishment. "On July 26, 1947, President Truman approved the National Security Act of 1947, which created the National Military Establishment, including the Office of Secretary of Defense and the Departments of the Army, Navy, and Air Force."[44] The United States Air Force became an independent service on September 18, 1947.

4

"COUNTING" THE CHANGES IN PERIOD ONE

AS I HAVE TRACED IN THE PREVIOUS CHAPTER, OVER THE years from 1907 to 1947 the United States Air Force finally gained its independence as an equal arm of the U.S. military. Throughout the period a series of external events resulted in an increased level of pressure that eventually influenced how and when airpower would experience a major organizational change. As the external events required internal perspectives to change, the overall culture shifted from its original characteristic in 1907 to its final orientation in 1947 (from an Army ground-operations perspective to an airmen's bomber-operations perspective). Moreover, those responsible for making organizational decisions, determining how money would be spent, and operationalizing airpower for war equally evolved throughout the period. All of the changes observed and measured were incremental in that they advanced the cause, perspective, and leadership of airpower closer toward a major organizational change at and following each significant external event.

AIRPOWER LEADERSHIP 1907–1947

Once the realization set in, in 1907, that powered, heavier-than-air aviation had the potential to support military operations, the U.S. Army began assigning personnel to the Army Aeronautical Division. During this time, officers were taught to fly and were given aeronautical ratings. Normally, a new Army weapon system would have a hierarchy of leadership responsible for the supervision and operational requirements. Furthermore, it would be assumed that the advent of a new and potentially valuable weapon system would require leadership to become fully qualified and capable of operating within the parameters of the new system. However, the officers qualified for aviation service (those who had received training and passed flying courses) were all lieutenants, with the exception of two captains. Although one could argue that a new and unproven system such as the airplane would be first manned by young officers, it also develops some important questions. How could senior Army officers responsible for supervising this new emerging airpower appreciate or even understand the complexities of flight if they themselves were not being trained to fly? From 1907, when aircraft were first brought into Army operations to 1913 (nearly six full years after the inception of airplanes into service), there appears to have been ample time for senior Army leaders responsible for supervising flying operations to have been appropriately trained as pilots. However, beyond the lieutenants and two captains, the new Army air arm was devoid of any pilot-qualified leadership. Although there are a number of possible reasons, one is that the Army wanted to control aviation but not at the expense of ground operations. If senior leaders perceived airpower as an auxiliary to ground forces (which has already been shown to be the case), then senior Army leaders would not want to stray too far from what they saw as the true nature of their profession. Only the young Army officers who had not yet assimilated or developed a cultural devotion to a ground-operations perspective were willing to transition and put full support into becoming pilots. This explanation may not be fully explanatory; however, there remains the fact that no officers above the rank of captain became qualified to fly – and why this was the case should not be ignored.

Further consideration should be given to how the number of qualified aviators increased from 1913 to 1917. The increased technology from 1907 to 1917 and the external realties of war brewing in Europe provided incentive for the Army to increase their number of pilots and aircraft. By 1917 approximately 161 officers and enlisted personnel were qualified to some level of aeronautical service; however, as figure 4.1 illustrates, there is a characteristic lack of any senior officers on aeronautical duty.[1] The large majority of those qualified are 2nd and 1st lieutenants, while only 10 captains and 2 majors are among the ranks. However, we know from the previously offered historical narrative that there were considerable

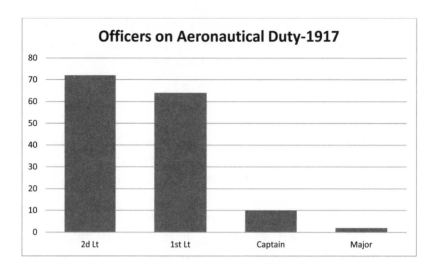

Figure 4.1

numbers of senior ranking Army officers associated with the decision making, procurement, and budgetary considerations of airpower. What this data partially suggests is that none of those senior ranking Army officers responsible for the supervision of airpower were qualified for aviation service. Because the Army was dominated by a ground-operations culture early on in the period, those senior officers who had reached the level and rank for command would have "grown up" within the traditional Army culture. It appears that the leadership perspective viewing airpower as merely a support system for the grander strategy of ground operations may have kept senior officers from taking the necessary steps to qualify in the very systems they would be responsible for commanding. Fortunately, one of the majors was Billy Mitchell. When the United States entered World War I, Mitchell was given the temporary rank of colonel in order to lead and command airpower at the appropriate rank. However, even with Mitchell holding a temporary rank of colonel, no general officers were qualified or had any experience in airpower by the time the war began. Airpower senior leadership, even in World War I, was dominated by a ground-operations Army culture.

In contrast, by the end of Period One (1947), the USAF had officer representation across all ranks from four-star general to 2nd lieutenant (five stars, if you consider Hap Arnold's rank after the war). Over the entire period (1907–1947), officer rank representation went from nearly no qualified senior officers to hundreds of qualified senior officers who were active airmen. The obvious ramifications to organizational change is clear – if senior officers responsible for airpower supervision transitioned from a ground-operations group to an airmen group, then those making the decisions by the end of the period regarding how best to organize airpower would have equally transitioned. The ramification, as we saw in the previous chapter, was a major organizational change in 1947 where airmen took over independent command of military aviation and reorganized into the USAF.

Another method for determining to what extent airpower perspective might have changed over the course of Period One is to examine the number of personnel associated with airpower operations. Not all personnel in Army aviation were flyers. Many had the responsibility of mechanics, air controllers, supply, administration, and all the basic services associated with airpower logistics. What is important is the understanding that personnel cost money, and that when one arm of a military service gains in personnel, an associated loss in personnel in another arm can be expected (unless an overall increase is underway). Determining the extent to which Army leaders were willing to commit personnel away from traditional Army operations and into airpower operations will help in assessing the Army's perspective of airpower relative to their normal ground-operations priority. In other words, examining the numbers of personnel authorized and attached to Army aviation service over the period can offer insight as to how important Army leadership considered airpower to the overall Army mission. The number of personnel attached to Army aviation duty continually increased throughout the period.[2] In 1907, only 3 personnel were assigned to aviation duty. By 1917 that number had increased to 1,218, and within a single year, the total had increased, in 1918, to 195,023. Following the end of World War I, total aviation personnel decreased and remained steady at around 15,000 to 20,000. However, the number grew in 1941 to 152,125 and to 764,415 in 1942. By 1944, aviation personnel in the U.S. Army grew to 2,372,292. Interesting to note are the massive increases that occurred leading up to and during World War I and II. As external events, these wars are shown in this data as extremely influential in regard to the impact made on airpower. Clearly, these numbers during each war would not have been what they were if airpower had not been evolving into an important and necessary force. The expenditures for the personnel assigned to aviation were a significant draw on the traditional Army budget. Given that nearly all senior Army leaders with the rank and authority to make budget decisions were not qualified aviators, the increase in personnel may well reflect the emerging influence that the airmen's culture and leadership had on the traditional Army perspective. Clearly the Army was challenged by airpower's demands for appropriate levels of personnel. The fact that the Army authorized these increased numbers throughout the period reflects the changes airpower as an organizational unit demanded.

One can ascertain from these figures, along with the previous narrative outlining the emerging internal cultural changes, transitional leadership, and external exigencies, that the face of military airpower over Period One changed significantly. Over the forty years from 1907 to 1947, airpower emerged from its infancy and grew into an independent service supporting overall U.S. military strength. The significant organizational change that occurred in 1947 is predictable using organizational change modeling that suggests changes in external realities, internal culture, and leadership drive organizational and institutional level change. Leaving Period One, it is clear that the newly formed USAF was dominated by a bomber-centric perspective, led by senior bomber pilots, and positioned to continue its independent and decisive capabilities on the foundation of strategic bombardment operations. What started in 1907 as a new weapon system dominated by a ground-centric perspective concluded in 1947 as an independent force dominated by a bomber-centric perspective. It is from this position of strength that the USAF entered into a new era – Period Two, 1947–1992.

To conclude the analysis of Period One, figure 4.2 illustrates the transition in this period from a ground-centric perspective to a bomber-centric perspective. As noted, the dominant culture in the beginning of the period slowly transitioned due in large part to the external exigencies that forged a new internal perspective in the expanding airmen community. Each external event increased the disequilibrium between the

Period I
(1907-1947)

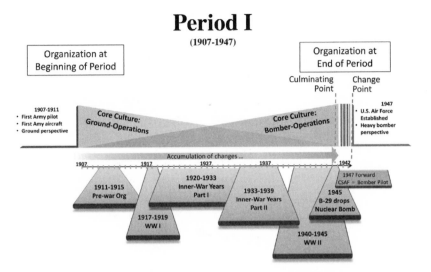

Figure 4.2

divergent perspectives of ground and air to new levels. Throughout this period, although not depicted in the illustration, transitional leaders such as Billy Mitchell, Giulio Douhet, and others enforced the development of a new and unique airpower identity. This emerging identity resonated in the hearts and the minds of flyers and propelled the organizational dynamics of airpower further away from its original ground-centric tether. However, as depicted, the culminating point of Period One organizational change came after the bombing of Japan in 1945 which validated the decisiveness of airpower to secure victory in war apart from the other traditional services (the U.S. Army in particular).

PERIOD TWO: 1947–1992

OVER NEARLY FOUR DECADES THE USAF STRUGGLED TO GAIN the recognition and independence it so strongly desired. Airpower and the new domain of air were rightfully established within their own service, separate from the original ground-centric origins. Through the external dynamics of two world wars, the internal development of a unique airpower culture, and formidable leadership that provided both vision and direction, the USAF entered into Period Two as an independent arm of the U.S. military. What is clear in the analysis and historical narrative that follow is that during the early years of USAF independence the bomber-centric perspective dominated the organization. Although airpower, in general, was a new and recognized domain for modern war, the specific bomber mission, bomber leadership, and bomber culture dominated nearly every USAF organizational decision. However, as Period Two unfolds, the evidence is clear that the emergence of the fighter-centric perspective increases in both importance and power. By the end of Period Two, a significant organizational change minimizes the once-dominant bomber perspective and passes the mantle of control to the new and dominant fighter-centric perspective. Understanding how and why this organizational change occurred is paramount to understanding and anticipating the possibility of future USAF organizational change.

Flying fighters is fun, flying bombers is important.

GENERAL CURTIS LEMAY

5

THE RISE OF BOMBER
DOMINANCE: 1947–1965

IN THE FIRST FEW YEARS FOLLOWING THE END OF WORLD
War II and the subsequent independence of the USAF in September of
1947, the organizational structure of airpower was formally developed.
The leaders of the new military service were faced with managing and
operationalizing the new atomic weapon, countering the emerging and
ever-increasing Soviet threat, and continuing to maintain the traditional
missions of strategic bombardment, transport, ground support, and air-
to-air pursuit and attack.

During these early years from 1947 to 1950, the first Secretary of the
Air Force (SecAF), W. Stuart Symington, and the first Chief of Staff of
the Air Force (CSAF), Gen Carl Spaatz began the process of developing
the organizational structure of the USAF:

> The Air Force adopted the basic organization that has persisted over the years:
> a headquarters, with a staff consisting of deputies who both advised and carried
> out policy and special assistants; a network of major commands and lesser agen-
> cies, both operating and supporting; and the operational commands overseas . . .
> the Air Force . . . assumed certain responsibilities, among them the deterrence of
> nuclear war. Deterrence, however, was but a single aspect of an evolving national
> policy, and the Air Force had to devote its resources to the others.[1]

Within this new structure, three major commands were developed:
Strategic Air Command (SAC), Tactical Air Command (TAC), and Air
Defense Command (ADC); however, "Strategic Air Command emerged
as the *most important* of the three."[2] Furthermore, "Strategic Air Command enjoyed a clear primacy within the Air Force . . . as its prestige rose,
that of tactical aviation [fighters] declined."[3] Within SAC, the operations
and the leadership were dominated by bomber pilots, and the doctrine

of strategic bombardment encouraged and even forced nearly all senior leadership positions throughout the USAF to be filled by World War II bomber pilots.[4] Under the strong influence and aggressive style of the new commander of SAC, Lt Gen Curtis LeMay encouraged and won the argument for strategic bombing to be the USAF's "primary mission."[5] With the organizational structure of the USAF dominated by bomber pilots and strategic bomber doctrine, the future and viability of TAC became questionable.

Describing the relationship between the bomber community that dominated the USAF and the subordinate fighter community, Worden asserts that

> most of the fighter community willingly conceded doctrinal preeminence to the bomber enthusiasts in the interest of autonomy. The achievement of autonomy, however, came too late to arrest the trend toward strategic tunnel vision and dogmatic doctrine. The postwar doctrine differed from prewar doctrine in little more than incorporation of long-range escorts.[6]

Because the bombing campaign in Europe and the dropping of the atomic bomb on Japan provided the catalyst for an independent air service (by proving decisiveness), the bomber mission and all those with bomber experience became the central and most influential aspect and group within the new USAF. The beginning of Period Two is dominated by a bomber-operations culture (values, beliefs, norms, and agreed best practices), and bomber pilot leadership (bomber pilot CSAF).

This bomber-operations organizational structure had significant consequences on missions that fell outside of the strategic doctrine agenda. For TAC, whose capability centered on close air support to ground troops and air-to-air dog-fighting to gain or maintain air superiority, existing in the shadow of SAC was extremely difficult:

> By 1949 TAC was truly a pawn in a game of chess between the Army and the Air Force. Continued budget limitations threatened TAC's existence. Some in the Air Force headquarters wanted to give TAC to the Army. Others saw TAC as a luxury whose budget should be trimmed to free more money for SAC. Fighter lieutenant general Otto P. "Opie" Weyland recounted that SAC should have priority, yet SAC wasn't satisfied with most of the chips . . . they wanted them all. The tactical community, Weyland argued, had to fight "just to preserve a force structure." Furthermore . . . TAC's primary mission was "to support operations of SAC . . ."[7]

The environment outlined by Worden suggests that because the bomber-operations community was in charge and dominated both the culture and the leadership of the USAF, secondary missions not directly in line with SAC's primary mission were at risk – TAC in the infancy of the USAF is a prime example of this organizational reality. However, SAC's emphasis on strategic bombing caused a further degree of myopia in the analysis of the possible political constraints and limitations that might surface in future combat environments.

In the years between the end of World War II and the Korean War, the newly established USAF charged ahead, believing in and preparing for its strategic bombardment capability. Leadership within the USAF believed that because the world had witnessed the ability of airpower to overfly enemy defenses and attack the industrial hubs needed to wage war, nations would be deterred from forcing the United States into any type of military conflict. Worden quotes William W. Momyer's recollection: "Our preoccupation with the strategic concept of war did more [than anything else] to frustrate any thinking on the employment of other aspects."[8] Further, the USAF leadership believed that the "air-atomic" (a common term used after the bombing of Japan) capability would virtually ensure that no nation would push a conflict too far.[9] However, as is often the case, the realities and lessons learned from previous conflicts do not always carry over directly into new conflicts.

In World War II, the political climate was such that President Roosevelt and then President Truman were able to call for unconditional surrender from both Germany and Japan. This pushed the Allied objectives of the war beyond a limited engagement constrained by political pressures, into an environment where nearly any combat operation or target was considered legitimate if it could be argued as being connected to the enemy's war-making capacity (unlimited war). However, in the years following World War II, the internal and domestic context was characterized by emerging political realties such as concerns regarding upsetting balances of power (specifically China and the Soviet Union); international concerns from a world population tired of war; and political constraints at home in the United States, where Americans were ready to enjoy the peace promised by victory in World War II.[10] Unfortunately, the USAF failed to appreciate or fully recognize how these

contextual realities could produce a politically constrained context for
a future war.

KOREAN WAR: 1950–1953

The USAF had proven its strategic bombardment doctrine in World
War II (an unlimited conflict); however, in the Korean War, where political constraints and neighboring belligerents limited the bombing
options, a tactical airpower requirement emerged that the USAF had
to scramble to meet. Leading up to the Korean War, the leadership and
nearly all those within the newly formed Department of Defense failed
to focus on the requirement for engagement in small scale, limited warfare and instead focused almost exclusively on large scale war.[11] When
confronted with the responsibility of engaging the North Koreans in
a politically constrained environment that required greater emphasis
on tactical rather than strategic operations, the USAF continued their
unwavering support for the strategic bombardment perspective. The
attitude within the USAF was that strategic bombardment would apply
in any context where the enemy had central industrial locations whose
destruction they would not want to risk. However, the failure of USAF
leadership (and nearly all U.S. planners) to consider the possible constraints deriving from political realties (limited war) was simply "na-
ïve."[12] The myopic focus on a world where strategic bombing would always have a place in warfare resulted in "a SAC dominated Air Force that
was building jet fighters to fly higher and faster to escort and intercept
critical bombers . . . not building technologies conducive to close air
support [supporting ground troops in battle]."[13] Confronted with new
and unforeseen political constraints that produced an environment of
limited engagement and tactical requirements that required air-to-air
superiority and close air support for ground troops, the USAF entered
into the Korean War.

Entering the war in June of 1950, the USAF believed strongly in its
strategic bombardment strategy, and it was this belief that influenced
nearly all USAF decisions. From the bomber-operations perspective, the
USAF would simply need to bomb the North into submission. Nearly

all of the USAF general officer leaders were shaped by their World War II experiences and believed that the Korean conflict could be won and decided by a massive bombardment of the North. Worden suggests these bomber leaders are best described as "absolutists" who grew up in the pre–World War II debates that centered on airpower's decisiveness. Most had read or studied Douhet either directly or indirectly, and all were aware of Billy Mitchell's zeal and arguments for airpower's dominance. To the bomber leadership within the USAF, limited war was a mistake and a strategic abuse of appropriate military capability:

> Absolutist views coincided with a strategy of annihilation that could envision only suitable total ends by way of massive means. The perspective was unambiguous, simple, and easy to embrace. If the nation decided to declare war, it should use all means in this punitive crusade, unhampered by political interference, to achieve total military victory quickly. Simply put, air absolutists believed resolute strategic bombing was decisive in and of itself.[14]

However, as Boyne points out, within the context of the Korean War much of the war-making capability of the North was coming out of China and the Soviet Union. Therefore, in order to bomb the enemy's war-making industrial hubs, targets within China and the Soviet Union would have to be selected, which would clearly expand the war – a move the Truman administration was not willing to make. Although the leadership of the USAF could simply frame the context of any engagement (including Korea) within their pre-framed structure of strategic bombardment, the failure to consider and account for the political realities and associated constraints was problematic. Had the USAF been prepared and considered the challenges of a possible limited war responsibility, a greater emphasis on tactical operations might have been organizationally encouraged. Instead, the USAF was confronted with a political context in the Korean War that they were not appropriately equipped nor organizationally aligned to take on.

Unfortunately, in the face of what was clearly a new dynamic different from the context of World War II, the USAF bomber-operations leadership failed to recognize the possible need to change or adapt. For the bomber generals in SAC, the Korean War was not a new type of limited engagement that required a strategy different from the strategic bombardment they promoted. What they saw as different was the inappropriate intervention of politics into war. The problem, as they saw it, was not with the strategic bombardment doctrine, but with the political constraints that kept the doctrine from being properly used.[15] Regardless, the political context was simply reality, and the USAF had the responsibility to act on the orders of and within the political dynamics forwarded by the Commander in Chief. Subsequently, the USAF was forced to fight a war in a way that required operations outside of their formidable and accepted strategic bombardment perspectives. Fighting a tactical air war under the organizational and cultural rubric of a bomber-operations structure caused significant challenges and resulted in the emergence of internal USAF organizational friction between the dominant SAC commanders and the subordinate TAC commanders that would last for many years.

In the early months of the conflict, because of political concerns and fear of escalation, several of the northernmost targets were kept off-limits to ensure Chinese airspace was not crossed, giving sanctuary to enemy fighter aircraft both in China and in several parts of North Korea.[16] Moreover, the USAF was so dominated by their strategic bombardment perspectives that their tactical pursuit and fighter capabilities were inadequate for the requirements confronted in the early stages of the war. The lack of appropriate consideration for tactical airpower (air superiority and close air support) became evident when U.S. airmen faced new Soviet built jet fighters: "The greatest threat to American air superiority, the Soviet-built MiG-15s, was first seen on November 1, 1950, when they attacked a flight of Mustangs and a T-6; all managed to escape, but it was immediately obvious that the MiGs were superior to any UN aircraft in the theater."[17] Although the Fifth Air Force, stationed in Japan, provided some level of tactical airpower, at the outbreak of war the USAF was at a clear technological and organizational disadvantage and "efforts to improve tactical capabilities proved too little, too late."[18]

> Although the Fifth Air Force gave the impression of aerial might located near the scene of the fighting in South Korea, this was largely an illusion. Most of its aircraft were F-80 jet fighters, which did not have the range to intervene effectively from their normal bases in Japan ... [and] airmen had little practice supporting troops in combat. *This deficiency resulted from the recent emphasis within the Air Force on strategic bombardment.*[19]

As the war developed, the USAF would be forced to put much greater emphasis on tactical requirements, even to the point of using the heavy B-29 bomber to tactically carpet bomb enemy troop locations.[20] The use of heavy bomber aircraft for tactical missions was not acceptable to many of the USAF leaders, but the realities and requirements of the war demanded their use. A leading USAF general officer responsible for air-power operations over Korea "complied but objected to the use of the big bombers against targets better suited for fighter-bombers."[21] The CSAF even met with Supreme Commander Gen MacArthur to argue the important differences between the tactical and strategic use of airpower in order to persuade MacArthur regarding the appropriate use of the B-29. "MacArthur conceded that it was indeed wasteful to use B-29s against the hard-to-locate targets normally hit by fighter-bombers, but in the present emergency he felt he had to hit the enemy with every available airplane."[22] However, "[Air Force] Generals Walker, Stratemeyer, and Partridge all insisted that the B-29s be used only against known targets, no matter how serious the emergency; dumping bombs blindly onto the countryside was not likely to do any good."[23]

This conflict regarding the proper use of heavy bombers, weighed against the real-time requirement for tactical capabilities, suggests that the external pressures encountered in the early stages of the war required flexibility and diversion from the USAF standard operating procedures – a flexibility the USAF bomber community was reluctant to offer. It appears that the external exigency of a limited, politically constrained war did not balance with the internal bomber-operations culture that dominated the USAF at the beginning of the war. Important to this analysis is the observation that the emerging disequilibrium between the organizational dominance of bomber operations and the external requirements for tactical capabilities brought about the first measurable sign of organizational conflict in the newly formed USAF. Unfortunately, this was not the last challenge the USAF would face due to the discrepancy between their bomber-operations perspective and combat tactical requirements.

Although the initial lack of tactical capability at the beginning of the war was overcome with the introduction of the new F-86 Saber jet, which could match the capabilities of the MiG-15, the lack of organizational structure at the tactical level created other problems as well. Perhaps the most serious came in regard to a lack of appropriate and codified tactical command and control. Going into the Korean War, the USAF internally lacked not only a tactical organizational capability, but also a coordinated unity of command agreement with the other services. Although an established "coordination control" agreement for Korea was designed to effectively focus airpower across the theater of operations, the Navy chose only to see the word "coordination," while the Air Force saw only the word "control."[24] Regarding the coordination control directive for Korean air operations, Robert Futrell writes:

> Hardly was this directive issued than Air Force officers discovered that the magic formula of "coordination control" had no officially assigned meaning. It meant one thing to FEAF [Far East Air Forces] and quite another thing to NavFE [Naval Forces Far East], and, although asked to give some clarification, CINCFE [Commander-in-Chief Far East] never saw fit to explain just what "coordination control" did mean. Time itself would give some meaning to the newly coined phrase, but until it did so there would be differences of opinion, misunderstandings of channels of communications, and disagreements over the wordings of important operations orders.[25]

As the war progressed, the Navy would only participate in air operations when it believed the operation fit into its own battle objectives.[26] However, the lack of centralized control and the neglect of unity among airpower leaders at the tactical level improved with the emergence of the Joint Operations Center (JOC).

The JOC was formed in Korea as early as July of 1950; although numerous communication and doctrinal problems kept it from being immediately effective, the JOC eventually became an important airpower command and control organizational center. The "center was intended to facilitate the coordination of air and ground operations in the theater."[27] Because close air support characterized much of the air operations in the Korean conflict, the JOC's intended design was to control that process. Once again, however, there were considerable differences between what the Navy believed "close air support" meant and subsequently required, and what the Air Force believed it meant.[28]

Unfortunately, the demands of war were often overshadowed by the continued disagreements over service roles and missions. Significant pre-war organizational structure that could guide tactical air operations in the war among the services was nearly nonexistent; the ramifications of this lack of organizational consideration were problematic throughout the Korean conflict.[29] The pre-war overemphasis in developing a dominant strategic bombing organizational structure left the USAF without the required tactical command and control requirements that could govern airpower responsibilities in Korea. In this regard, and for the purpose of this analysis, the external event of the Korean War appears to have introduced disequilibrium regarding bomber versus fighter organizational command and control requirements.

The challenges regarding a lack of appropriate tactical airpower technology and organizational control in the Korean War did not keep the overall actions of airpower from being vitally important to the outcome. As Boyne describes the situation:

> Although airpower did not win the war for the United Nations, it certainly prevented defeat. In essence, the United Nations was not willing to commit the millions of troops that would have been necessary to win a ground war and relied upon airpower to contain the Communist forces. For their part, the enemy realized that without air superiority, it could never win the war through its massive advantage in numbers on the ground. Airpower had brought about the tactical stalemate that permitted the armistice to be negotiated.[30]

However, perhaps the most insightful comment offered by Boyne in his analysis of airpower during the Korean War is captured in the last sentence concluding his historical review: "The effects of the Korean War would be felt throughout the world for many years, *not least in the very organizational makeup of the United States Air Force.*"[31]

According to Worden, there were two major consequences the USAF faced following the Korean War. The first was that a new group of younger airpower officers emerged that had little if any World War II experience. Furthermore, much of the airpower operations in the war were at the tactical level and were within the fighter community rather than the strategic bomber community. Although the long-term ramifications of this emerging new group would not be fully felt until they reached the senior officer level in later years, the new perspective resulting from experiences in a limited war environment clearly differed from the status quo bomber-operations perspective held by the senior USAF leaders at the end of the war in 1953. Second, Worden points out that "the Korean

War heightened a growing split between the bomber and fighter communities" from both an operational and an organizational perspective.[32]
However, because SAC remained the dominant culture after the war,
enjoying the greatest degree of influence within the USAF, little would
change other than a formal recognition of TAC and its role in Korea. As
a result, "By 1953 TAC and SAC began to march farther apart institution-
ally and philosophically."[33]

The dominance of SAC through its control of all aspects of USAF
organization, both during and immediately following the war, cannot
be disputed. As Thompson points out, the expansion of SAC relative to
all other subordinate groups within the USAF was stark:

> Deterrence continued to form the keystone of national military policy and
> the Strategic Air Command, as the principal deterrent, tended to attract the
> best the Air Force had. Numbers as well as quality reflected the importance of
> the command, which during the Korean War acquired more men and newer
> aircraft, even though none of the organization's first-line strategic bombardment
> squadrons took part in the fighting. LeMay, who led the Strategic Air Command
> throughout the war, carefully honed the cutting edge of the atomic strike force
> and provided just a few groups of B-29s, equipped solely for conventional
> warfare, to form the Bomber Command of the Far East Air Forces. Despite the
> limited participation in the fighting . . . the Strategic Air Command increased
> during the fighting from not quite 59,000 officers and enlisted men to more than
> 153,000, a rate of growth that slightly exceeded the overall increase in the Air
> Force from 411,000 to 978,000.[34]

Although TAC had performed with tremendous skill and had overcome
significant technological and organizational shortfalls, SAC would continue to call the shots and determine the organizational requirements
of the USAF.

BOMBER ORGANIZATIONAL DOMINANCE: 1953–1965

Following the end of the Korean War, the leadership within the USAF
continued on their quest to build SAC into the most powerful and lethal
military organization possible. The challenges brought on by the politically constrained limited war that characterized the Korean engagement
were no longer at the forefront of the USAF, and SAC leaders could now
spend all their time and resources building a strategic bombardment

force. Fortunately for the USAF and SAC in particular, President Eisenhower perceived the marriage between airpower and nuclear bombs to offer tremendous deterrence capability. The catalyst that propelled SAC to new heights was the Soviet Union's August 20, 1953, detonation of a thermonuclear device. With the knowledge that the Soviet Union had a nuclear bomb capability and the clear message in the Korean War that the Soviets (and Communists in general) would willingly fight against the United States, the Cold War began with SAC squarely at the top.

Following the Soviet detonation in 1953, the National Security Council under the leadership of President Eisenhower "directed that the nation's first line of defense should be an air atomic strike force, one that would deter the Soviet Union from attacking."[35] Eisenhower presented his "New Look" plan to Congress, which passed appropriate legislation that began the process of building a nuclear deterrent force. Per Eisenhower's guidance, the USAF would receive the greatest share of the defense budget, the Navy second, and the Army the least. The New Look involved a codified plan of action that prepared the military, industry, and organizational processes across the government for a deterrence strategy that would keep the Soviets at bay.[36] Furthermore,

> the New Look, which emphasized the threat of massive retaliation, not only incorporated the view that airpower could deliver a genuine paralyzing blow but also assumed that the Soviet Union, considered the master of the communist world, shared this belief and would react accordingly when menaced by the overwhelming power of the Strategic Air Command. In this scheme of things, the Air Force was dominant among the military services and the *Strategic Air Command ascendant within the Air Force*.[37]

Within this emphasis on deterrence and nuclear strike, SAC grew in both stature and numbers. In 1953, SAC had approximately 158,000 officers and enlisted men, and by 1961 that figure grew to over 254,000 while the overall Air Force dropped in numbers from 978,000 to 815,000.[38] Considering the overwhelming support from the president and both total dollars and numbers of personnel, SAC and the perspective of strategic bombardment at this point in Period Two were clearly in charge.

Unfortunately, the lessons learned from the Korean War regarding the need for tactical capability were lost in the shadow of SAC and the New Look, which emphasized massive destruction as a form of national deterrence. In this regard, SAC and the strategic bombardment perspective continued to dominate USAF organizational structure. In fact,

> even while the Korean War raged, and long before the "New Look" called for it, the U.S. Air Force was firmly focused on the task of making the Strategic Air Command's bomber fleet so powerful that it would deter the Soviet Union from aggression. Hard internal decisions were made relative to the scope of effort to be applied in Korea, the allocation of resources to be spent on air defense [tactical capabilities], and, perhaps the most contentious of all problems, the amount to be spent on the Tactical Air Command. [Leaders of both SAC and TAC] had a thinly veiled hostility of long standing.[39]

Although the Korean War escalated the need for tactical capabilities, "Within the Air Force, the natural rival of the Strategic Air Command was the Tactical Air Command."[40] As SAC continued to grow and build its influence, TAC had to fight for everything it needed. In nearly all cases, TAC was authorized expansion only when this could be tied directly to a supportive role with SAC. "During the decade, the organizations came to share the nuclear mission, though not always harmoniously."[41]

An additional problem developed that further separated the elite SAC officers from the rest of the non-SAC officers. Under the leadership of Gen LeMay, a "spot promotion" system was established that commanders (especially LeMay) could use to promote a SAC officer up one or even two ranks immediately. This opportunity was a tremendous motivator for those in SAC, but it further strengthened the disdain of those not in SAC who were not given spot promotion opportunities (TAC in particular). The spot promotion reinforced the in-group versus out-group dynamics building within the organizational context of the USAF. Not only was there a philosophical disagreement as to the importance of strategic and tactical capabilities, there was an unbalanced dynamic between how personnel in and out of SAC were treated. Within this environment, the developing and consequential rift between the two internal cultures of bombers versus fighters continued to grow.

Many of the Korean War senior officers who participated in the tactical operations of the war believed that TAC should be given equal status with SAC (an argument reminiscent of Army versus airmen).[42] When significant decisions were debated regarding how the United

States should deal with world issues that involved possible military engagement, SAC wanted only to talk in terms of their massive retaliation doctrine – an argument that fit neatly into their capabilities. TAC commanders, however, understood the realities of limited wars, territorial disputes, internal civil wars, and conflict based on divergent political perspectives. Many of the TAC leaders did not believe that a massive strike with nuclear bombs should be the solution to conflicts with clear, limited aims. One such debate took place in 1954 with respect to the United States becoming involved in the French conflict in Vietnam:

> Ho Chi Minh's communist Vietminh had surrounded the French forces at Dien Bien Phu in northern Vietnam in the spring of 1954, and France called on the United States for help. General LeMay quickly drew up plans and desired to "up the ante" with his superior SAC. General Twining [CSAF] favored a onetime atomic strike with three small atomic weapons: "You could take all day to drop a bomb, make sure you put it in the right place . . . and clean those Commies out of there and the band could play the 'Marseillaise' and the French could come marching out . . . in great shape." However, pragmatic general Earle E. Partridge, commander of FEAF and a fighter general with extensive experience in the European theater of World War II as well as the Korean war, had a different view. As the theater commander, he recognized that "this is basically a civil war, with pacification and unification (as opposed to destruction) being the prime objective. Air operations, without the required political and psychological programs, can be regarded only as destructive." This difference of opinion among generals reflected the philosophical difference growing within the Air Force between many in the strategic and tactical communities.[43]

The differing perspectives as to how wars in different context should be orchestrated and carried out could not be more stark. However, although SAC held nearly all the cards and would win nearly any debate based on numbers and position alone, the voice of the TAC officers (both senior and junior) were becoming louder and more demanding of attention.

Referring to possibly reorganizing TAC to carry a larger and more autonomous role in global security, Vice Chief of Staff Gen White acknowledged in 1955 that "our tactical air forces, with enormous firepower, global mobility, operational invulnerability and versatility, have become a deterrent to aggression and a decisive force in war. As such, our Tactical Air Command assumes a place alongside our Strategic Air Command as a potent force for peace."[44] However, it appears clear that this sentiment regarding the importance of TAC was more rhetorical and aimed at encouraging TAC personnel than it was reinforcement for new organizational considerations. Worden goes on to assert that TAC "remained underfunded and poorly supported" for some time.[45]

In terms of TAC receiving and developing new research and development funds, SAC clearly limited any progress. "SAC had complete dominance in the selection of new technologies, and usually the best TAC could do was to accept SAC rejects."[46] By late 1959, TAC Commander Gen Weyland went so far as to suggest that TAC could not support the mission it was called to support. Weyland, at his retirement later in 1959, suggested that "the Pentagon's preoccupation with strategic bombing and long-range missiles may soon leave us unprepared to fight a limited war."[47] Furthermore, as Worden points out with measurable evidence, "SAC received clear budgetary, procurement, doctrinal, and personnel preference" throughout the 1950s and mid-1960s.[48] SAC dominance overwhelmed USAF organizational structure such that by 1962, "SAC's methods had become Air Force methods."[49] According to Builder,

> Strategic Air Command was being forged into a complex of forces, *culture,* plans, bases, and doctrine that would dominate the Air Force and strategic thinking for almost two decades, worldwide. LeMay's SAC would own the Air Force; SAC *was* the Air Force; and SAC was the world's most awesome and respected military force.[50]

The consequence of such a dominant, one-sided relationship, such clear divergence in perspectives, and the observable and vocal disagreement between SAC and TAC general officers prompted one Air Force observer to suggest that "In the early sixties SAC and TAC were like two rattlesnakes. They would hardly talk to each other."[51] Furthermore, the dysfunctional relationship between SAC and TAC had serious operational consequences in that a myopic perspective regarding strategic bombing at the expense of all other airpower capabilities affected *unity of command* – a codified element in the strategy of modern warfare:

> The SAC dominated Air Force consumed itself so much with its chief challenges – the growing nuclear target list, the missile threat, alerts, and dispersals – that it had little time for conventional or nonstrategic considerations . . . the monolithic mind-set of bomber generals divided the Air Force into SAC and all others, undermining the indivisibility of airpower . . . by the early 1960s . . . bombers remained at the top of the Air Force's procurement list.[52]

Within this environment characterizing the 1950s and early 1960s, the organizational structure of the USAF was clearly dominated by the bomber-operations perspective.

The fighter-operations subgroup that existed in TAC did not see itself as a second-class group, although they knew the USAF did. An interview with Maj John Cotter (retired), conducted in December of 2009, revealed a number of interesting and insightful experiences. Cotter was drafted into the USAF in 1952 in support of the Korean War effort; however, because he enrolled in college, he received a waiver and did not enter service until 1956, as an officer. As a trained navigator, he should have been assigned to a SAC aircraft; however, due to a number of administrative events Cotter was sent to work for TAC. During his time in TAC Cotter described what he called the "fighter-pilot syndrome," where all fighter pilots shared a common narcissistic attitude and openly portrayed their own in-group versus out-group dynamic (you were either a fighter pilot or you were not). Cotter suggested that most fighter pilots considered themselves "superior" to other pilots . . . especially SAC bomber pilots. This insight from a primary source regarding the group dynamics of those in TAC is important to note; understanding the dynamics between the two groups of TAC, and SAC and the impact these two groups had on USAF culture in the 1950s and 1960s, is paramount to understanding how each group evolved and eventually affected the organizational structure of the USAF in Period Two. Cotter's observations of a strong "self-identity" for those who were fighter pilots suggests not only that TAC was voicing discontent as to its organizational position and relevance, but also that it had the characteristics of an emerging and formidable culture that could challenge the superiority of SAC (beliefs, values, norms, self-identity). At this point in the analysis of Period Two, the missing element that might offer TAC and its fighter-operations personnel greater opportunity appears to be an external event that could highlight their relevance and force greater attention (resources, personnel, technology, etc.).

For the purpose of this analysis, tracing the conflict (both internally and externally driven) between the two opposing perspectives of strategic versus tactical capabilities (bombers versus fighters) leads to the conclusion that the USAF was dominated by the bomber culture and

SAC organizational scheme, but that TAC, as an emerging subgroup, was continuing to push its agenda and requests for greater emphasis. This struggle between the dominant status quo and the emerging subgroup parallels similar struggles between the Army ground-operations leadership and the emerging subgroup of airmen witnessed in the Period One analysis. Although the historical record shows that SAC was clearly dominant, the mere presence of and continued call by TAC leadership for greater recognition and development posed a challenge to the accepted USAF bomber-operations culture and bomber-operations leadership.

6

BOMBER DECLINE: 1965–1992

IN THE YEARS LEADING UP TO THE VIETNAM WAR, SAC WAS clearly the dominating force behind all airpower organizational and operational decisions. However, as previously described, TAC and the fighter perspective continued to call for greater resourcing, developed scenario-based arguments in a limited war framework that required tactical capabilities, and refused to allow SAC's dominance to silence their views. Furthermore, with the advent of Kennedy's "Flexible Response" approach to foreign conflicts, the USAF was being pressured to develop more operational options than the traditional deterrence-based massive retaliation strategy of SAC and the bomber-operations advocates. As the Vietnam War emerged, it became clear that a limited war characterized by significant political constraints was developing. Dennis Drew, a professor and widely recognized expert on airpower in Vietnam, offered the following assessment of early USAF planning for operations in Vietnam:

> When planning for full-scale intervention by US airpower began, it focused on North Vietnam rather than the struggle in the South. The original Air Force plan called for a classic strategic bombing campaign against the so-called 94-target list, designed, among other things, to destroy "North Vietnam's capacity to continue as an industrially viable state." Such was not to be, at least not to the degree that the US airmen envisioned an aerial "blitzkrieg" against North Vietnam. Fears of escalation, Chinese intervention, and even nuclear confrontation with the Soviet Union convinced the political leadership that a "slow squeeze" was more appropriate than aerial blitzkrieg.[1]

Moreover, within the new Flexible Response policy and the limited war characteristics of Vietnam, the USAF was called to perform expanded tactical operations including close air support, interdiction, surveillance, and air-to-air combat – roles and missions well outside of SAC's traditional and focused capability.

The challenge for SAC to respond to this emerging environment was extremely difficult. Worden (1998) offers that fighter leadership at the time "complained of 'the curse of bigness,' which promoted a 'status quo attitude' and a tendency to hold what we have rather than risk untested organizational and doctrinal changes."[2] The fighter-operations community was not alone in this perception. An independent audit of the USAF (interestingly called for by the newly appointed CSAF Gen Curtis LeMay) suggested that "today there is little evidence of any substantive conceptual change nor is the Air Staff now organized so as to best generate and process proposals for change" and, further, that the Air Force had "defensive, status quo, reactionary positions on most issues."[3] It was from studies such as these that the Kennedy administration developed their Flexible Response policy and pressured the Department of Defense to change:

> Kennedy's new national defense policy of Flexible Response challenged the Department of Defense to bolster conventional and counterinsurgency capabilities to master the full spectrum of warfare. Kennedy wanted more options to achieve political objectives. He desired survivable, flexible, and cost-effective forces and weapons whose judicious use could send effective political signals, preserve maximum political options, and retain initiative at all levels of warfare. He desired a close, cooperative relationship between the State and Defense Departments to achieve a more coherent policy.[4]

The DoD under the leadership of Secretary McNamara wasted no time in pressuring (forcing) the services to develop new "flexible" capabilities. Of all the services, the leadership of the USAF under the guidance and dominance of SAC was the most combative of these new initiatives.

Of significant insight for this work is Worden's observation that "the Air Force self-image and definition of purpose seemed directly challenged."[5] He further suggests that

> the senior World War II generation had deep emotional roots in this doctrine [strategic bombardment], and the perceived revolutionary change facing them threatened who they were and what they had stood for ... They perceived the threat of doctrinal change as sacrificing a method they had proven with great investment, all for something unproven and championed by young civilians. The senior cohort generally held a suspicious attitude towards civilian defense analysts and intellectuals as well as OSD civilians.[6]

Such a reaction to the new emerging policies – an emotional perception of threat to self-identity – is characteristic of a challenge to one's
culture (beliefs, values, and standard and accepted procedures). In fact,
in an interview with then Secretary of the Air Force Zuckert, the Secretary explained that "to try to change the culture of an organization that
had been the dominant defense organization throughout the 1950s was
not easy."[7] These observations clearly suggest a direct challenge to the
bomber-operations culture. This environment greatly upset the CSAF
Gen LeMay, widely regarded as the father of SAC, and resulted in the
development of serious ill-will between USAF leadership, DoD, and the
administration. However, the new CSAF, Gen John McConnell, who
replaced LeMay in February of 1965, would attempt to ameliorate the
divisions created by his predecessor.

It important to observe that since the inception of the USAF as an
independent force, the CSAF position was dominated by a bomber-operations perspective; at no time was this truer than the appointment of
Gen Curtis LeMay. However, with the new Flexible Response outlined
by the Kennedy and later Johnson administrations and with the pressures from DoD for the services to develop and offer limited war capabilities, new CSAF McConnell was appointed to the top USAF position.
Remarkably, Gen McConnell had fighter pilot experience and a much
more flexible view of TAC than his predecessor. With the appointment of
McConnell, a clear message was sent to the USAF – it was time to change.
Fortunately for the USAF,

> The new chief hoped his friendship with the president, as well as his political
> acumen, would serve the interests of the Air Force better. He realized that the
> divisiveness and some archaic methods had to change if the Air Force were
> to regain its sway. [He] desired to widen the perspective of the Air Force....
> Broadening and reunification became a top priority; the challenges of Vietnam
> would provide the opportunity.[8]

The challenge and reaction to the bomber-operations culture, McConnell's desire to "widen the perspective of the Air Force," and the catalyst
for change that the Vietnam War would provide (as Worden observes)
together offer direct support for the modeling that suggests a correlation among leadership, culture, and external pressures in regard to organizational change. At this point in the analysis of Period Two a clear

emerging transformation between the bomber-operations and fighter-operations perspectives can be observed.[9]

As the model suggests, organizational change is slow; however, the trio of a changing culture, leadership, and external exigencies starts the process. Although the CSAF leadership within the Air Force was no longer in the hands of a fully dedicated bomber pilot, and although external forces were demanding a significant change to the operational and organizational structures within the USAF, the dominant SAC generals spread throughout the key leadership positions within the USAF remained unchanged:

> SAC's institutional imperative for nuclear war was amplified by senior absolutists dominating SAC who strongly resisted committing resources to Southeast Asia ... SAC commander Gen Power told the Air Staff not to "talk to me about that; that's not our life. That's not our business. We don't want to get in the business of dropping any conventional bombs. We are in the nuclear business, and we want to stay there." The feeling permeated the SAC staff.[10]

Furthermore, SAC's deputy director of plans is quoted as saying that "he would have put anyone in a straight jacket [sic] who had told him a few weeks before that he would be using B-52s to drop iron bombs on guerrillas in Vietnam."[11] The internal and external pressures of "the Vietnam challenge slowly eroded the traditional insularity and rigidity of SAC."[12] According to Trest,

> post-Korean nuclear thinking was evident in the decision to undertake this campaign of graduated response against North Vietnam, placing the Air Force in the untenable position of conducting conventional strike operations with a nuclear-oriented doctrine and aircraft designed for tactical nuclear operations against targets with little or no strategic value.[13]

The result of this disequilibrium between the internal perspectives and the external requirements associated with the Vietnam War is best outlined by Builder:

> The crisis came in 1965 when the United States entered the Vietnam War and the bombing of North Vietnam began. American airpower doctrine was found to be bankrupt in Vietnam because its underlying assumptions were untrue in that situation. Strategic bombing doctrine assumed that all U.S. wars would be unlimited wars fought to destroy the enemy and that America's enemies would be modern, industrialized states. Both assumptions were crucial to strategic bombing doctrine. They were reasonable and valid assumptions in the 1920s and

1930s, but invalid in the 1960s in the age of limited warfare in the third world. The results were frustration, ineffective bombing, wasted blood and treasure, and eventually the renaming of Saigon to Ho Chi Minh City.[14]

However, the SAC leadership argued that effective strategic bombing of the North would have ended the war in 1965 and saved the lives of over 50,000 U.S. service personnel. Unfortunately, the political realities did not warrant the operations that SAC leadership demanded. The disequilibrium between the internal perspectives and the external realities (regardless of who or what was right or wrong) frustrated the USAF organizational structure.

As the war progressed, a major new dynamic emerged that further challenged the traditional bomber-operations leadership within the USAF. The development of precision guided munitions (PGM) gave fighter-type aircraft the first opportunity to strike strategic targets. In fact, the capability of even the earliest PGMs carried by fighter-type aircraft was superior in terms of accuracy to anything that the World War II bomber pilots could have accomplished. With the advent of this new bomb-dropping precision capability, TAC expanded their missions and roles to include strategic bombardment without sacrificing their tactical capabilities. As Worden contends, "Previously constrained to lesser missions, fighters with air refueling and PGM were gaining access to the 'decisive' and sacred mission of strategic bombing."[15] In a summary of the major airpower lessons taken from the Vietnam War, Worden suggests that "the real lesson [from Vietnam] for the future of strategic bombing had been exhibited by the fighter-bombers. They had demonstrated greater versatility, survivability, and the ability finally to achieve that long-elusive 'precision' strategic bombing – a capability particularly relevant to limited war."[16]

Throughout the war, the leadership in SAC continually complained that the Vietnam War was the wrong war at the wrong time, fought in the wrong way, and beyond the deterrence strategy and doctrine that defined nearly all USAF operations. War planners outside the military argued that the underlying assumptions of the USAF bombing doctrine were flawed, in that North Vietnam was not an industrialized country and the objective of the war was not the destruction of the North but the establishment of Vietnam under a non-Communist government both of which were not conducive to a punitive or massive destruction campaign.[17]

However, in terms of this work, the most important insights to come out of the Vietnam experience can be summarized in six observations:

1. Nuclear deterrence under the banner of the Cold War would not decrease in importance; however, tactical and flexible operations well below the level of nuclear war would rise in both influence and operational necessity.
2. External forces (presidential policy and DoD initiatives) resulted in a decrease of SAC bomber-operations dominance and an increase of TAC fighter-operations authority.
3. Fighting a limited, politically constrained war was a reality the Air Force would have to be prepared to accept.
4. The advent of PGM technology afforded TAC a role in decisive bombing operations at the strategic level.
5. The disequilibrium between USAF capabilities and external responsibilities was codified, and organizational changes would be required.
6. Combat airpower experience coming out of the war was internalized predominantly by TAC officers who would later rise to senior USAF positions.

It is clear that the external event of the Vietnam War had tremendous influence on USAF organization. While before the war the dominance of the bomber-operations perspective was total, the post-war Air Force gave considerably more credence and authority to the fighter-operations perspective. Within the analysis of Period Two, this time frame is considered a transformational point, at which internal culture and leadership are no longer dominated by a single entity (SAC).

POST-VIETNAM TO THE FALL OF THE SOVIET UNION: 1975–1989

In the years following the Vietnam War, all of the U.S. military services were faced with new domestic challenges, fiscal realities, and a continued

concern regarding the Soviet Union and nuclear war. The political realities witnessed in the Vietnam War, although considered inappropriate by
many in and out of the military, forced the U.S. military to redefine and
widen the spectrum of war in which they might be called upon to engage.
The USAF, now acknowledging its responsibility to provide operational
capability in limited war as well as the continuing nuclear posture that
characterized the Cold War, began the process of numerous organizational changes in order to meet the emerging requirements. The historical record outlining USAF initiatives and changes between 1975 and 1989
offers important data in the analysis and assessment of organizational
change during Period Two. Borrowing the words of Worden's 1998 book
title, these years in the history of the USAF can best be called the "Rise
of the Fighter Generals."[18]

Following the war, USAF CSAF Gen David Jones commented, "Post-
Vietnam was a traumatic period where it was clear that a lot of things had
to change . . . It was a time of some real fundamental looking at where we
[the USAF] were going and to try and rebuild confidence in ourselves,
in the country, and in the military."[19] The Vietnam War as an external
event forced the USAF to reexamine its vision, mission, and overall organizational structure. The tactical requirements of a limited, politically constrained conflict, the emergence of PGMs, which opened the
door for fighter-based strategic bombing, and the fighter leadership that
dominated the combat experiences in the war all coalesced to force organizational change. However, due in large part to the continued nuclear
threat and the ongoing Cold War responsibilities that remained a large
part of the USAF mission – a SAC responsibility – this change fell short
of driving major organizational restructuring. Although SAC would continue to drive and determine much of the USAF organizational directives, TAC was no longer in their shadow. USAF changes over the next
fifteen years would continue to highlight and increase the prestige and
authority of TAC.

An interview conducted at Air University with Col Steven Chiabotti
(retired) revealed several important insights from his early career experiences.[20] Chiabotti, who entered the USAF in 1968, asserted that following the Vietnam War, "the Air Force was in the process of changing from
a bomber to a fighter dominant organization." He further recalled that

the "fighter dominant culture had not yet taken place completely but it was clearly in the process." Throughout the late 1970s, pilots graduating from pilot training still believed that the best place to build an effective career was in SAC; however, many pilots went into TAC with the understanding that the flying would be more exciting but the career opportunities might be limited when compared to being a bomber pilot. Chiabotti recalled that this paradigm began to change in the early 1980s. Chiabotti offered that "TAC had a reputation for eating their own" and that entering the world of TAC required one to "buy into the fighter culture or die trying." His perspective outlined a bifurcation between the bomber and fighter communities that was often hostile and combative.

As TAC began to gain more authority and relevance as a community equal in importance with SAC, the loss of power realized by the SAC leadership of the time created tensions that were counterproductive organizationally. The internal dynamics between the decreasing SAC culture and the increasing TAC culture (in terms of influence and authority) produced an internal disequilibrium that would eventually require both recognition and solution in order for the USAF to appropriately advance organizationally. As Chiabotti suggested, the years leading up to the fall of the Soviet Union chipped away at the traditional bomber-operations dominance and replaced it with an emerging fighter-operations dominance. Many of the small, incremental changes came in identifiable phases throughout this time frame.

According to Boyne, there are phases that the USAF went through in the years following the war. The first he calls "Rebuilding from Within: 1973–1976," outlining how even in the last few years of the war, the USAF began making organizational changes within. The USAF supported the end of a draft and encouraged the all-volunteer force. Leadership further began integrating a "Total Force" organizational scheme, where the USAF Reserves and National Guard would hold a more formal and integrated posture within the active duty USAF hierarchy. Finally, during this time period, the USAF began the process of analyzing procurement needs for the future of airpower. At the center of much of the discussion was the need for improved and more capable fighter aircraft.[21]

The next time period Boyne calls the "Difficult Years: 1976–1980." Much of the turmoil in this time period was the result of a contentious and often combative relationship between the U.S. military and the Carter administration. President Carter, upon taking office, cancelled the USAF B-1 bomber program and called for a massive reduction in the nuclear triad arsenal. As the keeper of much of the nation's nuclear posture, SAC was clearly a target of this new policy. The combination of the TAC fighter-operations realties that came out of the Vietnam experience with an administration that withdrew the foundational support enjoyed by SAC as the "Keeper of Peace" set the stage for continued organizational change within the USAF and DoD in general: SAC continued to decrease in authority and influence, while TAC continued to increase.[22] It was during these years that the new F-15 air superiority fighter came into active service. The capability of the new Eagle was far superior to anything the USAF had in Vietnam and would become the backbone of the USAF future frontline fighter force. Combined with exponentially improved PGMs, the F-15 was produced in both an air-to-air and an air-to-ground version (F-15C and F-15E respectively). The F-15 provided TAC with the ability to gain and maintain air superiority over an enemy (control the sky over the battle space), target with precision strategic locations deep within the enemy's territories, and refuel with the KC-135 for extended range and aloft durations. These capabilities provided exceptional flexibility to DoD planners and USAF leadership for nearly all considerations of what might be expected in the years to come.[23]

Also during these formative years, the F-16 Fighting Falcon became operational. The F-16 was designed as a low-cost, highly flexible fighter that could win the air-to-air battle but also provide significant air-to-ground capabilities. Although much smaller than the F-15 (both in size and cost), the F-16 was designed to provide a mass production opportunity with contracts offered to numerous U.S. allies throughout the world. The F-16, like the F-15, was a technological jump that significantly increased the capabilities of TAC at both the tactical and strategic levels of war. In the shadow of all this new and impressive innovation within TAC, SAC continued to stand alert with its aging (1950s) B-52s and nearly three-decades-old doctrine.

Boyne calls the next of his time periods the "Years of Plenty: 1981–1985." It was President Ronald Reagan who campaigned on and promised to renew the strength and posture of the U.S. military. Reagan brought back the new B-1 bomber program as well as a number of initiatives that flooded DoD with the opportunity to expand. USAF leadership's focus during this time was modernization, where the all-volunteer force (personnel), aging equipment (readiness), and standard operating procedures (doctrine) were all targets for extensive review and improvement. Fiscal budgets allowed for a number of emerging research and development studies to go forward, alongside significant increases in basing infrastructure (housing, services, work centers, family advocacy centers, etc.). All of these initiatives took away much of the rigor and stringent dominance of a once-authoritarian SAC whose main focus was on building and preparing for a nuclear confrontation with the Soviets. Although SAC continued to retain its strategic bombing mission and nuclear deterrence still hallmarked the nation's relationship with the Soviets, the understanding and subsequent changes required of modernization brought considerable opportunity to nearly all USAF agencies outside of SAC. No longer did budget meeting and procurement talks center on securing and advancing SAC's roles and missions; the USAF had a much wider spectrum of focus.[24]

The final segment outlined by Boyne he calls the "Leaner Years: 1985–1988." During this time, hard decisions were needed in order to downsize the USAF to a manageable peacetime force size. Several within the USAF leadership chain saw the decay within the Soviet Union and knew that a future without the formidable threat of the Cold War would make for a very different DoD posture. In an interview with USAF active duty Col Rob Ehlers, airpower professor at the School of Advanced Air and Space Studies, Maxwell Air Force Base, he commented that in the years leading up to the fall of the Soviet Union, the USAF began to rely more heavily on the small, faster, more survivable fighter aircraft to meet the tactical and strategic needs of the world environment. Ehlers suggested, as other had previously, that the advances in PGM technology allowed fighter aircraft to strike strategic targets at night, in any weather, and at extremely high speeds. The traditional B-52 strategic bomber, Ehlers suggested, was not capable of surviving in disputed airspace. Fighters, on the other hand, could maneuver, defend, and strike even in the context of encountering enemy aircraft. For the bombers, and for SAC overall, the fighters had successfully taken over the strategic mission and did so with increased capability that the bombers could not match. The missing element that could support a reorganization within the USAF, a reorganization that would propel the fighter pilot perspective into a place of dominance, was some type of major external event (or events). Enter the fall of the Soviet Union and the end of the Cold War.

Although the exact date for the end of the Cold War is debatable, the effect of the 1991 fall of the Soviet Union on DoD was unarguably profound. With the major external threat of a nuclear encounter with the Soviets no longer feasible and the further recognition that traditional proxy wars (where the United States supported one side and the Soviets supported the other) were no longer affordable by the Soviets, the fighter community within the USAF was in the perfect position to take over. According to Worden, the Vietnam War had produced fighter generals with combat experience primarily at the tactical level of war. Many of the SAC generals had not seen significant combat, and much of what they did experience was at the tactical level using bombardment in support of ground forces.[25] Worden adds, "In each year of the 1970s, a greater number and percentage of fighter pilots were promoted below the zone [early] than bomber pilots."[26] The combination of combat-experienced fighter generals and a core of fighter officers who were promoted ahead of their bomber peers strengthened the fighter community vis à vis the bomber community. The influence of the fighter-operations perspective had, by the late 1980s, surpassed the bomber-operations perspective, and to some extent, taken over the bomber-operations mission with PGMs. Within this context and in the presence of a dissolving Soviet Union, SAC was viewed by fighter generals as an anachronism. However, as distinct from past conflict between the two USAF groups, the fighter community now had the authority and strength to determine the consequences that the changing world security environment would bring.

As a summary to this time frame within the analysis of Period Two, the best description is presented by Worden in his concluding chapter:

> The insularity and narrow doctrinal focus of SAC on its all-important mission, coupled with the rigid discipline and centralized control demanded by that mission, hampered the dominant bomber generals' ability to contend with the realities of limited war in Vietnam ... the absolutists remained convinced of the efficacy of manned strategic bombers (despite new technologies) and assumed

a national willingness to use atomic weapons that exceeded political realities . . .
More pragmatic views that considered airpower a decisive element in joint warfare prevailed more often with the previously subordinated fighter community.
While they too believed in the massive use of airpower, they possessed better
equipment for the complex challenges of limited war in the Vietnam era.[27]

Worden makes it clear that the perspective of the dominant bomber
leaders was not in balance with the external realties of a limited, politically constrained war. Although USAF bomber leadership strongly suggested that Vietnam-type wars were not appropriate wars to be in, their
argument did not match the political authority that had the final vote.
Worden continues his analysis:

Flexible Response in the Vietnam War offered this more broadly experienced
and educated community the budget, force structure, and combat experience to
challenge for senior leadership positions. The fighter community also enjoyed
an internal climate that encouraged innovation and delegation. It demanded
aggressiveness, flexibility, and versatility – cultural characteristics more attuned
to Flexible Response and cultivating future leaders. Additionally, technology
increased the range, payload, survivability, accuracy, and flexibility of their
systems – even granting access to the sacred strategic bombing role. [SAC's]
homogeneity, as defined by shared experience, limits a total view of the institution's legitimate role. This organizational condition leans towards myopia and
monistic thinking, often manifested in a consuming focus on a purpose or mission that favors the dominant culture. When these organizations face inevitable
environmental or contextual change that challenges the existing paradigm, they
fail to recognize the need for change because of their uniformity of perspective.
This perspective also limits alternatives and adaptability to the change.[28]

Again, Worden's insight as to the dynamic that was occurring within
the core culture of the USAF is important. The bomber community had
enjoyed the highest honor in terms of dominant culture and leadership
positions. However, as the external realities of warfare changed and the
internal experiences of airmen changed (especially those in TAC), the
imbalance within the USAF became apparent.

Worden concludes by offering sage advice for how institutions, and
specifically the USAF, should and must contend with observed organizational changes:

Broad education and experience and a diversity of views at the senior executive
level are necessary to cultivate visionary leaders. These leaders must appreciate

obvious immediate concerns and manage and anticipate change with a view towards a greater, more holistic, enduring contribution to the future. These concerns include an understanding of how both internal and external forces influence the institution. For the military, battlefield victory embraces only one dimension of its professional requirements . . . military leaders must develop political and social insights to function successfully in today's security environment. In today's time of geostrategic change, as reflected by the end of the cold war, institutions that maintain broad, pluralistic, and pragmatic perspectives can better recognize and adjust to the new paradigm or realities.[29]

In Worden's work outlining the rise of the fighter leadership within the USAF, he clearly recognizes the internal and external dynamics of organizational change.

GULF WAR I AND MAJOR ORGANIZATIONAL CHANGE: 1991–1992

Although the years that followed the Vietnam War showed clear signs of a significant shift in USAF organizational structure, the timing of the Gulf War initiated by Iraq's invasion of Kuwait on August 2, 1990, delayed any major USAF organizational changes. The USAF was a central service in the war against Iraq and, as outlined in the previous segment of this analysis, the fighter community was increasingly in charge of airpower operational decisions. For the first time, TAC would be the dominant command authority responsible for planning and conducting the war from the beginning to the end of hostilities. The Gulf War offered fighter pilot leadership the opportunity to exercise their operational capabilities and to test their newly (post-Vietnam) obtained dominance.

Operations under the banner of the Gulf War are often split into two major segments: Operation Desert Shield, and Operation Desert Storm. Desert Shield primarily consisted of ensuring a rapid military presence within the Arab world in order to deter Iraq from extending its offensive into neighboring countries beyond Kuwait (Saudi Arabia specifically). The flexible and near-immediate response capability of TAC airpower provided the initial defensive cover, while a concerted and massive effort began to move the required equipment and personnel into the area in preparation of the anticipated operations required to remove Iraq from

Kuwait. Although the focus of this analysis centers on the dynamics between the bomber-operations culture and the fighter-operations culture, it is important to note that apart from the initial deterrence offered by TAC aircraft in the early weeks of Desert Shield, the mobility community (another USAF subgroup not previously mentioned) accomplished astounding airlift of personnel and equipment unmatched in speed and size:

> Supplies of all types came by airlift. Indeed, airlift was the critical factor in Desert Shield's success. Although sealift carried the bulk (approximately 85%) of the heavy equipment during Desert Shield/Storm, airlift hauled 99 percent of the personnel. The swift deployment of troops via aircraft enabled a significant combat force to be on the ground in time to forestall further Iraqi incursions southward.[30]

It is further of interest to note that while the Navy was responsible for roughly 85 percent of cargo movement to the region, the USAF provided 100 percent of all personnel and cargo in the first seven days following Iraq's invasion of Kuwait. This fact emphasizes the capability of speed and global reach that only airpower is capable of providing. However, although the mobility community deserves considerable accolades for its superior accomplishments, their performance did not produce an environment that threatened to any degree the dominance of the fighter community in terms of USAF organizational directives. In this regard, the fighter community remained the central and dominant organization that led airpower operations in the Gulf War.

Operation Desert Storm began on January 17, 1991; however, prior to military operations and direct engagement with Iraq, military planners worked day and night in preparing an Operational Plan (OPLAN) that would meet President Bush's objectives. Under the leadership of Col John Warden at the Pentagon Checkmate office, initial plans were developed that called upon airpower to dominate Iraq and force Iraqi troops out of Kuwait:

> Using new military technologies that promised to make the predictions of Douhet, Mitchell, and the AWPD-1 war planners come true, Warden's staff expected to demonstrate the decisiveness of modern airpower and fulfill America's political objectives, while essentially ignoring the Iraqi army in Kuwait. The combination of technology, doctrine, and strategy proposed in Instant Thunder

[name of plan] would impose "strategic paralysis" on Iraq and either convince
Saddam Hussein to capitulate or bring about his removal by the people of Iraq.[31]

In the planning for air operations, the most threatening aspect that airmen would have to contend with was the air defense capabilities of Iraq.
Strategic bombardment by traditional B-52s was simply not possible,
given the significant and networked layers of Iraq's air defense systems.

> Iraq's extensive air defense network consisted of radars, hardened and buried
> command and control facilities, surface-to-air missiles, interceptors, and prodi-
> gious amounts of antiaircraft artillery. It has been estimated that Iraq had 3,679
> command guidance missiles (plus an additional 7,400 shoulder-fired or mobile
> missiles), 972 antiaircraft artillery sites, 2404 guns, and 6,100 self-propelled
> guns. This network was patterned upon standard Soviet practice of an inter-
> twined, redundant, and "layered" air defense system. Baghdad's defenses, with
> 552 missiles, 380 antiaircraft artillery sites, and 1,267 guns, were so concentrated
> that it was thicker than the most heavily defended Warsaw Pact target of the
> Cold War . . . The network, however, depended almost wholly on centralized
> control, a vulnerability to be exploited.[32]

The only survivable airpower operations in the early stages of the
war would have to come from airpower systems capable of first accessing and then destroying key elements of Iraq's air defense systems. The
mission of suppression of enemy air defenses (SEAD) fell on specially
equipped fighter aircraft with the capability of detecting and destroying
key radar facilities. Furthermore, stealth fighter (F-117) aircraft capable
of access into highly defended areas were needed to destroy key command and control targets that would "blind" Iraqi defenses and cut off
their ability to communicate or receive commands from their highly
centralized structure. These initial actions would be the first step in
controlling the skies over Iraq. Not until the USAF reached a level of air
superiority (freedom to accomplish air operations without prohibitive
enemy interference) would non-fighter, heavy bomber aircraft be able to
reach and strike targets deep within Iraq's homeland.

It is vital to this analysis to acknowledge what the context outlined
above reveals. Strategic bombardment as a theory, operational mandate,
and established cultural perspective did not change in the Gulf War.
What changed was who in the USAF and what organizational system was
capable of accomplishing the strategic bombardment of Iraq. Previously,

heavy bombers were considered the panacea of strategic bombardment operations. However, with the advent of PGMs, fighter aircraft more maneuverable and survivable than heavy bombers began to take up the strategic bombardment missions. Furthermore, the exponential increase in air defense capabilities (surface-to-air missiles, antiaircraft artillery, radar, etc.) required new counter–air defense technologies in order to provide access. The SEAD mission was squarely in the hands of TAC. With specially developed aircraft that could not easily be detected by traditional radar (F-117), highly specialized s equipped with radar-seeking missiles that could detect, track, target, and destroy ground radar sites, and F-15E aircraft capable of jamming enemy radar and dropping precision munitions day or night in nearly all weather conditions, TAC had the airpower capability to access and bomb Iraqi strategic sites in the midst of exceptional antiaircraft defenses. These realties left SAC with the primary mission of dropping a nuclear bomb (a role that missiles could accomplish with less risk) or supporting ground troops in tactical engagements.

The air campaign witnessed in the Gulf War provided the last shred of needed evidence that fighter-operations capabilities (SEAD, close air support, air superiority, strategic strike, PGMs, interdiction, etc.), combined with a global reach due to air refueling, would need to cement major change from the traditionally heavy-bomber-operations organizational structure to a new fighter-operations organizational structure. Even the perspective of what constituted "strategic bombardment" had changed from the early definition supported by the pioneers of SAC. Mann suggests that

> Instant Thunder also differed significantly from the SIOP [Single Integrated Operational Plan, SAC's nuclear OPLAN], even though the latter was a strategic air campaign. Specifically, the SIOP called for the destruction of adversary nations, while Instant Thunder only aimed to create national strategic paralysis, which would allow the quick rehabilitation of Iraq after the coalition achieved its objectives. Thus, Instant Thunder entailed targeting and weaponeering procedures that differed significantly from the ones that had developed during the Cold War.[33]

TAC and the strategists within the USAF developed a strategic airpower plan, utilized the newest and most advanced fighter-operations airpower technologies, successfully operated at all levels of war (strategic, operational, tactical), and provided a decisive victory in the Gulf War as yet unseen in modern warfare. Even to this day there is tremendous debate as to whether or not the USAF and airpower alone was sufficient and decisive in the Gulf War. Regardless, there was then, and is today, no argument as to the significance and overwhelming capabilities that airpower afforded in the war. The organizational ramifications were certain: the fighter-operations community and culture would take over the organizational directives of the USAF.

Following the end of the Gulf War in February 1991, the USAF was riding high on its proven capabilities. TAC leadership knew there was no turning back to the traditional ways of SAC, and preparations for major organizational change began immediately. According to Col Ehlers, "the term heavy bomber was replaced with strategic bomber," and the ramifications for SAC could not have been clearer. Ehlers further offers that at the end of the Gulf War, USAF change was inevitable for a variety of reasons: "Strategic uncertainty after the end of the Cold War propelled fighter leadership into key positions; heavy bombers were less reliable than missiles; and survivability of fighter aircraft decreased the political risks of limited engagement." Ehlers recalls as well that the fighter general officers had a grudge against the SAC leadership for how they had been treated as second class citizens throughout the dominant years of SAC. Finally, Ehlers concludes that the Gulf War was the "culminating point" when organizational change within the USAF became certain.[34]

MAJOR ORGANIZATIONAL CHANGE: 1992

On June 1, 1992, Strategic Air Command was abolished and Air Combat Command was activated. From 1947 to 1992, the USAF was organized and dominated (to varying degrees) by SAC and the bomber-operations leadership that maintained it. However, given the external events over the years from 1947 to 1992, the changes in internal culture, and the emerging fighter-operations leadership, SAC and its traditionally dominant mission could no longer appropriately express nor reflect the needs of the new global context. In each war following World War II, tactical airpower grew in importance. Although SAC would continue to be a necessary hallmark through much of this period, by 1992 the perspectives developed from World War II had been rendered obsolete by the wars that followed. As the next section of this analysis shows, the leadership changes that occurred throughout this period equally reflect and suggest that by 1992 organizational change was certain. With the deactivation of Strategic Air Command, the era of World War II absolutists and the supremacy of the heavy bomber had come to an end. With the activation of Air Combat Command and the subsequent dominance of fighter-operations leadership throughout the USAF, a new era began.

7

THE CHANGING LEADERSHIP
OF PERIOD TWO

PREVIOUS CHAPTERS OF THIS STUDY OUTLINED THE INCRE-
mental changes from 1947 to 1992, focusing most of the analysis on the
external events and internal cultural dynamics of the period. As was
the case in the concluding analysis for Period One, in this chapter I will
present methods to measure and focus specifically on the variable of
transitional leadership. Organizational models suggest that changes in
leadership can have an influence on organizational structure; therefore,
knowing that there was significant organizational change in 1992 (as
previously presented), one should be able to trace an empirical change
in leadership throughout the period leading up to 1992. As an assessment
for this proposition, this chapter is presented in two parts. In the first
part I offer an examination of three specific timeframes within Period
Two: 1960, 1975, and 1990. At each point, an analysis of key USAF leadership positions will be examined to include the number of general officers
in key positions and their airpower primary backgrounds (SAC or TAC).
Analysis with fifteen-year increments provides data to help determine
whether any trends in the leadership change existed throughout the period. In the second part of this chapter I will present specific analysis
regarding the changing demographics and experiences of those selected
to the top Air Force leadership position – the Chief of Staff of the Air
Force. By tracing throughout the period the general officers selected
to be CSAF, one can assess what experience base was deemed to be the
most important; what specific group within the USAF was considered
dominant enough to hold the top decision-making position; and, most
importantly to this work, what changes or trends can be observed re-

garding the type and selection of the CSAF from the beginning of the period to the end. As modeling suggests, senior leadership often parallels the dominant culture within an organization. For this period's analysis, one would expect to find that a bomber-operations background characterized early CSAF officers while a transition to a fighter-operations background would dominate by the end of the period. If it can be shown that the top leadership position changes in parallel with the internal culture (as outlined in previous chapters) and ultimately reflects the dominant culture, then the correlation between changing leadership and changing culture will be an important indicator when attempting to anticipate future USAF organizational change.

PART ONE

Leadership in 1960

Following World War II and the subsequent establishment of the USAF as a separate and independent military service, the bomber community rapidly began to build the organizational structure of the USAF. As discussed earlier, in the period leading up to, during, and immediately following the Korean War, the USAF fell under the authority of SAC. Worden observes that during these early years of a bomber-operations USAF organizational structure, "SAC and TAC never were farther apart than under the *leadership of the bomber generals.*"[1] Up until the point when the Kennedy administration forwarded the Flexible Response doctrine that emphasized military operations short of nuclear war, SAC built its force with near unimpeded support and strength. Examining the leadership posture in 1960 suggests an assessment for how the USAF initially organized in the first fifteen years of independence and can further act as a baseline to determine change in leadership structure over the entire period.

Developed from the list of senior leaders in key positions,[2] figure 7.1 displays the primary airpower experience of Air Force leaders in 1960.[3] The bomber general officer leadership clearly dominates the overall senior officer representation. These percentages align with the previously offered assessment of a bomber-dominant culture at this point in the

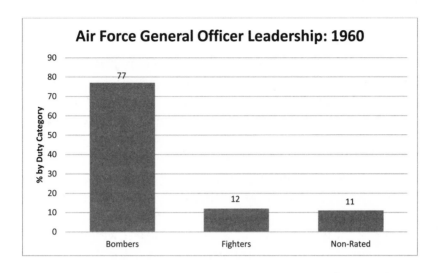

Figure 7.1

period. As organizational models suggest, leadership often reflects the dominant perspectives within an organization; in this case, it appears clear that the bomber-operations culture not only was dominant, but was reflected in who rose to the rank of general officer and who held the key leadership positions. As is the case in most organizations, those in the key leadership positions are the decision makers, and they have the greatest influence on shaping and developing the institutions structure. One can interpret these percentages to suggest that at this point in Period Two, the bomber community determined the organizational structure. Without an external event that could challenge the efficacy or relevance of the bomber culture, leadership would have no need to modify its characteristics. However, in the previous chapters I have presented evidence that the Vietnam War had significant influence on the organizational equilibrium of the USAF and that, in the fifteen or so years following 1960, the dominance of SAC was challenged by an emerging TAC. Furthermore, the external exigencies (Vietnam in particular) were shown to have had traceable influence on the internal culture of the Air Force. In light of the previously offered analysis, it appears important to examine how the leadership after 1960 may have changed in parallel with the external events and internal culture.

Leadership in 1975

The years that followed 1960 were directed in large part by the Kennedy administration's Flexible Response, which called for a wider variety of military options rather than the doctrine of traditional deterrence through exercising overwhelming force and instilling fear of annihilation. Small-scale contingencies that possessed some level of U.S. concern (often proxy conflicts between the United States and the Soviet Union) did not call for or render appropriate the massive retaliation option characterized by SAC doctrine. As the Vietnam War showed, political realties often dictate and constrain military options. In the case of the USAF, the constraints of limited war did not balance with the primary organizational structure that had been built around SAC's bomber-operations perspective. The Vietnam War required air-to-air dominance and fighter aircraft to engage and support ground troops. Furthermore, with the advent of PGMs, fighter aircraft were able to take on strategic strike missions, often in hostile airspace where the traditional heavy bomber aircraft (B-52s) could not fly without significant risk.

During the years of conflict in Vietnam, TAC officers gained significant combat experience, realized additional and important mission capabilities, and gained significantly greater relevance from leadership outside the USAF. As Builder asserts,

> the Vietnam war brought TAC into full bloom and put TAC pilots into the senior leadership of the Air Force for the first time . . . fighter aviators, who had long been suppressed by the bomber aviators under the tenets of airpower theory [strategic bombardment], were suddenly released to pursue their own interests and, as aviators who were more removed from airpower theory than their bomber brethren, eventually came to dominate the Air Force leadership.[4]

Furthermore, Worden suggests the Vietnam conflict reveals that "combat experience provided fighter pilots with a significant advantage over the bomber cohort in competing for future leadership positions in a military that prized combat and command experience."[5] As the analysis in the last section highlighted, the years from 1960 through 1975 changed the internal culture of the Air Force from a one-sided SAC-dominated service to a more balanced SAC and TAC service: by 1975 a transition occurred where TAC was no longer in the shadow of SAC; fighter-op-

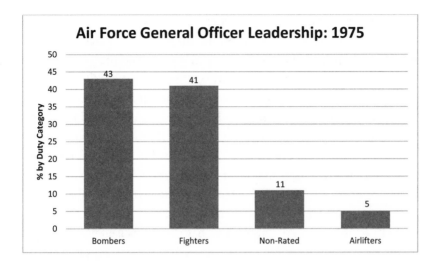

Figure 7.2

erations perspectives were openly regarded as paramount to successful airpower operations; and rising USAF leadership with the most combat experience was squarely within the fighter community.

Examination of the percentages of general officers in key leadership positions in 1975, presented in figure 7.2, shows a clear increase in fighter generals and a more balanced comparison with bomber generals. I have presented evidence in earlier chapters that the conflict between the SAC generals and the emerging TAC generals was often dysfunctional, and it was only after the external demands of the Vietnam War revealed the exigencies of tactical realties that bomber leadership was pressured to extend additional considerations to the fighter perspective. Worden offers that

> top executives supposedly stand where they sit. They comprehend well the complex nature of diverse internal dynamics [culture] which define their organization. From education and breadth of experience, they grasp how external forces influence within the organization. The struggle for . . . the leadership of the Air Force . . . differs little from that of other large institutions that attempt to cope with change.[6]

Worden further suggests of this transitional time that the successful Vietnam-era generals were those who effectively "exploited internal institutional dynamics [culture] and grasped new external demands on the military profession."[7] In this regard, from the percentages offered in figure 7.2, it appears that the fighter community and the generals who were raised within it were successful in many respects. On the other hand, Worden further suggests that the "insularity and narrow doctrinal focus of SAC on its all-important mission . . . hampered the dominant bomber generals' ability to contend with the realities of limited war in Vietnam."[8] In both cases, by 1975 the leadership within the USAF had begun to transition, and clear evidence exists to suggest that the bomber-operations leadership declined in stature and in numbers, while the fighter-operations leadership increased in both.

Although this may not necessarily have been a cause-and-effect situation, one can see the leadership changes from 1960 to 1975 as a consequence of combined external and internal changes. The external requirements impinging on the USAF in Vietnam forced an increase in and an emphasis on tactical airpower; this increase and emphasis encouraged and strengthened the internal group dynamics of the fighter community and its cultural relevance; the increased and strengthened posture of the fighter culture began to shape and demand internal fighter-operations leadership. In summary,

External Event → Internal Cultural Changes → Leadership Changes

The evidence outlined in the previous chapters suggests that the organizational change models appropriately explain and might even predict USAF institutional change.

Leadership in 1990

Over the fifteen years that followed 1975, the USAF underwent a number of important transitions. The development and procurement of the F-15 and F-16 fighter aircraft and the expansion of new PGM technology afforded the fighter community significant capability in all levels of airpower operations (tactical, operational, strategic). Additionally, the post–World War II bomber-operations absolutist general officers were

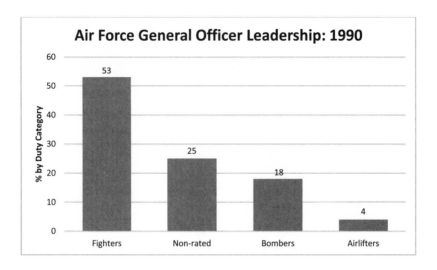

Figure 7.3

retired, and most of the combat experience within the USAF resided in those fighter pilots who drew their experience from the Vietnam War. The final external exigency was the collapse of the Soviet Union and the formal end to the Cold War. The context of a fighter-operations culture that had increased in both stature and relevance and the decline of the bomber-operations culture that was based on the Soviet threat combined to provide the fighter-operations community the path needed to dominate USAF leadership positions. The leadership posture of the general officers within the USAF in 1990 reflects the end of the Cold War but does not include the ramifications of the Gulf War. Although the culminating point driving organizational change within Period Two was determined to be the Gulf War, the leadership structure did not show significant change between 1990 and 1992. But by 1990 the dynamics and changes in leadership were almost fully representative of the overall organizational changes that were positioned to occur eighteen months later, after the Gulf War.

Figure 7.3 shows the changes that had taken place in the percentages by category of general officers over the past fifteen years since 1975. Perhaps the most striking change is not the fact there are now significantly

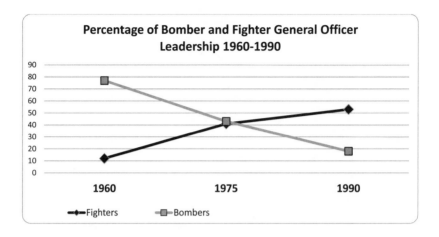

Figure 7.4

more fighter-operations general officers than bombers; rather, it is that there are even more non-rated general officers in key leadership positions than there are bomber generals. In a service that is dominated by pilots, the fact that non-rated officers (nonpilots) now hold more of the key leadership positions than the bomber pilots is significant, suggesting that the decline of the bomber-culture and the rise of fighter dominance by 1990 were nearly complete. Moreover, the Gulf War, which occurred in the months following this timeframe, further reinforced the relevance and the validity of having a fighter-dominated leadership structure.

When all three timeframes are graphed together, the change in the leadership characteristics is even more evident. Figure 7.4 illustrates the changes that occurred in the bomber-operations leadership and the fighter-operations leadership in 1960, 1975, and 1990. (Non-rated and airlift officers are not considered in the comparison). The graph suggests that the leadership developed from 1947 up to 1960 was clearly dominated by the bomber community. However, by 1975, a transition point was reached where the emerging strength of the fighter community equaled that of the bomber community. By 1990, just eighteen months prior to the known major organizational change in 1992, the percentage had nearly completely reversed from what it was at the beginning of the period. By 1990, fighter generals dominated the key leadership positions.

PART TWO

Chief of Staff United States Air Force: 1947–1992

Although the previous assessment of overall key leaders is significant for analysis, the characteristics of who fills the CSAF position can offer additional information in that the CSAF is often a reflection of the dominant culture. The CSAF is also a reflection of the leadership outside of the USAF in that DoD leadership, Congress, and the President all have an important part in determining who the CSAF will be. In this regard, what those outside the USAF believe are the most important characteristics and how they see the challenges of the world will normally be reflected in who they choose to fill the top USAF leadership position.

In a highly hierarchical organizational structure such as the USAF, it would be consistent with organizational models to see the top leadership position parallel the dominant culture within the organization and possibly even foreshadow future organizational changes. However, because the CSAF is determined by decision makers outside of the USAF, consideration is not wholly made on background and experience. As with most appointments, a common world view, personality, and previous relationships often play a major role in selection. A USAF general officer who has been an outspoken critic of certain policy is likely to be overlooked unless the administration shares in his perspective. On the other hand, a particular general officer may be in a good light with the current administration but fall out of favor when the presidency changes hands. The point here is that an examination of the primary experience base of those selected to be CSAF is important, but this perspective must remain constrained by the understanding of a complex and often politically determined context.

Notwithstanding the analytical limitations, it remains important to consider that all of those selected to hold the top position in the USAF up until 1982 were bomber pilots (with the acceptation of Hoyt Vandenberg). Although several of the chiefs had some experience with tactical aircraft (McConnell, for example), their primary responsibilities, whether in terms of flying or as a commander, was in support of a bombardment mission. Furthermore, prior to independence in 1947, nearly

all the senior leaders of the Army Air Forces were bomber pilots who
had extensive experience in World War II. From the war veterans available, the newly formed USAF naturally drew from the pool of bomber
pilots – a trend that lasted for over three decades.

The impact of having a specific subgroup within the USAF always
holding the top leadership position is an important observation. With respect to group identity and developing an "in-group" versus "out-group"
dynamic, whichever group can claim the top leadership position within
an organization has a significant and empirical advantage in terms of influence. Clark also examined the demographics of the chiefs throughout
the years since 1947. In his analysis he recognized the consistent line of
bomber-operations chiefs to hold the top position, but he further emphasized the organizational consequence this produced among subordinate
officers hoping to develop a highly successful career:

> A review of the biographies of the chiefs of staff finds that from 1947 to 1982
> every CSAF had an operational background in strategic bombers [except
> Vandenberg]. Not only were these individuals in a position to perpetuate the
> emphasis on nuclear deterrence and technology; their selection for the position
> also suggested to others that the nuclear mission was the path to the Air Force's
> senior leadership positions.[9]

As Clark points out, the appointment of only bomber pilots to the top
leadership position had more effect than simply to emphasize the nuclear
mission: it also sent a clear message that SAC was the path to a highly
successful career. However, throughout this period external challenges
outside of the USAF traditional nuclear mission continued to confront
USAF leadership. Beginning with the tactical requirements of limited
war in Korea, and further emphasized in Vietnam, the USAF was forced
to reconsider and widen its spectrum of possible conflict for which it
might be called to act. As a consequence of these external pressures
together with the emergence of PGM technology, in 1982 Gen Charles
Gabriel was appointed as CSAF. From Gabriel's appointment forward,
all those to hold the CSAF position up through 1992 were fighter pilots.
Gabriel's appointment sent a shock wave through SAC, and many within
the SAC command structure feared that the emerging organizational
changes looming within the USAF would not favor their SAC-dominated
experience base.[10]

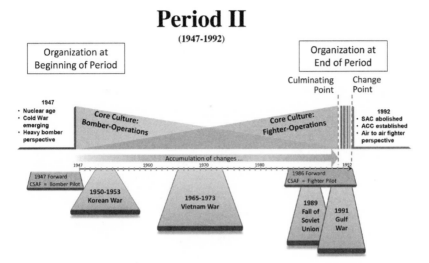

Figure 7.5

As depicted in figure 7.5, the internal changes of culture from a bomber-centric perspective to a fighter-centric perspective resulted from a series of external exigencies that drove internal changes in culture. Although in the aftermath of Vietnam the fighter community had already made significant advances relative to the bomber community, the combination of the fall of the Soviet Union and airpower's capability in the Gulf War ushered in the culminating point where major USAF organizational change was imminent.

PERIOD THREE: 1992–2030

THE PURPOSE OF PRESENTING THE PREVIOUS CHAPTERS, highlighting Periods One and Two, was to offer a historical reference for how and why the USAF has undergone organizational change in the past. Assessing how external responsibilities, internal culture, and organizational leadership all played a part in USAF organizational change will help inform and guide the analysis of current and future USAF changes. Just as the previous periods of change were presented chronologically, so too will Period Three be offered in terms of how the years unfolded. As noted from the analyses of the first two periods, a timeframe of approximately forty years passed between the beginning of the period and its end, when major USAF organizational change occurred. In order to appropriately predict future organizational changes, the research approach that effectively described and modeled the historical change in the first two periods is also used within Period Three analysis. However, two major timeframes within the period are considered: the historical portion from 1992 through 2012 and the future portion from 2013 through 2030. In this way, objective consideration can be applied to the entire period, providing USAF leadership with important insights for what changes might need to be debated today in preparation for tomorrow.

The first, the supreme, the most far-reaching act of judgment that the statesman and commander have to make is to establish . . . the kind of war on which they are embarking; neither mistaking it for, nor trying to turn it into, something that is alien to its nature.

CARL VON CLAUSEWITZ

8

FIGHTER PILOT DOMINANCE: 1992–1994

FOR USAF PERSONNEL, THE LAST FEW YEARS LEADING UP TO 1992 could not have been more challenging. The fall of the Soviet Union in 1991, the end of the Cold War, and the fighter-operations success of Gulf War I were precursors to the change the USAF would soon face in 1992. According to Boyne,

> the biggest hurdle, emotionally and organizationally, was still to come: the disestablishment of Strategic, Tactical, and Military Airlift Commands and the subsequent reorganization of their functions into new commands. Other commands were also affected, and for their members there was the same sense of uncertainty and nostalgia. But for the public at large, the loss of SAC, TAC, and MAC was almost sacrilegious.[1]

Of particular note was the deactivation of SAC, ending the formal hold that the bomber-operations community had on the USAF since its early days of independence, together with the activation of Air Combat Command (ACC), with its fighter-operations dominance, that had stood in the shadow of SAC for so many years. Important to note is that all of these events came within a three-year time frame. Officers who had a strong career developing in SAC were sidelined, and those officers who were leaders in TAC were elevated into the new ACC organizational dominance. Boyne suggests that "the net effect of a massive change entailing the transformation of three proud and distinguished commands into two new organizations is not measured merely by insignia and thoughtfulness," and, further, that the organizational change was "a visceral challenge to humans whose jobs, reputations, promotions, and futures are on the line." One of the tragedies of the reorganization, Boyne adds, is that "well-qualified people with outstanding records suddenly found themselves forced to leave."[2] Unlike the major organizational change in 1947 that brought independence to the USAF, an event celebrated by nearly all airmen, the change in 1992 formalized a clear split in the USAF – between fighter pilots and everyone else.

Although the changes associated with external events, internal culture, and leadership throughout the period helped explain the organizational change witnessed in 1992, as the analysis of Period Two clearly revealed, it remained true that integration, cooperation, and camaraderie within the overall USAF after the change were low – and in some contexts, nonexistent. Just as in the days when SAC leadership successfully "SACumized" the USAF, now the fighter community under the newly formed ACC would "TACumisize" all USAF operations. As Boyne points out, "even the last SAC commander prior to the 1992 change was a fighter pilot."[3] The dynamics within the USAF below the senior-ranking officer levels was frustrated and openly concerned about how the new fighter-operations Air Force would take shape. In fact, in the months just prior to the 1992 organizational change, a "brown paper" (anonymous essay not endorsed by the USAF) was passed around the Pentagon and spread throughout the entire service. Titled "TAC-umsizing the Air Force: The Emerging Vision of the Future," this essay was a parody presenting the fighter-pilot as the "Manly Man" that all USAF personnel should strive to emulate or worship. Commenting on the actions of the fighter operations in the Gulf War, the brown paper suggested that "those remembering the 1991 hyperwar of the desert will remember the young pilots and their younger aircraft. After all, the goal of this group is air superiority, and who else can achieve superiority but Superman himself?"[4] Moreover, this informal brown paper received considerable attention. The *Air Force Times* in November of 1991 ran a story titled "The 'Brown Paper'"; even *Defense Week* covered the story in its October 1991 issue and questioned CSAF Gen McPeak about its impact. However, the most detailed coverage came from the *Chicago Tribune*, October 4, 1991 when they ran an article titled "Report Lampoons Air Force's 'Manly Men' – Fighter Jocks."[5] All the coverage focused on the essay's point that the fighter-operations community was not only in charge but saw itself as superior to all those who were not fighter pilots. The paper further suggested that the organizational structure being developed by the newly "crowned" fighter community was designed specifically to give priority in promotion to fighter pilots and to keep the non–fighter pilots out of the leadership tracks.[6]

This in-group versus out-group dynamic could not have been more prevalent, and it was within this context that the fighter community was given full authority over the organizational construct of the USAF. Within this environment of us versus them (fighter pilots against everyone else) the new organizational structure would proceed and develop in the 1990s and early 2000s. Important to note here is that the brown paper criticizing the fighter-operations perspective was developed from unnamed subgroups (non–fighter pilots) within the USAF. The analysis reveals an emerging competition for organizational dominance at the beginning of Period Three, with the fighter-operations community contending against some other yet to be identified group. Identifying the "other group" that can eventually and potentially challenge the fighter-operations perspective will be the objective of the analysis that follows.

FROM MCPEAK TO SOMALIA: 1992–1994

In the months that followed the major reorganization of the USAF, CSAF Gen McPeak began taking significant actions that overtly and covertly enhanced the fighter-operations perspective. McPeak was "another of the group of fighter pilots that had supplanted the more bomber-oriented chiefs of the sixties and seventies," and he remained a "fighter jock" even after he became CSAF.[7] In several speeches, according to Boyne, "McPeak emphasized that the changes [he was making within the USAF] should not be regarded as a paring-down of the old Air Force, but instead as the building of a brand-new Air Force from the ground up to meet the challenges of the next century."[8]

The deactivation of the old commands and the newly established dominance of ACC were "accompanied by further changes down the administrative hierarchy."[9] Bases were now entirely commanded by those in flight suits, and nearly all were fighter pilots. McPeak further developed what he dubbed the "composite wings," where fighters, bombers, refuelers, and airlifters were all stationed together. Interestingly, it was normally a fighter pilot who was given control of these composite wings.[10] It was of increased concern to non–fighter pilot officers within these wings that their opportunity for promotion was in jeopardy.

Organizationally, the process for promotion to the higher grades (especially those beginning at the major and lieutenant colonel levels and above) was based on receiving a "definitely promote" (DP) recommendation from the senior officer on the base. However, the number of DPs available to be given out was a percentage of all those up for promotion at the time. For example, if the senior officer had ten majors who were up for promotion to lieutenant colonel, then he would be authorized 30 percent DPs (three DPs) to award among the ten officers. (Receiving the DP was a near guarantee to promotion in the primary promotion zone.) In the past, prior to the organizational development of the composite wing, bombers would compete for a DP recommendation among peers within their bomber community, and the same process went for most of the specialty groups. However, within the organizational construct of the composite wing, the senior officer with the authority to award the DPs was a fighter pilot, and his "pool" of officers was now larger due to the inclusion of non–fighter pilot officers into the calculus of DPs as a percentage of officers available to promote. From this context, more DPs by percentage were available to award; those DPs could then be given to fighter pilots rather than to the non–fighter pilots that helped to increase the DP percentages. This observation was addressed in several follow-up brown papers and was a central point of concern for the non–fighter pilot community. Furthermore according to studies conducted at Air University, "the composite wing reorganization lacked proper analysis, planning, and attention to fiscal constraints."[11] However, the records on the impact of this organizational construct are difficult to interpret or determine in that the awarding of DPs was often subjective, based on what the senior officer believed was important. Therefore, the argument was always that if fighter pilots were promoted at a higher rate in composite wings than were non–fighter pilots, it was because the fighter pilot deserved the promotion more, was considered a better officer or a harder worker, or had a greater potential for higher levels of command – all of which are highly subjective.

As is normally the case, perception is often considered reality; and for those who served during this time and were not fighter pilots, the reality was that the composite wing was a scam intended to place the fighter community in charge of all airpower. In one Air Force blog site where officers can provide their perspectives, a blogger wrote,

> Many of us recognized the "reorganization" for what it was – nothing more than a shell game, designed to preserve command billets for the pilot community. With force down-sizing after the Cold War, the Air Force lost both aircraft and units. Implementing new wing organizational structures allowed the service to retain commander's positions that would have otherwise been lost. Under one variant of the McPeak plan, virtually every wing in the Air Force was led by a brigadier general, despite the fact that colonels had been filling those positions for years. McPeak and his minions also had the bright idea of consolidating operations and maintenance functions under flying squadron commanders. Overnight, hundreds of enlisted airmen and maintenance officers were placed under the control of ops commanders [fighter pilots] who had little, if any, experience in managing aircraft repair, or the specialists who performed those tasks. As you might expect, the "merger" of maintenance and ops created numerous headaches, and more than a few maintenance officers got passed over for promotion, usually because their boss – the flying squadron commander – favored aircrew personnel in the appraisal and selection process. But, directing a larger squadron certainly looked good on a commander's resume, so the marriage of ops and maintenance continued long after McPeak's departure.[12]

This blog post was followed by a number of officers all agreeing that McPeak's plan was to enhance the promotability of fighter pilots at the expense of everyone else. Much of this argument appears to derive from perception on the part of non–fighter pilots; little to no empirical data could be found to substantiate these claims other than personal opinion of officers who experienced the composite wing reorganizational structure. However, the elements of perspective are often important in determining cultural characteristics in that beliefs are a large part of what makes up the culture of a group. In the case of non–fighter pilots who were in the USAF at the time that McPeak began constructing composite wings, they believed it was a direct assault on their potential for promotion – enhancing an us-versus-them dynamic.

Finally, in terms of the McPeak years of change, there was at least one more significant organizational conflict worth noting – the move toward a new Air Force uniform. McPeak decided that the traditional uniform that the USAF had worn for so many years no longer represented the newly emerging streamlined service.[13] He proposed, developed, and mandated a new uniform for the USAF that most believed looked too much like the Navy uniform or the uniform worn by airline pilots. The controversy and conflict brought about by the new uniform cannot be understated. Perhaps because a major element of culture relies on ac-cepted artifacts and norms, the new uniform was the tipping point for many who believed the USAF was moving too far away from its tradi-tional and historical roots. However, once again the perspective was that the fighter-operations community, under the leadership of its greatest supporter (Gen McPeak), was going to change everything that those outside the fighter community held sacred. In discussing changes in the USAF, one reporter at the *Tampa Tribune* recalled,

> McPeak wanted the Air Force organized around, and run by, fighter pilots like him. For those who flew bombers and cargo aircraft, this was a bitter pill to swallow. McPeak thought changes in appearance were needed, so he ordered a redesign of the blue dress uniform. Among the most significant changes, epaulets were removed and rank insignia was put on the sleeve. If McPeak's goal was to be distinctive, he scored. The result was a cross between what a bus driver and an airline pilot would wear. One officer privately complained he looked like Ralph Kramden. Perhaps McPeak's most controversial move, however, was to ban the wearing of crew neck T-shirts under the open-necked, light-blue uniform blouse. McPeak thought the combination was unkempt. V-neck tees were acceptable. For rank-and-file airmen, however, this was more of McPeak's machismo run amok. A series of underground brown papers began circulating inside the Pentagon poking fun at the general. In them, his reforms were mocked as "The Emergence of the Manly Man": "What this type of undershirt hides is the amount of chest hair of the USAF member," one paper says of the crew-neck decision. "The implication, of course, is that the more chest hair, the better." McPeak retired in November 1994. His replacement, Gen Ronald Fogleman, wasted little time in reversing many fashion decisions.[14]

Again, the conflict surrounding the changing of the USAF uniform at first may appear trivial when compared to the traditional external events this book has offered. However, within the USAF, McPeak's changes were perceived as anything but trivial. Many of the changes were attacking the core beliefs of those who had spent many years serving in the USAF. The combination of a fighter-operations-dominated organizational structure, the clear perspective of an in-group versus out-group dynamic between the fighter community and everyone else, and the changes that the "chief fighter pilot" was forcing, culminated in an internal USAF environment characterized by conflict, distrust, and increasing tribal allegiances. During these same years, another external event was unfolding that would further challenge all the services.

Although not considered a traditional airpower engagement, the events that the United States experienced in Somalia from 1992 to 1994 had a significant impact on all the military branches, including the USAF. This outline of the events in Somalia offers that the experience indirectly and tacitly started a new global security reality by which the USAF found itself organizationally and operationally challenged. Under the leadership of the United Nations and President George H. W. Bush and in reaction to considerable political and social unrest in Somalia, the international community began humanitarian relief efforts there in the early 1990s. The U.S. involvement began as a food and medicine airlift effort led in large part by USAF C-130s, providing considerable amounts of needed cargo to the starving Somali population.[15] However, as the Somali government continued to decay and multiple clans fractured into separate armed militias, the humanitarian operations required significantly greater defensive capabilities and considerably more combat military presence. After a series of diplomatic setbacks, increasing evidence that the food and medicine delivered through the UN was being stolen by warlords, and increased reports of massive murders in what was becoming a civil war, the UN and the United States decided to take more forceful actions to ameliorate the Somalia problem.[16]

Analysis of the conflict regarding the various factions within Somalia concluded that the warlord Mohamed Farrah Aidid was the primary problem. Under the approval of the UN charter and Security Council resolution 814 (1993), the United States developed plans to capture Aidid while he was meeting with tribal leaders in Mogadishu. Led primarily by U.S. Army forces using a combination of helicopters and ground forces, the plan was initiated on October 3, 1993. Although the details of the operation are beyond the scope or purpose of this work, the outcome and failure of the operation are directly related. In summary, the Army forces failed to locate Aidid and instead were confronted by a considerably larger and more heavily armed group of combatants than they had anticipated. Moreover, the combatants were armed with rocket-propelled grenades (RPGs) capable of downing Army helicopters. U.S. Army personnel as part of the operation were air-dropped by Army helicopters into the area where Aidid was supposed to have been residing. After extensive firing into the location where Aidid was thought to have been meeting with tribal leaders, it was discovered that Aidid was not present but that dozens of tribal leaders had been killed (a failure of intelligence).

During the early stages of the operation, Somali combatants using RPGs downed two Army helicopters. At some point within the operation, the actions turned from an operation to capture Aidid to a rescue operation to retrieve the helicopter crews as well as the Army troops that had been dropped into the area. By the time the conflict was over on October 4, eighteen American service men had been killed and eighty-three had been wounded.[17] However, perhaps the worst consequence of the war came when the bodies of the U.S. helicopter crews were paraded through the streets in celebration after the United States withdrew following the directive of President Bill Clinton. The images of the U.S. service members being dragged through the streets amid cheering Somali rebels had a significant impact on the American public and equal impact on the services. However, it was the Clinton administration's emerging policy in reaction to the events in Somalia that would affect the services and their organizational structure.

In a presentation aired on the PBS program *Frontline* in late 2001, William Cran produced a story examining the politics and policy that resulted from the Somalia conflict. Among those interviewed were Army troops who participated in the failed operation; general officers who commanded the actions of October 3 and 4; Senator Richard Lugar, who sat on the Foreign Relations Committee at the time; Robert Oakley, ambassador to Somalia 1992–1993; Gene Cullen, CIA special agent; and several others directly involved in the operations and follow-on policy directives.[18] It was suggested by nearly all the respondents that the Clinton administration had a "tense" relationship with the military services during his early months in office. Following the failed missions on October 3 and 4, President Clinton gave the following address on October 7:

> My fellow Americans, today I want to talk with you about our nation's military involvement in Somalia. Let me express my thanks and my gratitude and my profound sympathy to the families of the young Americans who were killed in Somalia. My message to you is your country is grateful, and so is the rest of the world, and so are the vast majority of the Somali people. Our mission from this day forward is to increase our strength, do our job, *bring our soldiers out and bring them home.* Thank you and God bless America.[19]

Those interviewed for this *Frontline* story who had direct contact with the Clinton administration all commented that the Somalia failure had significant impact on the decisions that Clinton would make in the future.

As Cran suggested, "After Somalia, Washington was even more reluctant to be drawn into foreign conflicts. The United States held back in Bosnia and stood aside while a million people were massacred in Rwanda."[20] Walter Clarke, deputy special envoy, commented, "The ghosts of Somalia continue to haunt U.S. policy. Our lack of response in Rwanda was a fear of getting involved in something like a Somalia all over again."[21] What is portrayed is that the United States feared the dynamics of urban, guerrilla-type warfare where traditional military operations were not dominant. However, the objective of this Somalia overview is not to point out or target the Clinton administration's policy or its unwillingness to engage in urban combat environments; rather, there is an underlying and vitally important element that the Somalia experience highlighted and even fostered regarding the USAF.

The Somalia experience took the lesson of Vietnam to a new level. During and following the Vietnam War, the military, and especially the USAF, were confronted by the realities of politics and how political constraints can affect military operations. Furthermore, and equally important, the USAF realized that war would not always be defined or framed within the characteristics of the last war. The bomber community during the Vietnam War wanted to fight the war as they did in World War II; however, the context of the Vietnam War, the changes in the global security environment, and the political realities, both foreign and domestic, were not conducive to the unlimited war that characterized World War II. The bomber community found themselves facing a war in Vietnam they were neither prepared for nor capable of fighting with the organizational, technological, or cultural dynamics they had developed. So too, in Somalia, the USAF received its first glance of what the future would hold in terms of urban and insurgency warfare.

In Somalia, there were no "centers of gravity" that some state-centric leadership would not want destroyed, leaving it susceptible to threats or deterrence. The tribal clans and numerous warlords of Somalia lived among and with the people – combatants were ordinary citizens who could not be identified separately from noncombatants. Within this urban environment, what place did the fighter aircraft have in terms of military combat operations? Other than the traditional airlift that continued to be vital yet secondary to the dominant fighter community, what could the USAF offer in the Somali environment? In fact, although not formally recognized as a sign of things to come, the humanitarian airlift operations during the Somalia experience would eventually characterize the majority of the USAF global operations throughout the 1990s. The humanitarian airlift requirements, together with the challenge of how to airlift in an area where nonidentifiable combatants fire sporadically at arriving and departing mobility aircraft, created a problem for which the USAF did not have a solution. Nonetheless, following the Somali conflict, the questions offered here were not brought up; the vision was still clearly on how the USAF would be used to win another Gulf War–style conflict where strategic targets are identifiable, competition to control the air is present, and clear lines between civilian and combatants are apparent.

The "crack in the dam" that the Somali engagement started is subtle but vital: *fighter operations and the associated fighter-centric organizational structure are only appropriate when the conflict requires air superiority, the enemy is identifiable, and the enemy has coveted infrastructure that can be threatened.* In an urban environment where civilians and combatants are the same, infrastructure is not "coveted" by enemy leadership, and traditional strategic and tactical operations are challenged by asymmetric insurgency operations, the superiority of the advanced air-to-air fighter and PGM capability is limited in the best cases, and irrelevant in the worst. In other words, just as the earlier s a c bomber-operations per-spective required an unlimited war, the fighter-operations community requires a conventional war with identifiable targets and combatants. In war, context matters. However, it will take several more years and a number of additional pressures before the u s a f is forced to confront the increasing disequilibrium between the traditional and dominant fighter operations and the emerging external threats of counterinsurgency and counterterrorism conflicts.

The new security challenges of urban war, civilian combatants, and non-state actors is clear in retrospect; however, these emerging contex-tual changes were not nearly as visible during their initial time of occur-rence. Few if any in the u s a f saw Somalia as an issue for which the u s a f had any concern or reason to consider its capabilities. To the u s a f, other than airlift, Somalia was not on the radar screen. Most indications are that the u s a f was continuing to prepare, posture, and organize to fight the type of war that they had so recently dominated – Gulf War I. No one, as far as could be determined, was considering the Somalia challenges a precursor to what the u s a f might need to be able to address in the future. The realization that the context offered suggests a tacit or indirect challenge to the fighter-operations status quo is difficult to capture and support. Until the u s a f is physically required to perform within a new or emerging "non-Gulf War-like" conflict, the status quo will prevail. However, based on the outline of this time segment, there is support to suggest some degree of organizational disequilibrium is building.

9

FROM BOSNIA TO ALLIED FORCE: 1994–1999

ALTHOUGH THE CONFLICTS IN THE FORMER YUGOSLAVIA HAD begun in the 1980s, the United Nations and the North Atlantic Treaty Organization (NATO) did not become fully involved until the early 1990s. As was the case in Somalia, much of the conflict initially started as a humanitarian relief in the midst of what was building up to an internal civil war in the area. However, as in Somalia, the "peacekeeping" and humanitarian efforts of the world community were challenged by the instability, factions among various armed subgroups, and widely divergent political perspectives across the international community. For the USAF, Bosnia would be an example of the limits of the fighter-operations perspective within the context and realities of a complex international and political environment.

According to political scholars who closely followed and examined the Bosnian crisis, the Clinton administration "inherited a U.S. – indeed Western – Bosnia policy that was in complete disarray."[1] Daalder describes best what the United States under the international authority of the United Nations had to deal with in the early 1990s:

> The previous year had been witness to the most brutal war in Europe since 1945. It was a war marked by concentration camps, massive expulsions of Muslims and Croats from their homes in a self-described Serb campaign of "ethnic cleansing," widespread incidents of rape, and unrelenting shelling of cities, including the capital, Sarajevo – together accounting for the deaths of tens of thousands of people, mostly civilians, and well over a million refugees. The Western response to these atrocities had been to condemn Serb actions and impose a total economic embargo on Serbia and Montenegro to force an end to their involvement in the Bosnian war, to deploy a UN peacekeeping force to protect humanitarian relief supplies being transported to affected communities, and to scurry around

to find a diplomatic solution acceptable the warring sides.... By the time the new [Clinton] administration took office, these international efforts were producing limited results.... Conspicuously lacking, however, was U.S. engagement in – let alone leadership of – the international effort in Bosnia ... the Bush administration had effectively deferred the design and implementation of the Western policy to the Europeans. The Europeans ... eagerly seized the policy reins ... only soon to realize that the breakup of Yugoslavia represented too large a challenge for them to resolve on their own.[2]

By 1994, the unrest within the former Yugoslavia had increased to the breaking point.[3] Atrocities committed by a number of internal groups were being televised across Europe and the United States. These images, together with concern for how the conflict might foster or expand hostilities beyond the regional boundaries, forced additional action in an attempt to control the growing escalations. In February 1994, President Clinton reported that the United States would expand its participation in the region; he allocated approximately sixty U.S. military aircraft and accompanying support personnel. Later that very month, U.S. fighter aircraft flying for NATO shot down four Serbian Super Galeb aircraft in support of a no-fly zone mandate established through the United Nations and Security Council.[4] The airpower strikes within Bosnia had begun. Throughout the remainder of 1994 and 1995, U.S. and coalition air forces attacked both airborne and ground targets within the region. However, the classic fighter-operations perspective that was so dominant and successful in the Gulf War was not nearly as applicable within the context of Bosnia.

Within the U.S. military establishment, considerable debate existed regarding what should be accomplished and expected from airpower. The Vice-Chairman of the Joint Chiefs, Admiral David Jeremiah, publicly commented, "Hitting tanks spread out in the desert is one thing; hitting artillery near barns, schools, and civic centers is another. It is not a simple or easy thing to use airstrikes against guerrilla warfare units spread round the country."[5] Furthermore, and especially of interest in the context of this work, there appear to be parallel considerations between the challenges in Somalia outlined previously and those confronted in Bosnia. In both cases, a peacekeeping objective was at the heart of the U.S. engagement; also, in both conflicts the United States struggled with how to provide effective and needed humanitarian supplies to civilians while avoiding the ground-to-air threats posed by groups within the country that did not want the United States to intervene. Additionally, the belligerents were often intermixed among the noncombatant populations, and when valid military targets could be located, they were often strategically placed in civilian areas where their targeting would likely result in collateral damage to innocents.[6] Moreover, as the region continued to collapse into civil war and instability fostered the growth of armed factions, "the distinction between 'humanitarian' and 'peace-keeping' activities, and even military intervention, became blurred."[7]

What is clear is that the context of Bosnia was not anything like the context of the Gulf War, where clear objectives were established, enemy targets were identifiable, and traditional force-on-force strategy gave the advantage to the U.S. military. According to Mason,

> assessments of and genuine concerns about the potential of air power to facilitate a resolution of the conflict in the former Yugoslavia were distorted by parochial interests or ignorance, or both: political wrangles within NATO; domestic politics in the USA; turf wars between armed forces faced with swingeing reductions and staking claims for their role responsibilities in peacekeeping; governments seeking peace dividends and loth to accept unexpected and apparently interminable new security burdens; and civilian audiences, overwhelmed by media coverage of atrocities demanding action, any action, from those same governments. There were also genuine fears, there were constraints and there were unexplored opportunities. *Significantly absent was informed, objective, public debate on the role of air power.*[8]

Furthermore, the authors of a RAND Corporation study regarding the airpower experience in Bosnia suggested that the tensions between the military and the political authorities were extensive and that the "complexities of political control" pressured the USAF at the strategic planning level.[9] However, despite the morass of political and contextual complexity, the position of the USAF was no different in the Bosnian conflict than it had been in the Gulf War. From the fighter-operations airpower perspective, all one needed to do was to ensure air superiority, select appropriate targets that were important to the continued resistance of the belligerents, and precisely bomb those targets until the enemy could no longer continue resisting and was forced to comply with demands. However, as outlined by Mason, and reminiscent of Vietnam, the political realities and physical context of the Bosnian conflict did not accommodate such traditional, conventional strategy – at least not in the early stages of UN involvement.

The context encountered in the Bosnian engagement required new strategy for dealing with new challenges. Specifically, and of greatest importance to highlight during this time in Period Three analysis, these include the emerging role of the concept and associated challenges of "peacekeeping." Again, unlike anything in any of the previous major wars, peacekeeping was not about victory, annihilation of the enemy, or the restoration of disputed territory to its rightful government. Peacekeeping involved appeasement, diplomacy, humanitarian aid, cooperation, and treaty/cease-fire agreements, all within the context of instability, armed conflict, war crimes, and divergent political demands from numerous interested parties. Mason again offers important insight as to how the emerging "peacekeeping" context challenged the current airpower perspective:

> The Bosnian theater presented quite different problems to air force planners ... there were constraints on the use of airpower which are likely to be met in all peacekeeping environments ... air operations in the modern peacekeeping continuum ... will have a supranational authority, usually the United Nations. The implications of such an authorization is that airpower must be applied with scrupulous regard to formal international agreements and in accordance with the principles upheld by the authorizing organizations. ... As a result, the peacekeeping is likely to be subject to more resource constraints, political control and narrow political sensitivities than traditional military activities. Failure on the part of airmen to recognize and accept such political realities and their operational implications would have serious consequences for the future. ... The final and most complex characteristic of peacekeeping operations is that reconciliation is the objective in all applications of force along the continuum. That implies seeking to reduce both the friendly and hostile casualties as far as possible. That may entail a maximum demonstration of force but the application of the minimum. That in turn risks tactical planning and weapon choices which by minimizing force could actually jeopardize friendly forces. All in all, it is not surprising that military commanders are frequently very loth to become involved in combat in a peacekeeping scenario.[10]

As Mason points out, peacekeeping operations are not anything like the engagement encountered in the Gulf War or, for that matter, in the previous wars where airpower was available. Interestingly, some in the USAF argued that the way the conflict in Bosnia was being conducted was not appropriate, and that combat operations should fall more in line with the traditional military strategy of overwhelming force that had proven so successful in the Gulf War.[11] This sounds very similar to the arguments made by the bomber community in relation to how the Vietnam War was waged. In this case, however, it was the fighter community that perceived the extensive political constraints as inappropriate and the source of frustration.

Within the context of an unstable region and armed resistance, the peacekeeping operation and need for humanitarian airlift of goods must also face the realities and risks of improved ground-to-air weapons systems.[12] According to Mason, the new mobile technology of hand-launched, ground-to-air antiaircraft missiles is easily obtainable on the international market from a number of vendors. Furthermore, these systems do not require significant training; they are easily hidden until needed; and the belligerents can vanish into the population immediately after their use. For cargo aircraft, the takeoff and landing phase is extremely vulnerable to these types of weapons. The downing of a single cargo aircraft will cause the humanitarian flights to either limit their capabilities, or stop them all together. The challenge to airpower cannot be understated in this context. Successful air operations require air superiority (the ability to fly and operate with impunity). In considering the handheld technologies available to even third-world combatants, Mason (1994) suggests, "such a threat would complicate proposals to introduce air power anywhere on the peacekeeping continuum, except in peacekeeping when truces or settlement terms had been agreed." However, "even then, the risk of attack by dissident minorities would remain. ..."[13] Attempting to support humanitarian airlift requirements within regions where airlift aircraft may be easy targets produces a problem to the USAF that the fighter-operations perspective is unable to solve.

Another important observation regarding the emerging realities in the peacekeeping environment that the USAF failed to appreciate in the Bosnian conflict was that airpower in a counterinsurgency operation is normally in direct support of ground operations. This perspective was not openly supported by the USAF and, when it was discussed, the default example often touted by airmen was that USAF had won the Gulf War (from the USAF perspective). Mason suggests that in peacekeeping situations such as Bosnia, "close co-operation between ground and air forces will be essential." He further observes that "the USAF may need to modify their traditional sensitivity to operations which appear to impinge upon their 'independence', even to the extent of placing operational control of combat aircraft in-theater under a foreign ground commander."[14] However, at this point in the 1990s (post Gulf-War dominance) the culture within the USAF fostered an environment characterized as independent of ground forces, capable of operations without the need for direct ground coordination, and having an overwhelming sense of sufficiency regarding what airpower brings to the operational planning table. This culture, especially exemplified and magnified within the "single-seat" fighter-pilot community, was not in line with the realities and demands of the peacekeeping context. As witnessed in the initial Bosnian experience, traditional fighter-operations may not be effective or appropriate for meeting the political objectives of regional stability. Instead, within the peacekeeping and humanitarian context, greater airlift capability in terms of survivability, increased understanding and capabilities for ground support, and significant attention to intelligence, surveillance, and reconnaissance (ISR) capabilities that can provide needed information to political leaders was essential.[15] Moreover, although the USAF did all it was capable of doing within the Bosnian context, its fighter-operations perspective and organizational norms for how war should be fought and how the USAF should organize, train, and equip fell well short of what the emerging peacekeeping context required.

Just as in the engagement in Somalia, where the USAF dominant culture (fighter-operations) was not conducive nor appropriate to the operational requirements, the Bosnian experience highlighted the disequilibrium developing between USAF organizational structure and the emerging nontraditional threats of the post–Cold War years. As Mason concludes, "If the Gulf War marked the apotheosis of late twentieth century air power . . . in the Bosnian fiasco . . . it reached an impotent nadir."[16] By mid-1995, this realization of U.S. impotence in the emerging peacekeeping environment was not acceptable to the Clinton administration or to the USAF. According to Burg, "what was needed was a *direct* display of US and NATO strength, through large-scale air strikes."[17] In other words, change the peacekeeping objective to a "peacemaking" objective. This change would allow the USAF to respond with its traditional and dominant operational standard – precision strikes using fighter aircraft against strategic and identifiable targets.

The complex and often divergent international political establishment finally reached a breaking point when it could no longer demand only limited military responses in the hope of bringing peace to the region. In reaction to what were called the Markale Massacres, where Serbian forces fired artillery shells into a crowded open market in Sarajevo, Operation Deliberate Force was initiated. In late August 1995, U.S. and coalition NATO airpower forces began what can only be described as a traditional target-based bombing campaign aimed at forcing the belligerents to capitulate or lose their most important internal infrastructure and command and control capabilities. The understanding was: peacekeeping plans had fallen short, and now peacemaking was required in order to stop the atrocities that continued to occur. For this, airpower was very well suited, and the operational capabilities of the USAF in particular were ready to succeed. By November of 1995, following a concerted and intense bombing campaign, the Serbian leadership capitulated, agreeing to the demands of the international community and signing the Dayton Peace Accords (signed in Paris December 14, 1995).[18] In large measure, the air campaign, strategic and precision strikes, and air superiority capabilities of modern U.S. airpower drove the Serbs to break from their intended objectives of territorial takeover and ethnic cleansing.

What is vital for the current study is the understanding that, in the situation of a military conflict that fits into the organizational structure of the USAF, the importance and capability of airpower cannot be discounted. However, when the traditional use of airpower confronts the emerging peacekeeping context, or humanitarian airlift requirements are blocked by armed belligerents, the traditional fighter-operations perspective fails to meet or address the needed response. *Instead of an independent airpower operation aimed at targeting an enemy's ability to wage war, fielded troops, or command and control centers of gravity, peacekeeping operations require a much greater reliance and emphasis on ground operations, airlift survivability, ISR, and the ability to remain engaged in a politi-*

cally constrained context. The significant take-away from this analysis of the Bosnian years 1994–1995 is that the USAF cannot afford to be prepared only for the type of conflict they are most comfortable or amenable to fighting. It appears, at least at this point in the analysis, that the USAF must be capable of fighting both in the traditional fighter-dominated context and in an environment where traditional fighter operations will be secondary if needed at all. This analysis appears to make this observation clear, however, only in hindsight.

In the mid-1990s the USAF leadership under the dominant banner of the fighter-operations community did not consider the emerging asymmetric, counterinsurgency, peacekeeping requirements (as in Somalia and Bosnia) as anything more than a distraction from their primary role of owning the skies and striking with precision the strategic targets that could win any war. As a partial explanation for why this myopia developed, Barnett sums up what he believes was the overall DoD hallmark across all the services – including the USAF:

> A new era was born with the collapse of the Soviet Union, but our being present at its creation was not nearly enough. America needed to embrace the new security environment in which it faced no peers, through its clear redefinition of both an enemy worth fighting and a future military worth building.... The Pentagon failed dramatically on both counts, and it did so primarily out of fear for its own institutional standing within the U.S. political system – or, to put it more bluntly, its share of the federal budget. The fear drove the military to cling to the dream of a "near-peer" which would justify its desire to retain a military fashioned primarily for great-power war, when the new era not only did not generate such a threat but instead challenged America's definition of "New World Order" by producing its exact opposite: the rise of the so-called lesser includeds.[19]

In Barnett's follow-on assessment, he defines the primary tactic of the "lesser includeds" as asymmetric war, in that they are forced to adapt their tactics to counter the hegemonic capabilities of the U.S. military. According to Barnett, if you choose to ignore or disqualify the lesser includeds, then you also choose not to develop a military capable of countering their tactic: asymmetric war.

Final analysis of this timeframe within Period Three suggests that the USAF was neither organizationally equipped nor prepared for a Bosnian-type war, where political constraints frustrated USAF planners. The record suggests that in 1994 and most of 1995, the traditional fighter-operations perspective did not inform or appropriately offer a diligent course of action that could effectively meet the needs of emerging peacekeeping responsibilities. However, by late 1995 when the political climate had turned to allow for a more traditional airpower campaign, the USAF under the banner of its dominant fighter-operations perspective was extremely successful. The consequence of this narrative resulted in recognition of a disequilibrium between operations that called for greater emphasis and support for non-fighter capabilities that could better support the peacekeeping requirements, and reinforcement of the traditional status quo with the successful air campaign that eventually resulted in the Dayton Peace Accords.

OPERATION ALLIED FORCE 1999

NATO began Operation Allied Force on March 24, 1999. The Federal Republic of Yugoslavia's unwillingness to cooperate or constructively negotiate forced the eruption of an international coalition air war in the skies over Serbia. Although the air war lasted only seventy-eight days, the lessons for airpower and the effects the war had on USAF organizational perspective are both relevant and important. However, as this analysis will present, the lessons taken from Allied Force at the time were very different from the lessons this work, in hindsight, proposes.

Analysis of Operation Allied Force requires an examination of not one air war, but two. The historian John Keegan asserts there were really two air wars, the first lasting a month, the second six weeks. He further suggests that the first air war was a failure, while the second was a success.[20] Ellwood Hinman agrees with Keegan's assertion, further explaining that the first thirty days of Allied Force saw a gradual escalation of tactical airpower, mainly against fielded forces. As a result, Yugoslav President Milosevic showed little reaction to the U.S.-led air strikes and continued his aggression into neighboring territories.[21] The first thirty days of air strikes did little to the industrial web or strategic infrastructure of the enemy. The tactical and escalating strikes, however, were not the idea of the USAF leadership in charge of planning and supervising the air operations. Most agree that in the first thirty days of the war airmen were not given the authority to fight the war they had been educated and trained to fight in terms of strategic strikes on key central targets using PGMs. Considerable disagreement between Lt Gen Short, Allied Force's Combined Force Air Component Commander, and Army officer Gen Wesley Clark, who was Joint Force Commander, erupted over the proper use of airpower. Gen Short asserted after the end of the war:

> [I] would have gone for the head of the snake on the first night. I'd have dropped the bridges across the Danube. I'd [have] hit five or six political headquarters in downtown Belgrade. Milosevic and his cronies would have waked up the first morning asking what the hell was going on.[22]

Although Gen Short voiced his frustration regarding what he perceived to be an air campaign overly harnessed by Gen Clark's inability to appreciate airpower's proper role and capabilities, the reality of Gen Clark's decisions were more complex than Gen Short appears to have realized. Although final authority rested with Gen Clark, the political regime within the UN and the United States and the fragile realities associated with keeping the NATO coalition together all had significant influence – influence that Clark did not have the luxury of ignoring.

By the end of the first thirty days of escalating air strikes aimed in large part at fielded forces, NATO political leaders concluded that the tactical escalating strikes were not having the effect they had hoped. On May 26 airpower planners received the green light to fight the air war based on the targeting and tempo established by Gen Short and guided by the dominant perspective of strategic precision strikes. The plan quickly shifted to strategic bombing of key military, production, transportation, and communication targets; Milosevic capitulated fourteen days later on, June 10, 1999.[23]

Clearly the change in air operations and the subsequent capitulation of Milosevic reinforced the prevailing fighter-operations perspective that airpower using PGMs and targeting a belligerent's key centers of gravity had a greater impact than tactical strikes against fielded forces. In a report offered before the Senate Armed Services Committee, Secretary of Defense Cohen and Chairman of the Joint Chiefs Gen Shelton summarized the result of Allied Force:

We forced Milosevic to withdraw from Kosovo, degraded his ability to wage
military operations, and rescued and resettled over one million refugees. We
accomplished this by prosecuting the most precise and lowest-collateral-damage
air campaign in history – with no U.S. or allied combat casualties in 78 days of
around-the-clock operations and over 38,000 combat sorties.[24]

However, it was also learned, by both Gen Clark and Gen Short, that
coalition and allied air campaigns require a high level of integration for
effective theater-wide operations. Gen Short commented that the most
difficult thing he had to do, yet the most important, was to "coordinate
with coalition forces." Gen Short shared that the relationships with coalition air forces were not mandatory based on combat requirements;
rather, coalition partners' political support of the war often depended
on their inclusion in the process. According to Gen Short, this taught
him the importance of learning as much as possible about the allies you
will be fighting alongside.[25] Despite the friction between Gen Clark and
Gen Short, and although the first several weeks of the conflict did not
go as most hoped that it would, the final assessment of Operation Allied
Force is that it was a prime example of a successful air campaign. Nearly
all objective observers at the time (and even through today) consider
Operation Allied Force as a prominent success for the decisiveness of
airpower.

Although the success of Operation Allied Force reinforced the
fighter-operations, precision-targeting perspective, it is equally important to consider what airpower was not able to accomplish. Within the
highly charged political environment that characterized the UN and
NATO coalition, airpower was unable to effectively meet the objectives
of the international community without turning the war into a traditional strategic bombing campaign. Within the fighter-operations organizational structure, strategic strikes and precision targeting of the
enemies key centers of gravity is required to ensure victory. However,
as witnessed in the early days of Allied Force, if strategic strikes are not
available (due possibly to political constraints, peacekeeping objectives,
nonidentifiable combatants, lack of coveted infrastructure, etc.), then it
appears that, under the umbrella of a fighter-operations perspective, the
USAF is unable to provide any significant solution or capability. Barnett
suggests, of the U.S. military at the time, that "most military leaders

wanted little to do with trying to manage this messy world, preferring instead to plan brilliant high-tech wars against brilliant high-tech opponents."[26] However, as was apparent in Somalia as well as the early years in Bosnia, if the USAF is organized to fight only in the type of engagements they prefer – where the enemy is identifiable, the enemy covets targetable infrastructure, and air superiority is challenged – then the emerging political complexities of the post–Cold War global environment may significantly challenge the USAF organizational structure. Non-state actors, terrorism, rebel groups, insurgents, and asymmetric warfare that purposely divert actions from traditional combat parameters may render the USAF, under the fighter dominated organizational structure, impotent.

Within the political realities of Allied Force, the objective of the international coalition was to stop the Serbs' ethnic cleansing, halt the exodus of refugees being forced from their Kosovo homeland, and do so without expanding hostilities into a protracted war.[27] Because airpower at the time appeared to policy makers as a panacea for engaging with the least amount of risk and the greatest amount of capability, it was politically rationalized that airpower could control events on the ground. The point is that the decision to use airpower as it was used in the opening stages of Allied Force was a political decision based on political concerns that were not necessarily in line with what military planners (e.g., Gen Short) might prefer or suggest. However, increased political complexities are the reality of modern war – Allied Force was not an exception. Many of the decisions made in the early days of Allied Force regarding the use of airpower were based on political objectives where other options (strategic bombardment) were simply not amenable to all those politically involved in the decision calculus. Airpower was used as it was because policy makers outside the military saw no other option that had the potential to meet their political objectives at a lower cost. Although this may have been a frustrating reality from a military perspective, from a political perspective it was rational. It is within this political reality that the USAF must be capable of operating to the best of their abilities. *It is also this context of political constraints that the USAF must prepare and organize for to be successful in the future.* If the USAF had its way, it would only engage in battles where there was a clear enemy, coveted enemy infrastructure, identifiable military targets, and an enemy that could respond to coercive pressure. However, within the increasingly connected global and international environment, politics in war will only increase. The USAF, as well as all U.S. services, must acknowledge and prepare for such realities.

Although there is little evidence the USAF leaders recognized in 1999 that their success was possibly closing them into a box where the enemy must have certain characteristics, they were not the only ones suffering from such myopia. Scott Cooper, U.S. Marine and pilot with significant combat experience including missions in Allied Force, asserted:

> At the outset of Allied Force, policy makers expected they could use air power to stem the flow of refugees out of Kosovo. They ought to have known and in fact soon learned that air power had little or no impact on the Serbs' efforts to expel Kosovars from their homeland, except perhaps to hasten them. Air power was chosen because it was something that could be done, and done quickly, even though it hardly related to the situation on the ground.[28]

Policy makers working within the confines of political complexities that increasingly characterize modern military engagements appear quick to believe that airpower is a low-risk option for meeting political objectives. Unfortunately, policy makers who do not understand the *specific contextual parameters* required of the USAF fighter-operations perspective could potentially make decisions to use airpower in conflicts neither appropriate nor conducive to airpower's capability. Cooper advises that

> Operation Allied Force should serve as a warning. After Operation Desert Storm, Eliot Cohen warned of the seductiveness of air power, comparing it to modern teenage romance. It offers political leaders a chance for "gratification without commitment." Air power is often viewed as the universal remedy when diplomatic means are exhausted. . . . Policy makers should be mindful that air power carries enormous risks and costs.[29]

Moreover, if USAF leaders believe they only need to be prepared to fight the kind of war they prefer (a war with strategic targets), then what will the result be when they are called to fight in an environment alien to their organizational structure or dominant capability? Cooper warns, "We cannot assume that the situation on the ground will lend itself to symmetrical battles or situations where coercive strategies will work."[30]

Although this imbalance between the USAF organizational structure and emerging asymmetric requirements is slowly building from Somalia, Bosnia, and now Kosovo, at the time immediately after Allied Force the USAF was not preparing for anything other than another Gulf War or Kosovo–type air-superiority and strategic-strike engagement. However, the emerging post–Cold War environment, even at this point in 1999, was one where belligerents knew better than to take on the United States in a conventional symmetric engagement. According to Cooper, in his reflection on the real lesson airpower planners should have learned from Allied Force, "Asymmetric competitors will stun us with new methods and measures . . . we will have to overcome the fog and friction of war and adapt to the inventive efforts of adversaries bent on feeling out our points of vulnerability. It is not enough simply to possess overwhelming firepower."[31] The lesson that is bubbling under the surface by this late date in the 1990s is that the fighter-operations, strategic-bombardment strategy is not *the* strategy for war; rather, it is *a* strategy. Although at this point an emerging new perspective or culture that can challenge the fighter-operations view is not yet identifiable, the disequilibrium between USAF organizational structure and the emerging global context is *tacitly* building.

One final significant observation that comes out of the Kosovo experience is the continued friction witnessed between USAF leadership and the political establishment when the USAF leaders do not agree with political decisions. As was the case in Vietnam, military planners often point to the war they prefer to fight rather than accept the war they are given. Within the calculus of war, it should not be a surprise that political constraints complicate what military planners would "prefer" in terms of context. Clausewitz could not have made this clearer when he suggested, "the political object is the goal, war is the means of reaching it, and the means can never be considered in isolation from their purposes."[32] However, as was characteristic in the early stages of Allied Force, Gen Short was emphatic that the war was not being fought the way he wanted. Rather than oblige the political community, whose coalition was weak at best and near collapse through much of the engagement, Short's myopia regarding how airpower could defeat Milosevic caused him to ignore the broader issues and political complexities. Whether Gen Short liked it or not, the political realties were such that had the first thirty days not played out as they did, lacking significant success, the coalition would likely not have supported the strategic targeting of Belgrade that followed. If, as Gen Short implied, the USAF had been given authority to "go after the head of the snake the first night," it might well have been the case that political rhetoric from Milosevic, media coverage of collateral damage, and the imbalance of power in the U.S. response would have broken the coalition's will and forced NATO to stop or indefinitely postpone further operations. Obviously this is a counterfactual; however, the point is clear – political realties in limited war are pervasive and cannot be ignored. The USAF is called to fight the battles our political leaders call us to fight – political constraints included. This knowledge is not merely hindsight, for it was evident during and after Vietnam, highlighted in Somalia, reinforced in Bosnia, and further established in the early weeks of Allied Force. Given this observation, it appears that by 1999 an emerging requirement is building to develop an organizational structure capable of training and equipping for engagements highly constrained by political complexities.

10

SEPTEMBER 11, AFGHANISTAN, AND IRAQ: 2001–2011

THERE IS NO QUESTION THAT THE EVENTS ON SEPTEMBER 11, 2001 (9/11), changed the United States and the world; interestingly, the terrorists on 9/11 used airpower as their weapon of choice. However, as history clearly outlines, the belligerents did not attempt to use air-power to challenge our Air Force for air superiority or attack our military ground forces; instead, *they operationalized an asymmetric strategy that fell outside of our traditional and symmetric status quo.* The attacks on 9/11 took America by surprise because they did not fall into our accepted paradigm of traditional national defense strategies. The use of an asym-metric attack on 9/11 challenged the defense establishment by exposing the existing disequilibrium between our national defense organizational structure and the potential for attacks outside of that established para-digm. Of direct importance to this work, the major events that followed the attacks of 9/11 called for significant effort by the USAF. Examin-ing those events and determining their influence on the organizational structure of the USAF is vital in the assessment of Period Three analysis. This chapter covers two specific post-9/11 timeframes: the first addresses the initial military actions in Afghanistan and Iraq up through May 1, 2003; the second addresses the sustained operations in Afghanistan and Iraq from 2003 to the summer 2010.

AFGHANISTAN AND IRAQ THROUGH MAY 1, 2003

Following the 9/11 attacks, President Bush called on the U.S. military to target what appeared to be the most visible source of the terrorist threat – Afghanistan. On October 7, 2001, the United States and several coalition allies began combat operations in Afghanistan to destroy the Al-Qaeda terrorist organization and the Taliban government that helped support it. As was the case with the first Gulf War in 1991, the initial attacks in Afghanistan were carried out predominantly by airpower, by both U.S. and coalition forces. A news report on the opening day of operations reported:

> The first strikes began about 8:45 p.m. Sunday and targeted the Taliban's air de-fense installations, defense ministry, airport-based command centers, airfields, electrical grids and other energy production facilities. . . . The mission included bombing runs by U.S. B-2 Stealth bombers flown from the continental United States, as well as B-1 and B-52 long-range bombers from the British air base on the island of Diego Garcia in the Indian Ocean. . . . The bomber force was bolstered by 25 strike aircraft launched from the carriers USS Carl Vinson and USS Enterprise, and about 50 Tomahawk Cruise missiles launched from four U.S. surface ships, a U.S. submarine and a British submarine. . . . Airdrops of hu-manitarian aid were set to begin shortly. . . . Packages of food and medicine were set to be expelled by two C-17 transport aircraft. . . . The United States planned to drop some 37,000 pre-packaged meals and medicines in the first stages of the operation. . . .[1]

The lethal combination of strategic strikes targeting key Taliban loca-tions (both governmental and military) rendered the Taliban ineffective in their attempts to defend their positions.

As the current fighter-operations perspective understood it, air-power unrestrained and used to strategically target an enemy's ability to wage war (communications, command centers, electrical grids, training facilities, and major transportation routes) will so decay the enemy's mil-itary options that further resistance by enemy forces will only prolong the devastation. In the war against Afghanistan, the Air Force declared on October 10, 2001, that it had "air supremacy" (unrestrained freedom for air operations) throughout Afghanistan – just three days into hostili-ties.[2] Within the next two months that followed, the United States and its coalition partners would continue to use airpower to target known enemy locations and to disrupt any attempt by the enemy to fortify or establish a defensive location.

By December of 2001, victory was being declared by the local Afghan tribal leaders opposed to the Taliban rule as well as by U.S. leadership. On December 16 the BBC reported:

> Tribal fighters in Afghanistan say they have taken the last al-Qaeda positions in the caves and tunnels of Tora Bora in eastern Afghanistan . . . "We cleared al-Qaeda from our land. We did the job," senior commander Haji Mohammad Zaman told reporters. . . . The reported victory comes after weeks of fighting and relentless bombing, with US warplanes dropping hundreds of bombs on al-Qaeda positions in the past couple of days alone.[3]

Just a few days following the announcement of victory, the new interim government was sworn in under the leadership of Hamid Karzai.[4] From all accounts, the United States and its coalition partners had broken the back of the Taliban, severely damaged al-Qaeda's ability to operate, and had won the military battle in Afghanistan – predominantly with airpower.

However, perhaps the best evidence of the years that would follow and eventually characterize the context developing in Afghanistan is offered in the closing lines of the same BBC news report on December 16, 2001:

> Key tasks for the new government include establishing security throughout the country, restoring essential services and beginning the process of reconstruction. Since the collapse of the Taleban, there have been reports of increasing numbers of armed men on the streets in some cities and of pockets of looting and lawlessness. Three men whom security officials described as Taleban fighters were arrested inside the Interior Ministry compound on Saturday morning.[5]

What the U.S. and coalition forces would face in the next several years – exactly what is described in this near-prophetic coverage – was a new and developing counterinsurgency (COIN) context that the USAF would be forced to deal with, a context well outside of the fighter-operations standard perspective. However, following the initial success in Afghanistan, the USAF once again believed that its capabilities and its fighter-centric perspectives were confirmed as the panacea for modern war. As was the case in Somalia, Bosnia, and Kosovo in the 1990s, the USAF failed to pay attention to the emerging imbalance between the organizational structure built around a fighter-operations perspective and the looming challenges of COIN operations. Although operations over the next several months would begin to clearly highlight the challenges of COIN operations, the USAF was preparing for another strategic attack in Iraq.

Despite the significant involvement in Afghanistan, U.S. policy under the leadership of President Bush saw Iraq as another threat that must be confronted. Armed with the argument that Iraq had weapons of mass destruction and that it was continuing to thwart the international community through its lack of cooperation with the United Nations, the United States, with a small coalition of other countries, prepared for yet another war in Iraq. On March 17, 2003, President Bush informed Saddam Hussein that he had forty-eight hours to leave Iraq or risk attack. On March 19, with authorization of the U.S. Congress, military operations against Iraq were initiated with the launch of Operation Iraqi Freedom (OIF).

The first actions of the conflict began with airstrikes against key command and control and air defense sites throughout Iraq; however, much of the targeting was centered in Baghdad. According to reports, the Pentagon characterized the operations as "shock and awe" and Secretary of Defense Donald Rumsfeld claimed that "the initial phase of the war is mild compared to what is to come: 'What will follow will not be a repeat of any other conflict. It will be of a force and a scope and a scale that is beyond what we have seen before.'"[6] The combat plan, however, was not a repeat of the 1991 war where airpower targeted Iraq's centers of gravity for several weeks before ground forces engaged. Instead, the shock and awe strategy in OIF is best described as a modern blitzkrieg, where air and ground forces attacked simultaneously and in rapid coordination. As concerns the airpower strategy, the only real difference in the standard perspective of strategic bombing with PGMs was that ground forces were immediately on the move at the same time the air campaign began.

The combination of massive cruise missile strikes, significant and persistent strategic bombing using PGM technology, and the pressure imposed by a rapidly advancing ground component all combined to quickly and decisively overrun Iraqi resistance. Although the United States and its coalition partners confronted some heavy pockets of resistance, the Iraqi military was outgunned, overwhelmed, and defeated in short order. According to the reported OIF timeline of significant events, on April 14, 2003, less than thirty days after the beginning of combat operations, "Major fighting in Iraq is declared over by the Pentagon...."[7] The following day, a U.S.-led group of military leaders and diplomats are put in place to begin establishing a new Iraqi federal government. On

May 1, President Bush, aboard the USS *Abraham Lincoln,* announced to the American people and the world that "major combat operations in Iraq have ended." As a backdrop to his announcement, a large sign hanging off the command tower of the ship read "Mission Accomplished."[8] As far as the President, Pentagon, and military were concerned, the heavy lifting in Iraq was over and only the cleaning up and establishing of a pro-Western government was left to be completed.

Like Afghanistan as described above, Iraq was viewed in mid-2003 as a complete success and more evidence of U.S. military capability and hegemony in the modern world. The USAF, in parallel with ground forces, conducted a near-flawless campaign and reached its objective of overturning the Iraqi government in remarkable time. In a military-developed report to Congress August 18, 2003, OIF was characterized as a successful "low-cost victory."[9] From all accounts in mid-2003, the Iraq and Afghanistan conflicts both supported and reinforced the dominant fighter-operations perspective that controlled the organizational structure of the USAF. The success of airpower in both theaters again proved to the USAF leadership (as well as most in the government) that the fighter-operations perspective, based on air superiority and strategic strikes with PGM technology, would continue to serve as the driving capability for ensuring U.S. victory in modern war. Although the events following 2003 would bring unforeseen challenges with significant organizational consequences, at this point in the timing of Period Three, the status quo of the fighter-operations perspective appeared near unchallenged.

Although not specifically addressed within the text describing the military action in Afghanistan and Iraq, the increased reliance by all services, and the USAF specifically, regarding the need for ISR, secure communications, space-based capabilities, pictures, transmission of data, and the increased requirement for effective command and control in a complex and rapid combat environment increased nearly exponentially in the 1990s and especially in the Afghanistan and Iraq conflicts. The USAF is predominantly responsible for the capabilities called upon by space systems, and ISR requirements are provided in large measure by both manned and unmanned aircraft flying in theater. However, the primary mission of the USAF under the banner of the fighter-operations perspective and culture continued to push these capabilities into a mere support role rather than considering them a primary mission. Short of a context where the fighter-operations strategic-bombing perspective is significantly reduced in necessity or determined to be altogether irrelevant, the USAF subgroups of ISR, space, and even cyber were considered to be secondary to the dominant roles and missions of the fighter community.

The reality in mid-2003 of successful USAF contributions under the dominant fighter-operations perspective provided no mechanism to suggest a need for organizational change. However, as was noted following the Somalia and Bosnia engagements and the initial stages of Operational Allied Force, "success" was a term used to describe only those events in which the USAF engaged under predetermined parameters for what constituted modern war. Given the context of strategic targets, identifiable combatants, and disputed control for the air, the USAF was in fact a very successful military organization. However, as the previous conflicts began to tacitly suggest, given a different context where these traditional assumptions do not exist, the capability of the USAF to effectively influence combat operations without making significant changes to their status quo organizational structure is questionable.

IRAQ AND AFGHANISTAN: 2003–2010

As presented, the initial operations by airpower in both the Afghanistan conflict as well as Iraq showed that given the predefined context of a traditional enemy with strategic targets, identifiable combatants, and the need to compete for air superiority, the USAF is remarkably competent and capable. What appears unfortunate, however, is that across the military as well as in the highest level of the U.S. government, the view was that major combat operations started and ended within this predetermined context. The April 2003 statement by the top U.S. military leader, Gen Tommy Franks (Commander-in-Chief of the U.S. Central Command, 2000–2003), that in Iraq the "assigned job had been completed," and President Bush's USS *Abraham Lincoln* "Mission Accomplished" pronouncement together suggest that what constituted "victory" was clearly inside the box of the traditional paradigm.[10] However, not everyone was so optimistic.

Defense analysts and many lower-level military strategists pointed out in both April and May of 2003 the concerns for an emerging asymmetric conflict. Thomas Ricks quotes Jeffrey White, a former analyst of Middle Eastern affairs at the Defense Intelligence Agency: "My worry is that we could see the beginning of some kind of resistance based on regime diehards, nationalists, disaffected tribal elements, etc."[11] Ricks reports that a retired Army officer stated at the same time:

> I suspect that serious people somewhere – probably hiding out in Syria – are planning the counterattack, which I suspect will take the shape of popular demonstrations against U.S. occupation, fedayeen attacks on coalition troops and Iraqis who cooperate with efforts to establish a new government, and general operations to destabilize and deny U.S. efforts to move to a secure and reformed Iraq.[12]

However, in April and early May, the majority of military and governmental planners believed that the worst was over.

Perhaps the best way to outline the decay of security and the eventual breakdown into insurgency, terrorism, and near civil war that followed in the months after May 2003 is to present an abbreviated timeline of events from May to December 2004. As developed and published by Brunner:

Apr. 14, 2003   Major fighting in Iraq is declared over by the Pentagon, after U.S. forces take control of Tikrit, Saddam Hussein's birthplace and the last city to exhibit strong Iraqi resistance. Saddam Hussein's whereabouts remain unknown.

May 1, 2003   The U.S. declares an end to major combat operations.

Aug. 19, 2003   Suicide bombing destroys UN headquarters in Baghdad, killing 24, including top envoy Sergio Vieira de Mello, and wounding more than 100.

Aug. 29, 2003   A bomb kills one of Iraq's most important Shiite leaders, Ayatollah Muhammad Bakr al-Hakim, as well as about 80 others, and wounds 125.

Sep. 7, 2003   Continued violence and slow progress in Iraq lead to President Bush's announcement that $87 billion is needed to cover additional military and reconstruction costs.

Oct. 27, 2003	Four coordinated suicide attacks in Baghdad kill 43 and wound more than 200. Targets included the headquarters of the Red Crescent (Islamic Red Cross) and three police stations.
Nov. 2, 2003	In the single deadliest strike since the Iraq war began, guerrillas shoot down an American helicopter, killing 16 U.S. soldiers and injuring 21 others. Other attacks over the course of the month make it the bloodiest since the war began: at least 75 U.S. soldiers die.
Feb. 1, 2004	About 109 Iraqis are killed by suicide bombings in Erbil.
Feb. 10, 2004	About 54 Iraqis are killed in a car bombing while applying for jobs at a police station. The next day an attack kills about 47 outside an army recruiting center.
Mar. 2, 2004	Suicide attacks in Karbala on Shiite Islam's most holy feast day kill more than 85 and wound 233 others. It is believed that the perpetrators are attempting to foment unrest between Shiites and Sunnis.
Mar. 17, 2004	At least 27 people are killed and 41 wounded in the car bombing of a hotel in Baghdad. The bombing came just two days before the anniversary of the first American attack on Baghdad that launched the war last year.
Mar. 31, 2004	Iraqi mob kills and mutilates four America civilian contract workers and then drags them through the streets of Falluja, a city west of Baghdad that is part of the Sunni triangle.
Apr. 9, 2004	An American contract worker, Thomas Hamill, is taken hostage. In all, more than 20 foreigners kidnapped in Iraq.
Apr. 17, 2004	The number of hostages taken by various Iraqi guerrillas reaches about 40.
May 8, 2004	Nicholas Berg, an American contractor, is beheaded by Iraqi militants, who claim the grisly murder was in retaliation for the treatment of Iraqi prisoners.
May 17, 2004	A suicide bomber kills the head of Iraq's Governing Council, Izzedin Salim, and six other people.

Jun. 1–17, 2004   Between June 1 and June 17, at least 100 people are reported killed in car bombs across Iraq. Among the dead are a senior Iraqi government official and a senior diplomat. Several other members of the new Iraqi government become the targets of gunmen.

Jul. 28, 2004   In the deadliest attack since Iraq's interim government took power, at least 68 are killed in a car bombing in Baqouba.

Sep. 7, 2004   The American death toll in Iraq reaches 1,000; about 7,000 soldiers have been wounded. In August, attacks on American forces reached their highest level since the beginning of the war, an average of 87 per day.

Oct. 14, 2004   Insurgents detonate two bombs in the Green Zone, home to Iraqi officials and the American Embassy.

Oct. 19, 2004   Margaret Hassan, British-Iraqi director of CARE International, is abducted in Baghdad. She is later presumed dead.

Oct. 24, 2004   Fifty new Iraqi soldiers are executed by insurgents loyal to Abu Musab al-Zarqawi.

Dec. 19, 2004   Car bombers target Shiites and election workers in brazen attacks in Najaf and Karbala. More than 60 people killed and 120 wounded.

Dec. 21, 2004   Bomb explodes in U.S. military tent at base in Mosul. At least 24 people die, including 19 American soldiers.

This abbreviated presentation only covers those events up through 2004 – the nineteen months following the proclaimed "victory" in Iraq. Additionally, the separate operations that the U.S. Army and coalition forces conducted throughout Iraq in COIN combat numbered in the hundreds.

As history records, the same and even worse occurrences of significant violence in Iraq continued over the years that followed; similar violence exists even through today. What can be taken from this accounting is that all involved who deemed Iraq a "victory" in 2003 were making that determination from inside the paradigm of traditional, symmetric, and status quo filters. In other words, they were all accurate if their assessments were bounded and framed within the traditional perspective of what constitutes a military victory. However, when the actual and full spectrum of the context is revealed, the realities confronting the United States in Iraq in 2003 were well short of what could be considered victory.

The missing element of the contextual picture was the same anomalous situation that had been building since the years of Somalia back in 1992. For the USAF in particular, victory appeared to be defined only in those contexts where an enemy was identifiable, strategic targets were available to strike, and coercive operations had the potential to convince the leadership within the belligerent group that continued resistance to U.S. demands would prove too costly.[13] However, when the above parameters are not present yet continued security requirements exist, what is the USAF, under the dominant banner of the fighter-operations perspective, left capable of providing? It is true that during the years from 2003 to 2012 the USAF has used PGM strikes on a number of high-value targets when intelligence pointed to specific buildings or locations where insurgents might be located. The USAF further used their fighter-operations capabilities to target enemy movements, in all weathers, day or night, when particular belligerents could be identified. However, it is equally clear that since 2003 the USAF has not operated in the traditional fighter-operations parameters that dominate its organizational structure. Fortunately, Secretary of Defense Robert Gates understood these emerging challenges. Gates offered, in a speech delivered in 2008:

> In a world of finite knowledge and limited resources, where we have to make choices and set priorities, it makes sense to lean toward the most likely and lethal scenarios for our military. And it is hard to conceive of any country confronting the United States directly in conventional terms ship to ship, fighter to fighter, tank to tank – for some time to come. The record of the past quarter century is clear: the Soviets in Afghanistan, the Israelis in Lebanon, the United States in Somalia, Afghanistan, and Iraq. Smaller, irregular forces – insurgents, guerrillas, terrorists will find ways, as they always have, to frustrate and neutralize the advantages of larger, regular militaries. And even nation-states will try to exploit our perceived vulnerabilities in an asymmetric way, rather than play to our inherent strengths.[14]

In the continuing conflict in Afghanistan, operations equally decayed from the traditional symmetric perspectives that were present at the start of the war. As was the case outlined for OIF, most government and military planners failed to recognize the challenges that might and eventually did emerge in Afghanistan after the traditional Taliban defeat. However, many military voices and defense analysts knew of the danger that would likely emerge when thousands of combatants were forced into hiding. In terms of the transition to an asymmetric context, where the United States and its allies would be out of their traditional symmetric element, several scholars recognized early in the 1990s that enemies can and will *adapt* to meet the challenges of war.[15] It is long recognized that every military force has vulnerabilities; for the United States, the vulnerability was asymmetric war. The Taliban and al-Qaeda recognized that the only way to confront the United States and its allies was to fight on their own terms using tactics that traditional U.S. military capabilities could not easily dominate. Unidentifiable combatants, limited logistical requirements, little to no required infrastructure, organic intelligence using the population, low-tech improvised weapons that are hard to detect but lethal and very capable of significant disruption, and the understanding that the American people (as well as its partners) had limited resolve – all these features developed a context in Afghanistan that was not conducive to the way the USAF under the dominant banner of the fighter-centric perspective was organized to fight. Within these conditions, only the U.S. Army and U.S. Marines had any significant capability.

The lessons learned from Vietnam regarding guerrilla war and counterinsurgency were still available to tap into; however, for the USAF much of the tactical ground support lessons learned in Vietnam had been discarded for the more decisive and more fighter-centric capabilities of air-to-air operations and strategic bombing. Barnett asserts that "we spent the 1990s buying one sort of military, only to realize after 9/11 that we needed another to wage this global war on terrorism, a threat that until recently was routinely considered the least of the lesser includeds."[16] Although fighter dominance was reinforced in much of the 1990s as well as in the opening operations of Iraq and Afghanistan, when the context shifted away from the preferred and preassumed symmetric context, the fighter-operations perspective upon which the USAF was built became increasingly ineffective and, to a degree, irrelevant.

As both theaters reduced to an environment of uncertainty, insurgency, suicide bombings, Improvised Explosive Devises (IEDs) and sporadic assaults by unidentifiable combatants in an asymmetric context, all the services were forced to adapt if security was ever to be realized. For the USAF, this new context highlighted the emergence of several important subgroups whose capabilities became, and continue today to be, of paramount importance in both conflicts – capabilities well outside of the dominant fighter-operations community.

Among the various groups that have surfaced and have risen to new levels of recognized importance are the nonkinetic attack applications. Nonkinetic attack capabilities include space operations, ISR, counter-IED, combat search and rescue, cyber defense and attack, mobility, and information operations. The USAF has a significant presence and capability in all of these vital areas; however, among all of them the capability of ISR appears to be in highest demand. ISR in both Afghanistan and Iraq has become the backbone for daily mission directives and counterinsurgency decision making, and is the driving force behind nearly all ground movements. Judy Chizek, a national defense fellow, suggested in her 2003 research that ISR is becoming and will further be the most significant capability in war.[17] Chizek suggests that a "transformation" within DoD is paramount in order for the United States to meet its twenty-first century challenges, contending that "a key component of this transformation is DoD's Intelligence, Surveillance, and Reconnaissance (ISR) capability."[18] Her study also determined that "Congress remains concerned that ISR capabilities may not be able to meet the needs of military force unless they [the military] also undergo significant change."[19] She cites the fact that "the Air Force is the largest military provider of surveillance and reconnaissance as it operates most surveillance and reconnaissance aircraft and is DoD's executive agent for space."[20] Within this responsibility, the USAF is faced with the requirement to adapt, reorganize, and develop an ISR capability appropriate for the current and future context.

In Chizek's assessment as to whether the USAF is appropriately "transforming" in order to meet the emerging ISR requirements, she concludes:

> Do the Air Force's activities in ISR support transformation? Judged by the
> standards of interoperability, support to changed methods of warfighting, and

ability to confront a wide range of threats, the answer is unclear. Interoperability stands at the top of the Air Force's stated priorities. The various changes in Air Force organization which have occurred since the end of the Cold War appear to be the most aggressive of all the services. The availability and applicability of space assets to warfighting has increased significantly, adding greatly to the services' access to a world-wide perspective as well as in-depth intelligence. As noted earlier, Air Force efforts appear to have played a large role in establishing the lauded ISR capabilities, particularly their persistent surveillance, for Operation Enduring Freedom. However, some observers believe the Air Force is primarily achieving technical improvements to established programs and operating methods, rather than a radical change appropriate to a potentially radically different enemy.[21]

This assessment suggests that as early as 2003 evidence and scholarship existed focusing on how ISR was becoming a vital capability that had strategic effect (effect across the entire battle space). Furthermore, the USAF was clearly at the center of this enterprise, in that ISR employs capability from manned and unmanned aircraft, space-based systems, and significant command and control networks responsible for turning collected data into information and then disseminating it to the appropriate user – all of which are central USAF capabilities.

In the years from 2003, there is significant evidence that the USAF has in fact accepted the responsibility of an increased ISR capability. According to Gen David Deptula, the USAF top leader for ISR operations and initiatives in 2007, ISR is a "critical requirement needed for today and the future."[22] Deptula further suggests,

> Today we need to ferret out our enemies from among civilian populations, mountain caves, tents in the desert, and the like. They're not massing on the other side of the Fulda Gap. They're diffuse, deceptive, and elusive. As a result, Air Force ISR is one of the most critical weapons we have at our disposal. . . . My point is that our focus needs to be not on platforms, but on providing optimal, maximized, and seamless ISR capabilities for the benefit of our nation, and that's where we're headed in our Air Force. . . . We need to figure out how to task our growing stable of ISR capabilities resident on platforms we generally associate with other tasks.[23]

Much of this recognition for increased ISR that Deptula expresses has resulted in a significant increase in unmanned aerial vehicle (UAV) capability. UAVs have made a tremendous impact on not only the way the U.S. military fights war, but also on how the USAF spends much of its time and resources. The former CSAF, Gen Norton "Norty" Schwartz, offered in a speech in March of 2009, that

> the demand for game-changing, UAV-borne capabilities is insatiable, and shows no sign of abating. General Petraeus has called these contributions "invaluable" in recent combat operations . . . we're flying them non-stop because of their extraordinary value. Our MQ-1 fleet has logged over 600,000 hours; and while this number by itself is impressive, the accelerated rate at which we've accumulated these hours is really the remarkable story. It took us 12 years from 1995 to 2007 to fly our first 250,000 Predator hours. In less than two years, we flew our next 250,000 hours; and, we are on track to log the next quarter million in only 13 months. As we continue significant investments in these aircraft – 320 in the next 5 years – and immediately deploy almost all of them to fly continuous combat air patrols, or "CAPs," for our Joint and Coalition teammates, these flying hours will only continue to multiply. We have come a long way since we started with only one CAP in 2001. After the Joint team realized how vital these aircraft were, they requested more; and, we have delivered, surging nearly everything that we have directly into theater. We're now flying 37 CAPs in Iraq and Afghanistan, and we're on track to provide 50 by the end of 2011.[24]

The chief further acknowledged that this increased emphasis and demand for ISR will require a "cultural shift" within the USAF. He remarked in his speech to recently graduated Air Force UAV pilots,

> Senator John McCain, of course, a former aviator, asked me about these implications [the importance of UAVs] during this May's Air Force posture hearing before the Senate Armed Services Committee. There, he noted that it was a "seminal time" in the history of the Air Force, and asked if the transition to unmanned aircraft would be a *significant cultural adjustment" for the Air Force.* I answered him then, in the same way that I do to you today: you are part of the major new Air Force development of the decade. *This cultural change for our Air Force has to do both with the future of these unmanned systems, and how we see ourselves as Airmen.*[25]

From the above discussion, it is clear that the secretary of defense, the CSAF, policy makers, and academics have all recognized that ISR has emerged over the past several years as a vital capability within the modern context of war. It is further realized that the USAF is at the heart of such capabilities and that organizational change will be required to prepare for increased ISR operations. As Deptula commented in a 2009 *USA Today* interview, "ISR has never been more important than it is today – and that importance will only increase for the foreseeable future."[26] The advent of UAV technology, the increased demand to outfit existing airpower systems with new ISR technologies, the incorporation of space systems, and the increasing need for an organizational structure capable of training, equipping, commanding, and controlling this complex mix of capability is now a major focus of the USAF – and, at this point, perhaps the most significant attribute it brings to modern war.

The salient observation that captures and considers all of the discussion regarding ISR, UAVs, space, cyber, and command and control is the idea that all of these attributes and operational requirements fall within the rubric of "information." Information on the battlefield has long been the desire of every military leader. Today, the context of insurgency, terrorism, unidentifiable combatants, organic enemy operations, and concern for civilian casualty all drive the need for significant information. No longer is it a matter of determining months before a war begins which strategic targets should be hit by airpower and PGMs. As an example of the importance of the ISR and logistical requirements that go into planning a strike in the complex urban war environment, Deptula offers,

> When we took out Abu Musab al-Zarqawi in Iraq last June, that operation consisted of over 600 hours of Predator time, followed by about 10 minutes of F-16 time. The find, fix, track and target part of the equation in this case took far longer, and was much more complex than the engage part. So, are operations supported by intel, or is intel supported by operations? I would tell you that in the 21st Century intelligence is operations.[27]

Within the context of urban war and insurgency operations as witnessed in Afghanistan and Iraq, strategic targets are time-sensitive and often discovered and identified for possible strike within a window of opportunity lasting only a few minutes. Single enemy actors planting IEDs at night, small civilian cars transporting explosives through town, and even suicide bombers who need only reach a crowded destination to instill fear into the entire city or country can only be countered with information – operational information. It is the requirement for information that drives the need for integrated intelligence, sustained surveillance, and responsive reconnaissance across the entire battle space – operational ISR. Integrating space, manned and unmanned aircraft, signal intelligence, human intelligence, integrated ground communications, and overall theater-wide command and control of massive waves of data is the new centerpiece of USAF operations. The fighter capability remains vital, within context; however, it is within this "information-operations" community that the USAF is providing the greatest impact within the context of modern twenty-first-century conflict. It is further within this information-operations environment that the future of the USAF may well be determined.

There is significant evidence that the Afghanistan and Iraq experience has forced the USAF to reevaluate its priorities and to refocus what it sees as its most dominant role. Although it will require additional analysis and scenario building to assess where these changing trends may lead (predictive analysis), at this point the emerging requirements of ISR, cyber operations, space-based capabilities, remotely manned attack platforms, and the command and control infrastructure needed to turn data into operational information are clearly challenging the traditional and dominant fighter-operations organizational structure of the USAF.

11

SIGNS OF CHANGE: 1992–2010

THE ISSUE OF THE DYNAMICS OF LEADERSHIP HAS ALREADY
been presented, in part, in the discussion regarding Gen McPeak and
Gen Fogelman. However, in line with the previous chapters measuring
changes in leadership demographics, further assessment will serve to
help identify trends that are not captured in the historical narrative.
Because leadership is often a reflection of the dominant culture, and
because organizational change models have shown the influence that
leadership can have on the change process, analysis of the leadership
changes that occurred from 1992 through 2010 should provide important insight regarding possible future organizational change within the
USAF. This chapter will examine the leadership characteristics (specific
operational specialty of senior ranking USAF leadership) over the period
from 1992 to 2010. Due to the shorter length of time for this analysis
(eighteen years), specific data will examine the leadership posture at
nine-year points: 1992, 2001, and 2010.

In the beginning of Period Three, the leadership of the top ranking
USAF three- and four-star generals clearly represented the dominant
fighter-operations culture. As figure 11.1 illustrates, the fighter community enjoyed the majority of senior officer positions. In fact, the fighter
community had greater representation at the senior officer level than all
other specialty areas combined. In light of the dominance of the fighter-
operations community within the leadership sector of the USAF, organizational change scholars suggest two considerations. The first is that
the dominant culture (beliefs, values, standard procedures, artifacts,
norms) within the organization is normally represented in the charac-

Figure 11.1

teristic of the leadership. This insight lines up well in the analysis of 1992 leadership and suggests that the leadership of the USAF at that time appropriately reflected the dominant perspectives within the overall institution. The second consideration drawn from the literature is that if organizational change is to occur, then leadership often trends toward the needed changes in the period prior to the actual change. As seen in the study of Period Two (1947–1992), as the analysis unfolded, over the years the dynamics of leadership slowly changed as well (from bomber to fighter). Both of these considerations suggest that analysis of Period Three leadership from 1992 to 2010 may offer important insight as to the trends and internal changes that the USAF may be experiencing in this current period. Using figure 11.1 as a starting baseline, any changes in the USAF leadership structure can be identified and possible trends can be considered to support the predictive analysis that concludes this chapter.

As presented in the historical narrative, the years from 1992 to 2001 saw a number of short-term conflicts that all required some level of air-power engagement. Further, as each conflict emerged, it was determined that the USAF had limited capability in asymmetric conflicts and only achieved success, in their own terms, when the context fit their precon-ceived parameters of conventional and traditional battle. It was noted

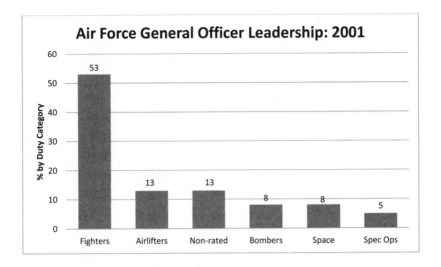

Air Force General Officer Leadership: 2001

Figure 11.2

that in each engagement throughout the 1990s the positive focus of the USAF was on the airpower campaigns that highlighted their strengths (Kosovo in particular). Because most of the USAF engagements ended with a traditional airpower success, the status quo of the fighter-operations perspective was reinforced. Within this timeframe, few external or internal challenges were observed that pressured the USAF to reorganize in order to meet some new or emerging condition for which they were not prepared. The events supported the fighter-operations status quo such that the USAF leadership chose not to focus or appropriately acknowledge the emerging external realities and asymmetric conditions. Therefore, one would expect, and organizational models would suggest, that the senior leadership measured in 1992 and compared now in 2001 would remain highly dominated by the fighter-centric community.

Accessing the demographics of the senior leadership through analysis of the USAF Statistical Digest published by the Secretary of the Air Force in 2002, there are a number of important observations that surface. As illustrated in figure 11.2, the fighter-operations community continued to dominate the overall senior leadership pool. Within the overall leadership hierarchy, the fighter community continued to have greater representation than all other operational areas combined. However, it is also important to note the emergence of two new operational categories: space and special operations (spec ops). Previous analysis demonstrated that both space and spec ops were filled with fighter or bomber personnel. However, with the advent of increased space technologies and the growth of airpower capabilities with special operations–specific roles and missions, senior officers with unique backgrounds in these areas emerged in the three- and four-star ranks. In addition, the airlifter community has increased in representation from its previous percentage of 4 percent in 1992. This also appears in line with the experiences of the 1990s, reflecting the significant airlift responsibility in response to increased humanitarian operations that the analysis of Period Three observed.

As the data suggests up through 2001, the fighter-operations community remains dominant in the top leadership positions. However, following the events of this phase, the historical record equally reveals that the USAF began experiencing pressure from new challenges falling outside the fighter-operations domain. One would expect that in the years from 2001 to 2010, the leadership of the USAF should show some signs of change reflecting the emerging challenges noted in the analysis of this particular timeframe of Period Three. Organizational models suggest that the significant challenges the fighter-centric perspective confronted in the 2003–2010 segment should have some level of indication in the data of USAF senior officer leadership. Although it is difficult to determine what amount of lead or lag the leadership representation has in relation to the emerging external responsibilities, it would be expected that the dynamic shifts over a nine-year time frame from 2001 to 2010, together with the clearly new conditions that were captured in the historical narrative, would show some sign of change regarding who occupies the senior leadership positions.

Drawing data from the list of senior USAF leaders who occupied the key three- and four-star positions, figure 11.3 offers the specialty demographics for 2010. As the data shows, the fighter-operations community has decreased by 20 percent, while each of the other specialties have increased in representation. Except for the fighters and the non-rated group, all specialty areas nearly doubled from the 2001 percentages. Of specific importance is that for the first time since 1982, the CSAF is not

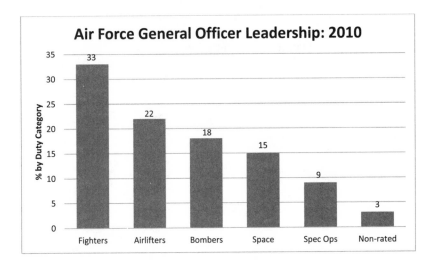

Figure 11.3

a fighter pilot; rather, Gen Norty Schwartz is a special operations pilot. This alone is a considerable observation, highlighted within the organizational change modeling, that suggests a significant shift in the USAF organizational perspective.

Taking the initial suggestion for Period Three that in 1992 there were two groups – fighters and everyone else – a graph showing the percentage and the changes in senior leadership from 1992 to 2010 helps illustrate the changes in leadership. As illustrated in figure 11.4, the percentage of fighter representation in the three- and four-star ranks remained consistent throughout the period leading up to 2001. This data parallels the observations made in the analysis that during this same time period, airpower and the fighter-operations perspective was continually reinforced (Kosovo, OIF, Afghanistan). However, as the previous section observed, the years following 2001 introduced contextual asymmetric challenges that the fighter-operations organizational structure was not prepared to address within its dominant perspective and accepted operating procedures. The increase in counterinsurgency, urban warfare, and terrorism, all elements of asymmetric conflict, led to the emergence and increased importance of various subspecialties (those specialties that under the fighter-operations perspective were traditionally and historically not

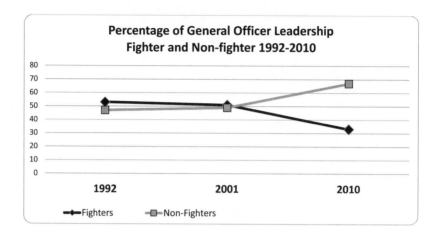

Figure 11.4

considered as primary). The increased need for ISR, space capabilities, and unmanned aircraft increased significantly, while the need for the traditional fighter-operations decreased. When the trend presented in figure 11.4 is considered together with the dynamic of having the first non–fighter pilot CSAF in over twenty-five years, organizational models would suggest that the potential for major organizational change is increasing.

ANALYSIS OF CHANGES: 1992–2010

As the historical record suggests, this period beginning in 1992 was dominated by the fighter-operations perspective and the organizational structure of the USAF followed with the rise of Air Combat Command. The conflicts throughout the 1990s introduced new challenges to all the services, and the USAF was no exception. In the post–Cold War years, internal unrest, civil war, terrorism, tribal discontent, power grabs, and rampant crimes against humanity characterized much of the global context. Within this context, the USAF was called to provide a range of capabilities from humanitarian to combat operations.

As previous chapters suggested, the USAF was successful in nearly all the conflicts for which they were engaged – within the context that airmen preferred. As long as the conflict fit the predetermined parameters that afforded the need for air superiority, strategic strikes, and uncontested airlift opportunity, then the USAF under the organizational dominance of the fighter-operations perspective was extremely capable. However, as was shown, *the underlying reality of the 1990s was one where an asymmetric environment was building and belligerents across the globe were adapting to U.S. hegemony.* Unfortunately, there is limited evidence that the USAF gave much more than cursory attention to the emerging asymmetric threat. In fact, through much of the 1990s, the USAF doctrine characterized and named the emerging asymmetric responsibilities as "Military Operations Other Than War" (MOOTW). The connotation that these operations were something "other than war" may well have led to imposing a secondary or lower priority on such operations. Although the USAF recognized their emerging responsibilities, they categorized them under the banner of "low-intensity conflicts," whose very nature, indicated by the title alone, placed them well below the primary mission of fighting a major peer competitor. However, as 9/11 showed, this new way of waging war against the United States turned out to be anything but "low-intensity."

It is interesting to note that the 9/11 terrorists did not need or require a recognized airmen's perspective or specific airpower culture in order to realize the advantage that the airpower offered in terms of access, time, and space. The airpower they used was not somehow part of their culture, a hallmark of their identity, or a characteristic that set them organizationally apart from other combatants. They simply used the advantages offered by airpower to deliver the effects they desired by exploiting the vulnerabilities of the United States. In other words, *they considered the context of what the United States had planned for in terms of possible national defense contingencies; creatively determined what "weapons" were at their disposal; and then organized themselves to exploit that weapon within that context.* On a larger scale, the events witnessed after 2003 in both Afghanistan and Iraq parallel this same 9/11 strategy: exploit U.S. weakness with whatever capabilities are available; in the context of COIN, combatants blend into the population; infrastructure is not coveted and therefore cannot be targeted for deterrence; and low-technology weapons (IEDs) and suicide/car bombs can instill enough fear and instability within a region that security operations are near impossible. The lesson here of an adapting enemy is not new in warfare and should not be an epiphany for military strategists.

It does, however, raise several questions as to whether or not the USAF has applied the same or similar insight in preparation for their responsibilities:

· Does the USAF organize, train and equip for the context they are given rather than the context they prefer to be given?
· Leading up to 2001, is there evidence that the USAF was actively preparing for counterterrorism, asymmetric war, or counterinsurgency all within a highly charged political environment?
· Was the USAF preparing for the possibility of another Somalia-type conflict, Bosnia engagement, or UN/NATO political war where strategic bombardment might not be appropriate?
· Was the USAF organizational structure prepared to effectively use airpower operations to support ground forces as their primary mission?
· Was the dominant fighter-operations culture within the USAF ready to operate within a context where air superiority was not a concern?
· Was the USAF leadership calling for an increased capability in survivable tactical airlift, or training for the possible need to coordinate intelligence, surveillance, and reconnaissance capabilities in support of ground operations?
· Did the USAF have a codified plan for operationalizing the unmanned aerial vehicle technology to include joint command and control agreements, interagency coordination training, or considerations for how the UAV technology might support a ground-operations COIN conflict?

It appears from the record that the likely response to all these questions is no.

Although an argument can be made that some level of operational preparedness actively addressed many of these questions, it is equally

clear that under the fighter-centric and dominant perspective that characterized the USAF during these years, these outlined concerns were
considered anything but primary – far from the central role of the USAF.
The evidence to support this assertion comes from the events and challenges confronted after 2003. As was shown, the fighter-operations organizational structure of the USAF was neither appropriate nor capable
within the politically charged, asymmetric, urban, and insurgency context of the two conflicts. Although some may argue that the USAF was
indeed flexible and was able to advance capabilities in support of the two
wars, most objective thinkers will agree that the events following 2003
are best described as a "pick-up game," where solutions to the emerging
challenges had not been fully considered prior to their occurrence. The
question at this stage of the analysis is: Why not?

Assessing why the disequilibrium between the USAF organizational
structure and the new asymmetric environment came to exist, Builder
highlights an important element that helps explain the evolution. In assessing the underlying perception of the decisiveness of airpower that
goes clear back to Period One analysis, Builder suggests,

> The claim of decisiveness should have been conditioned to certain kinds of war.
> . . . But that claim [decisiveness of airpower in war] was flawed . . . it didn't con-
> template different kinds of warfare such as we have seen increasingly in the last
> half of the twentieth century – irregular wars that are not dependent on highly
> organized industry and transportation for the provision of their means – where
> there is no heart of the enemy which can be struck decisively.[1]

Builder further suggests that a better axiom for the USAF is that "airpower can be employed decisively in war *when the enemy's essential means
for waging war are vulnerable to attack from the air.*"[2] This perspective,
as Builder points out, "leaves room about the decisiveness of airpower
depending upon the nature of the enemy's means for war and their vulnerability to attack from the air."[3] Taking Builder's argument further, the
USAF should have recognized the emerging asymmetric challenges as
they developed in the 1990s; should have begun organizing, training, and
equipping for such contingencies; and should then have refined those
capabilities for the specific context encountered.

Instead, the USAF appears to have held strong to the one facet of airpower that from the beginning in Period One was their Holy Grail – de-

cisiveness. This is not surprising; after all, it was decisiveness that eventually gave the USAF their independence in 1947; it was decisiveness that lifted Strategic Air Command under the banner of nuclear deterrence to the height of its glory in Period Two; and it was decisiveness that ushered in the fighter-operations dominance witnessed and exercised in the 1991 Gulf War, opening the door to Period Three. However, as events after 2003 revealed, it appears that the desire for decisiveness developed organizational blinders, resulting in a myopic organizational structure built around and for a particular type of war – one where airpower could be decisive. When confronted with an environment not conducive to the *decisive* perspective, the vulnerability of the USAF organizational structure under the fighter-operations dominance became apparent. This analysis at the point in 2010 suggests that Builder's axiom can be expanded: *"Airpower can be employed decisively in war when the enemy's essential means for waging war are vulnerable to attack from the air; when they are not, airpower must be prepared to support the operation with capabilities drawn from across the entire USAF spectrum."* "Prepared to support" means having an organizational structure in place well prior to hostilities that effectively develops capabilities outside of the dominant fighter-operations perspective – capabilities viewed and resourced as primary within the organizational structure of the USAF.

Some might argue that the foundational attribute of flexibility (a hallmark of airpower espoused for many years) allows the USAF to adapt to contingencies, and therefore there is no immediate need to prepare for specific types of warfare. However, as bureaucratic modeling has shown,[4] large organizations are subject to operating within the framework for which they are organized. Claiming the attribute of flexibility while at the same time being constrained within the fighter-operations organizational structure is another way of saying that one is free to move around within the box; however, when the event occurs outside of the box, flexibility in the box matters little.

Fortunately, as the analysis of the previous chapters revealed, there are signs that the USAF is moving toward major organizational change that will focus on the full spectrum of war rather than on a particular facet, context, or weapon system. Within the previous analysis, it was observed that the disequilibrium between the dominant organizational structure and the actual needs in combat has fostered the emergence of several subgroups within the USAF that are proving themselves vital and paramount to successful operations. Furthermore, the changes in the representation of these subgroups in the three- and four-star leadership structure suggest that their operational necessity is being recognized in the appointment of senior leaders. The combination of pressure from external events (post-2003), the importance, recognized internally, of groups outside the fighter-operations community, and the incremental changes observed within the leadership structure, all support the assertion (and the models) that organizational change in the USAF is likely in the near future. Presented again is the quotation from Clausewitz that opened Period Three analysis: "The first, the supreme, the most far-reaching act of judgment that the statesman and commander have to make is to establish ... the kind of war on which they are embarking; neither mistaking it for, nor trying to turn it into, something that is alien to its nature."[5] Being *prepared* to embark on the war that confronts one without attempting to "turn it into something alien to its nature" is the lesson learned from the post-2003 engagements in Afghanistan and Iraq.

Given this assessment, the analysis in this chapter suggests that the USAF appears to be transitioning from the perspective that all modern conflict must and will meet the USAF's own predetermined "decisive" parameters. As will be considered in the next chapter, the consequence of this recognition is likely to be major organizational change. Within this assessment, the objective of the next chapter is to anticipate further what the coming change may look like, to what extent and in what direction the changes may occur, and how future external exigencies might develop and affect USAF organizational structure.

The Nation's interests in the future, as in the past, are likely to be better served by the diversity than by the scale of capabilities offered by the Air Force.

CARL BUILDER

12

ANTICIPATING USAF CHANGE

THIS CHAPTER OPENS THE ANALYSIS OF PERIOD THREE BEGIN-
ning in the present day and attempts to map how the future organizational structure of the USAF might develop (2013–2030). In the view
of Bernstein, Lebow, Stein, and Weber, "Social scientists cannot afford
the luxury of only examining the past, they are deeply engaged in the
attempt to explain the present and think analytically about the future."
Moreover, "Our [social scientists'] interest is in the identification and
connection of chains of contingencies that could shape the future."[1]
Up to this point in the present analysis, I have deliberately considered
Periods One and Two in order to assess the explanatory power of the
outlined organizational change models within the context of the organizational elements of the USAF. Finding that the organizational modeling appropriately helped to describe, inform, explain, and anticipate
organizational change within the context of the USAF, I then used these
insights as a guide to examine the first eighteen years of Period Three
(1992–2010) in preparation and as a basis for continuing Period Three
analysis into the future.

The aim of this work, and this chapter in particular, is to provide
a relevant and objective guide aimed at helping USAF senior leadership effectively and appropriately prepare for an uncertain future. Unlike the previous case studies, where we knew in advance who the new
dominant group would be at the end of the period (bomber pilots, then
fighter pilots), in this future period analysis the emerging group that will
challenge and possibly gain new dominance over the fighter-operations
community is unknown and will need to be analytically determined. As

demonstrated in the previous analysis, organizational modeling suggests that external events, emerging culture, and changes in leadership will together help identify and anticipate this new competing group that will eventually challenge the fighter-operations status quo. This chapter uses data from a recent survey to examine the internal culture, to assess various perspectives, and to determine if any divisiveness or disagreement exists among the various operational groups within the USAF. If internal imbalance within the USAF cultural perspective is identified, this would suggest, in line with organizational change modeling, an environment of disequilibrium similar to those that developed prior to previous USAF organizational change in Periods One and Two.

USAF CULTURE: 2010

Transitioning from the previous method, where historical narrative was able to capture the internal culture of the USAF at various periods in time, the first challenge for mapping the future is to assess the internal culture of the USAF as it exists today. In order to determine the current state and trends of USAF internal culture, I used a survey developed and completed for this work to assess USAF cultural perspectives within the officer ranks (values, beliefs, norms, perspectives, accepted operating procedures). The survey sample was drawn from officers attending various military academic schools across Air University, Maxwell Air Force Base, Alabama.

Air University continually accommodates over one thousand Air Force officer students attending various military educational programs. Five major schools at Air University offer a diverse number of officers available for inclusion in such a survey. Each school is responsible for conducting courses designed to meet specific educational objectives for specific officers in terms of their rank and time in service. As officers move up in years of service and grade (the officer's rank), each school is designed to accommodate the new and increased educational needs of the officers. This made possible a sample across Air University that represents all Air Force ranks from 2nd lieutenant to colonel and that incorporated officers with years in service from less than one year to over twenty-five years. Importantly, the sample taken at Air University

Table 12.1

School	Average Officer Rank	Years of Service (Range)
Air and Space Basic Course	2nd Lieutenant	0–2
Squadron Officer School	Captain	4–8
Air Command and Staff College	Major	8–14
School of Advanced Air and Space Studies	Major/Lt Colonel	14–16
Air War College	Lt Colonel/Colonel	16–22

is highly representative of the greater Air Force population. Table 12.1 presents the various schools and demographics of the officers attending. As the table shows, surveying all the schools available created a sample including all officer ranks up through colonel and collected data on officers that represent various years of service from 0 to 25.

This sampling opportunity, when combined with statistical software, allowed for detailed examination of responses stratified and categorized along a number of different and diverse designators. Because each school is also represented and attended by a cross-section of various Air Force Specialty Codes (AFSC: codes that designate what operational skill an officer is trained in), additional stratification was accomplished regarding internal Air Force subgroups. These separate and distinguishable demographic elements allowed analysis regarding how opinions differ among certain AFSCs, gender, rank, years in service, and schools. By administering the same set of questions to each officer across the university, it was possible to obtain tremendous insight regarding Air Force culture, perspectives, and opinions about future Air Force organizational changes.[2]

The most important aspect driving the categorization of different survey responses is the comparison of how the participating members of the USAF responded to a question overall, and how that compares to the fighter community as the recognized dominant community from 1992 to 2010. In this way, assessing how the non-fighter subgroups perceive various issues in comparison with how the fighter community perceives the same issue will provide insight as to the differences in perspectives, changing of norms, values, and beliefs, and the determination of possible trends that may suggest an emerging subgroup (or groups) that might be challenging fighter-operations dominance.

Beginning with descriptive statistics, figure 12.1 presents the breakdown of officers responding by gender, officer rank, and AFSC. In total, 1,142 surveys were sent out and 530 were returned, for a completion rate of 47 percent. Other than the low number of lieutenant responders, the overall response percentages are close to the actual percentages by rank that are attending school at any given time throughout the academic year. Furthermore, the percentages in response rates by gender and operational specialty come very close to the actual percentages of these categories across the entire USAF population (18.4 percent female officers, 21 percent pilot officers). The officer rank percentages in the response rate also represent the overall population in that as the officer rank increases, the overall number of officers decreases by at least half (more when one examines the flag officer ranks). Overall, the sample drawn from across Air University schools appears a valid representation of the greater USAF population.

The responses are grouped into four major areas of inquiry, with each group of questions attempting to capture specific elements that might help inform and measure current USAF officer culture. In the following results a comparison is offered between what the responses from non–fighter pilot officers are versus the responses from fighter pilot officers. In this way, it can be assessed if any disequilibrium exists between the dominant group that started Period Three (the fighter community) and those outside the fighter community (everyone else). The first group of questions targets whether or not the dominant fighter-operations perspective (air superiority and strategic strikes) is supported across the officer ranks and whether the fighter-operations perspective is appropriate for an unconventional context. The second set of questions examines procurement perspectives, what airpower systems are viewed as most important, and whether the current Air Force policies are appropriate. The third set of questions addresses leadership issues, including opinion on what specialty code is appropriate for top leadership and whether the promotion system is consistent across all operational specialties (this group of questions acknowledges the relationship between culture and leadership). The fourth and final group of questions asked

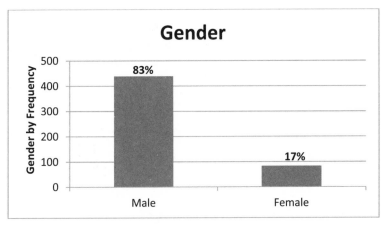

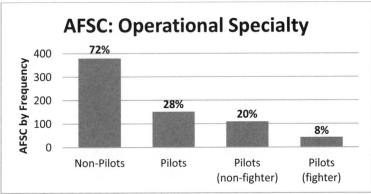

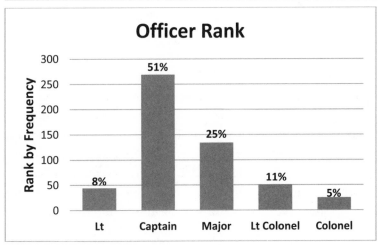

Figure 12.1

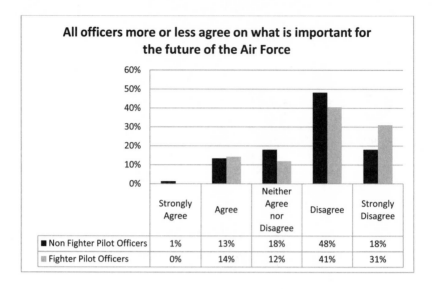

Figure 12.2

responders about possible unwritten cultural hierarchies within the Air Force among various specialties and any possible informal prestige that might exist within the various subgroups, as well as a final question asking responders specifically about the Air Force of 2030.

FIGHTER-OPERATIONS PERSPECTIVE
AND UNCONVENTIONAL WAR

The first group of survey responses follows a logical and connected path of inquiry. Each of the following four survey questions specifically aims to address the internal state of agreement or disagreement among officers regarding their perspective of airpower. Each statement prompts a response indicating, in part, the degree to which the overall non–fighter pilot officer population perceives the current use of airpower relative to the current challenges and then compares those responses to the fighter-pilot-only responses to assess any possible disequilibrium between the groups.

With the aim of measuring the degree of shared perspective, officers were asked whether they agreed or disagreed with the statement head-

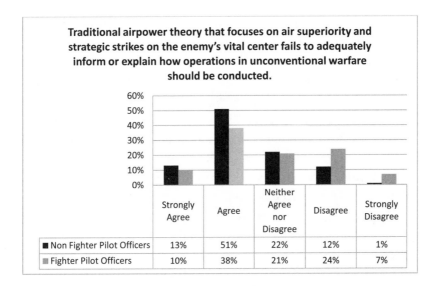

Figure 12.3

ing figure 12.2. The responses show that 66 percent disagreed to some level with the statement (they believe there is not agreement among officers on what is important). As previous analysis in Periods One and Two highlighted, when officers within the USAF disagree as to what is important, the potential for disequilibrium develops. It is of further interest to note that the fighter pilot officers also responded that there is not agreement among officers regarding what is important (72 percent either disagreed or strongly disagreed). This suggests that the dominant fighter community recognizes and acknowledges that differences among officers exist regarding what is considered important for the future of the service. If the large majority of officers across the USAF do not believe there is consensus as to what is important for the future of the service, then as the previous case studies showed and the models have anticipated, the potential for organizational change within the USAF appears likely.

In an attempt to assess the foundation of the fighter-operations perspective and overarching capability, officers were asked to respond to the statement at the head of figure 12.3. This survey item specifically addresses the majority of the airpower operations deemed successful throughout the 1990s and up through 2003. The responses to this survey statement indicate that 64 percent of non–fighter pilot officers either agree or strongly agree with the statement. In other words, the large majority of officers do not think that the traditional and accepted fighter-operations, strategic-strike perspective is appropriate for unconventional war. Comparing results for this survey statement within the fighter-pilot-only community, the response rate drops to 48 percent – a drop of 15 percent from the overall officer perspective. Given that this question goes to the heart of the fighter mission, the fighter-operations in-group is less convinced that this statement is true.

As group psychology theory suggests, when challenged by external pressures, the in-group is likely to resist and will be slow to recognize the need for change.[3] Furthermore, as Schein and others point out within organizational change theory, the dominant group within an organization is often reluctant to recognize the need for change due in part to the possible decrease in power, status, or influence that the change may bring upon the group.[4]

Given the high response from officers who agree that the traditional fighter-operations perspective fails to inform unconventional war, a logically consistent question follows regarding the officers' belief in the future frequency of unconventional war. Officers were asked to respond as to whether they agree or disagree with the statement at the head of figure 12.4. This survey item lines up well with the previous one; if the majority of officers believe that the traditional fighter-operations, air-superiority, strategic-strike perspective fails to rise to the challenge of unconventional war, and if most officers equally believe the future holds an increase in unconventional war, then a clear organizational disequilibrium is emerging. Figure 12.4 presents the responses, indicating that over 75 percent of non–fighter pilot officers either agreed or strongly agreed. Combining the responses to the statements in figures 12.3 and 12.4 suggests that most officers do not believe that the dominant fighter-operations perspective is appropriate for the expected future external context. Comparing this to the fighter-pilot-only group, a response of 55 percent is recorded – a drop of nearly 19 percent from the overall officer population. As with the last question, this suggests that the fighter community does not see nor acknowledge the same degree of disequilibrium

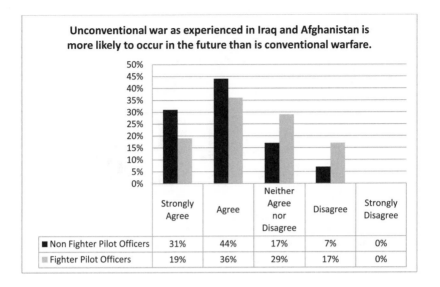

Figure 12.4

as the larger USAF population. The majority of fighter pilot officers do, however, see a future where unconventional war will increase over conventional war. This majority perspective among the fighter community might imply that the USAF is in a transitional time in terms of its potential for major organizational change.

Based on the response acknowledging the inadequacy of the traditional fighter-operations airpower perspective to meet the unconventional context of today's conflicts, and considering the belief held by the majority of officers that the future will see increased unconventional warfare, the logical next question is to ask what might be done in response. This question takes an even deeper look into the heart of the fighter community culture. The air-to-air mission is the soul of the fighter community, with the F-15C air superiority fighter and the new F-22 as centerpieces. Furthermore, the statement in figure 12.5, eliciting opinions as to whether the air-to-air role should decrease while the air-to-ground role increases, harkens back to the Period One analysis, which looked at the era when the Army battled over control of airpower. Within this question lies an underlying aspect of culture, historical institutionalism, and group identity. Figure 12.5 shows that 47 percent of

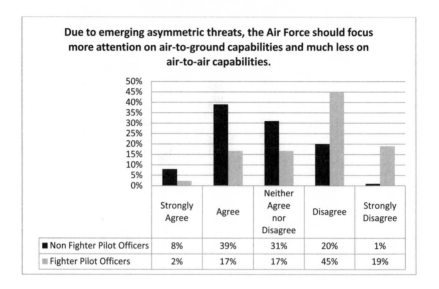

Figure 12.5

non–fighter pilot officers agree or strongly agree. Considering the responses of fighter-pilots only, 19 percent either agree or strongly agree.
Furthermore, within the fighter-pilot-only community, 64 percent either
disagreed or strongly disagreed, compared to only 21 percent in the non–
fighter pilot officer population. This divergence is substantial, suggesting
a further divide between what the dominant fighter-operations community believes and what the rest of the officer corps believes – a strong
sign of disequilibrium. Theory explains this divergence, in part, as the
resistance of the dominant group to relinquish power.[5] Given that the
dominant theme of the fighter-operations community is the air-to-air
superiority mission, a new focus where air-to-ground takes the primary
spotlight within the foreseeable future would naturally encounter resistance from the fighter community.

Overall, this first group of questions suggests that there is agreement
regarding disagreement: officers across the USAF do not believe that
there is consensus as to what is important. The majority of officers do
not believe that the traditional fighter-operations, strategic-strike, air-superiority perspective appropriately informs the current unconventional
war context. Furthermore, the majority of officers believe that uncon-

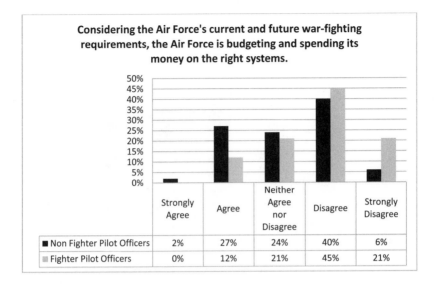

Figure 12.6

ventional war will characterize future engagements. Finally, given the requirements in unconventional war, the large majority of officers believe that the USAF should focus more on air-to-ground capabilities and less on air-to-air capabilities. However, for these same statements, in assessing responses from the fighter-pilot-only community, there appears clear divergence from the overall officer perspective. The most prominent difference is observed in responses to the statement regarding air-to-air versus air-to-ground priorities. The response patterns from the overall officer group and the fighter-pilot-only group form near-opposites. This suggests a significant disequilibrium between what the fighter community believes and what the rest of the USAF officer corps believes. What will be important in concluding this survey analysis is assessing how this difference may potentially affect future USAF organizational structure.

SURVEY: PROCUREMENT PERSPECTIVES

In this section, a group of statements is offered that further attempts to capture the current trends in officer culture, opinion, and perspective. These statements directly attempt to assess officers' opinions on

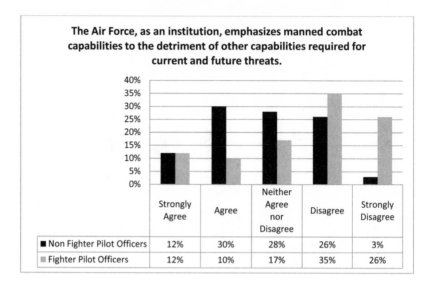

The Air Force, as an institution, emphasizes manned combat capabilities to the detriment of other capabilities required for current and future threats.

	Strongly Agree	Agree	Neither Agree nor Disagree	Disagree	Strongly Disagree
■ Non Fighter Pilot Officers	12%	30%	28%	26%	3%
▨ Fighter Pilot Officers	12%	10%	17%	35%	26%

Figure 12.7

procurement decisions for today and into the future based on perceived airpower needs. Planning for future spending requirements is another way to assess what officers believe will be important. As was shown in the previous Period One and Two analyses, as the majority of officers begin to see a different future than the current dominant group (in this case fighter pilots), the support, shape, and direction the USAF takes will begin to change. Figure 12.6 presents the results for both groups, which concur that the USAF is not spending its money on the right systems. The fighter community is stronger in this opinion, with the majority of fighter pilots either disagreeing or strongly disagreeing with the survey statement. What will be important to assess is specific areas where these officers believe that the USAF should be doing things differently and how particular capabilities should be prioritized.

Regarding specific system requirements, officers were asked to provide their opinion on the traditional manned flight capability that has characterized airpower operations from the earliest years in Period One. As recorded in figure 12.7, 42 percent of the non–fighter pilot respondents agreed with the statement. Although not reflective of a majority opinion, the fact that nearly half of the officer corps believes that the emphasis

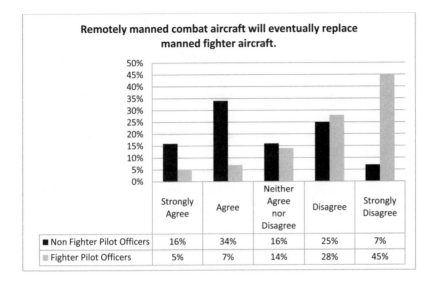

Figure 12.8

on manned capabilities is a *detriment* to other needed capabilities is a significant observation. Also of interest is that the fighter community agrees at a rate almost half that recorded for the non–fighter pilot officers perspective (22 percent). As was the trend in the previous group of survey questions, the fighter community appears to support the traditional airpower perspective more than the overall officer corps does. However, the fact that a large number of fighter pilot officers (22 percent) align with the other officers' perspective regarding the changing and emerging requirements of airpower in today's current context suggests that the USAF is in a transitional time where organizational change is likely and is potentially building.

Although a large number of capabilities within the USAF arsenal do not include manned flight, one particular area that is important to assess involves the emergence of unmanned flight – UAVs. As the Iraq and Afghanistan battles have highlighted, the need for UAVs is, echoing the CSAF Gen Schwartz, "insatiable."[6] The capability these new systems provide cannot be understated and nearly all U.S. and coalition forces from each branch of the service are now dependent on UAV technology. Given the emerging and clear importance that the UAV capability is providing in modern conflicts, inquiry as to how the officer corps sees the UAV versus the dominant fighter community will help determine what organizational impact may be developing as a result of this new technology.

Referring to figure 12.8, 50 percent of the non-fighter pilot officers believe that UAVs will eventually replace fighter aircraft. Again, this number does not ensure any organizational concrete changes at this point; however, the fact that nearly half of the officer corps believe that the manned fighter aircraft will eventually be replaced by unmanned combat aircraft might well have some degree of influence on the long-term procurement decisions and eventually on the organizational structure of the USAF.

Interestingly, the disequilibrium between the overall officer population and the fighter community is evident in that 73 percent of the fighter group disagreed with the statement compared to only 32 percent of the non-fighter officer corps. The difference in these two responses suggests a significant internal conflict between what the non-fighter pilot officers believes and what the dominant fighter-operations community believes. This internal imbalance parallels similar disagreement between the bomber community and fighter community in Period Two. As the Period Two analysis revealed, the increased imbalance between the then dominant bomber community with the emerging fighter perspective eventually led to a major organizational change. It may be that the building divide observed in this question suggests that the current fighter-operations dominance is eventually going to be replaced by an emerging new perspective that is deemed more appropriate for meeting the current and future needs of the USAF (just as in 1992).

The final assessment in this group of questions asks officers to rank order specific airpower systems in terms of how they would prioritize them for purchase. This assessment is extremely important in that it offers insight as to what the officers believe is important relative to other systems; it reveals what aircraft officers believe are the most relative to current and future requirements; and it offers an important comparison between the non–fighter pilot officers and the dominant fighter community regarding what decisions each group would make if it were up to them to decide. The officers were asked the following: Given the five aircraft systems below, rank order how you would prioritize them for

Table 12.2

Rank Order	Non-Fighter (Mean)	Fighter Pilots (Mean)
1	Refuelers (2.41)	Fighters (2.15)
2	CAS (2.71)	Refuelers (2.33)
3	UAV (2.80)	CAS (2.79)
4	Airlift (3.33)	Airlift (3.64)
5	Fighters (3.74)	UAV (4.68)

purchase. Number your priorities from 1 to 5, with number 1 being your top priority that must receive funding and 5 being the lowest priority for funding.

· Close Air Support
· Unmanned Aircraft
· Airlift Aircraft
· Fighter Aircraft
· Refueling Aircraft

Table 12.2 presents the responses from both the non–fighter pilot officers and the fighter-pilot-only group. The rankings for each individual aircraft were averaged among all responders and presented in order from highest priority to lowest.

Interestingly, the non–fighter pilot officers ranked refuelers, close air support, and UAVs in the top three for purchase priority. Moreover, it should be observed that refuelers, CAS, and UAVs are all significant requirements within the current conflicts. Given the previous assessment that suggested the majority of officers believe the future will consist of more unconventional warfare, the response here may also reflect their understanding of what will be required of the future USAF. However, within the fighter pilot group, fighter aircraft are considered the most important aircraft for procurement, with UAVs considered the lowest priority. The responses to this question reveal a complete imbalance between the ranking of number one and number five airpower systems between the two groups.

Taking into account the historical narrative and analysis of the previous chapters and considering the current state of operations in both Afghanistan and Iraq, one can perceive an explanation for why the non–

fighter pilot officers rank UAVs higher than fighters. In fact, the majority of Air Force officers deem fighters to be the lowest priority. However, this same evaluation is not held by the fighter community. The fighter pilots believe that UAVs are the lowest priority, and that their own fighter aircraft should receive top priority. The disequilibrium between opinions about what aircraft should be prioritized could not be more stark. Furthermore, this assessment and the responses from the fighter community appear to offer some level of support for Builder's 1994 assertions. The possible consequences of this divergent internal perspective to the future organizational structure of the USAF will be considered in the final analysis of this work.

LEADERSHIP AND UNWRITTEN HIERARCHIES

For this section of the survey, questions were designed to specifically address and emphasize various perspectives of leadership within the USAF. Just as previous case study analysis suggested the importance of leadership to the overall organizational structure, assessing what the officer corps believes regarding leadership in the current context will provide important cultural data from which to draw. The first of two leadership assessments in this group asked officers if they agreed or disagreed with the following: Because of the nature of what the Air Force is primarily responsible to accomplish in war, fighter pilots are best qualified to hold senior leadership positions.

This is an interesting question in light of the responses that were presented previously. As a reminder, when the non–fighter pilot officer and the fighter-pilot-only groups were asked if the traditional fighter-operations perspective was appropriate for unconventional war, both response groups believed it was not appropriate (63 percent and 48 percent respectively). Furthermore, as outlined in the previous chapter regarding the primary importance of ISR and space-based capabilities in modern war, there was clear evidence that subgroups outside of the traditional fighter-operations community were responsible for the primary USAF role in both Iraq and Afghanistan. In light of these observations, one would presume that the officer corps would begin to recognize that

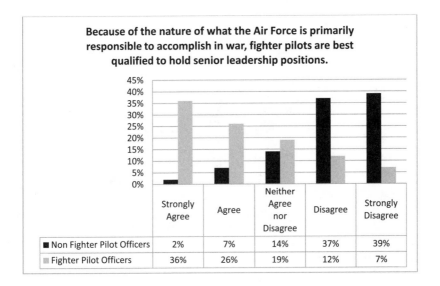

Figure 12.9

fighter-operations specific experiences may not be the best requirement for the top leadership positions.

Figure 12.9 presents the responses and provides another significant difference between the two groups. Only 9 percent of the non–fighter pilot officer corps believe that fighter pilots are the best qualified to hold top leadership positions. This is compared to the large majority of fighter pilots (62 percent) that believe fighter pilots are the most qualified given the current responsibilities of war. This divergent opinion within the officer corps between the fighter community and everyone else may have significant organizational consequences depending on who is selected for the top leadership positions.

Another important leadership inquiry involves how officers believe their operational specialty affects their opportunity to reach senior officer positions. Officers were asked whether they agreed or disagreed with the statement: Nonrated officers have less chance of making flag officer rank regardless of their overall air and space power strategic thinking capabilities. Put another way, this question asks officers if they think the USAF promotes officers to senior levels based on their operational status

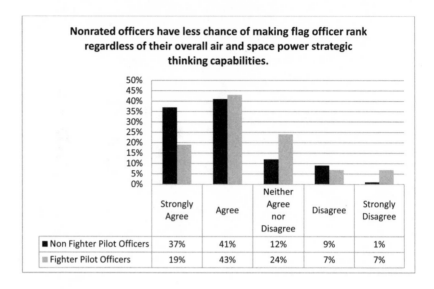

Figure 12.10

(pilot or nonpilot) rather than on their individual and proven strategic thinking skills. If it is found to be true that officers generally believe that flag officer selection (general officer ranks) is more a function of operational specialty and less a function of airpower intellectual or strategic thinking capability, then the USAF is promoting those less qualified in order to sustain a particular dominant culture. Figure 12.10 displays the responses for both groups and reflects that the majority believe the statement to be true. The consequence of this observation has the potential to be significant. If the majority of officers believe that only certain types of operational specialties are promoted to the highest ranks regardless of whether or not others have superior airpower thinking capability, then the idea of a "glass ceiling" develops.

One is forced to ask the question why such an environment (real or perceived) might exist. Could it be, as Builder suggests, that the USAF puts an irrational amount of significance on pilot-specific capabilities, to the detriment of other highly capable and required skill sets, and therefore leadership is selected that reinforces such bias? Furthermore, as Builder suggests, has the glamour and prestige associated with flying aircraft (fighters in particular) become so glorified that highly qualified airpower thinkers not within the in-group of the pilot community are considered less capable as strategic airpower leaders? Perhaps the answers may be easier to find in the results of further survey analysis in the responses to the next group of questions regarding whether any informal and unwritten prestige exists within the service.

UNWRITTEN HIERARCHIES

Up to this point in the survey analysis, it has become clear that there is a divide between the overall opinion and perceptions of the non–fighter pilot officer corps and that of the fighter-pilot community. In some cases, the differences were significant, indicating an imbalance great enough to suggest the need for organizational change. However, the missing element in this analysis comes from this fourth and last group of survey questions, which address whether there exists an informal prestige or an unwritten ranking of "who" and what operational specialties are tacitly considered superior to others. Considering the possible need for organizational change, it will be important to understand whether one group is inherently dominant over another group and whether individuals within the USAF organizational structure have a level of tacit prestige based solely on the operational group to which they belong.

The response from both the non–fighter pilot officer group and the fighter-pilot-only group, offered in figure 12.11, suggests that an overwhelming number of officers believe that there is prestige given to some AFSCs based solely on the operational specialty. Interestingly, the fighter-pilot-only group also agrees with the majority, though to a slightly lesser degree. The obvious question that comes from this observation: What is the unwritten hierarchy within the USAF that these officers all appear to believe exist?

Officers who agreed with the previous statement were asked to rank order two different sets of categories. The first ranking involved five general operational specialties. Officers were asked: If you agreed with the last question regarding an unwritten culture that places more importance and prestige on some AFSCs over others, then rank order the duty categories below in the order that you think this "unwritten" culture perceives different AFSCs. Number your perspective from 1 to 5, with

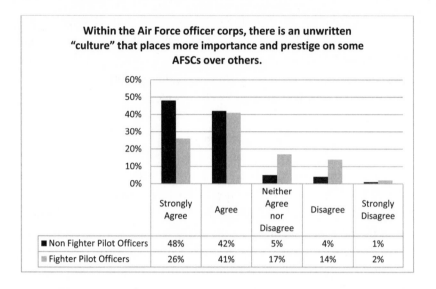

Figure 12.11

number 1 being the service area that receives the highest importance and prestige and number 5 being the service area that receives the lowest.

- Intel
- Pilot
- Space
- Support
- Missile

The responses to this inquiry are offered in Table 12.3 with the mean values determining the overall ranking across the groups. As presented, the data suggests that there is near-unanimous agreement among all officers. Other than a very slight difference regarding the rankings of space and intel between the two groups, both are nearly unanimous in their assessment. What is noteworthy is the overwhelming (almost 100 percent) agreement that the pilot community at large holds the greatest amount of unwritten prestige within the USAF. The question arises as to whether external events that drive the need for nonpilot capabilities

Table 12.3

Rank Order	Non-Fighter (Mean)	Fighter Pilots (Mean)
1	Pilot (1.04)	Pilot (1.03)
2	Space (2.88)	Intel (2.79)
3	Intel (3.00)	Space (2.97)
4	Missile (3.79)	Missile (4.10)
5	Support (4.28)	Support (4.10)

(such as those since 2003 in Afghanistan and Iraq) will change this prestige, or whether the tacit and dominant internal culture characterized by piloted aircraft will continue to receive this standing and the subsequent influence this ranking enjoys.

Although this specific type of data was not available for the 1960s, one can presume that in the middle of Period Two, when the bomber community dominated under the organizational structure of SAC, this same response would also place the pilot in the highest ranking. What more than likely has changed since the mid-1960s is the prestige within the pilot community itself. As theory suggests, the influence and power within an organization is normally held by the group that defines the dominant culture. In the 1960s, that group was clearly the bomber community. However, one would presume that in Period Three, following the major organizational change in 1992, the fighter community would hold the highest level of "unwritten" prestige. Determining one layer deeper in this inquiry into the unwritten prestige within the USAF requires analysis of the pilot community at large.

The next question is asked in relation to the previous question: Where within the pilot community do the various aircraft systems rank in terms of an unwritten pilot prestige? In other words, since the previous assessment determined an overwhelming majority believe that pilots hold the highest ranking in terms of prestige, how specifically within the pilot community does this prestige break down? In this regard, officers were asked the following: Among the various aircraft within the Air Force, pilots have specific specialties. If you believe that an "unwritten" culture exists among pilots that places greater importance and prestige on some pilots over others, then rank order the list of pilot specialties

Table 12.4

Rank Order	Non-Fighter (Mean)	Fighter Pilots (Mean)
1	Fighter (1.06)	Fighter (1.03)
2	Spec Ops/Helo (2.57)	SpecOps/Helo (2.26)
3	Airlift (3.61)	Airlift (3.74)
4	Tanker (4.03)	Tanker (4.26)
5	C2ISR (4.19)	C2ISR (4.73)
6	UAV (5.49)	UAV (5.00)

with 1 being the "most important and prestigious" and 5 being "the least important and prestigious."

- UAV Pilots
- Airborne Command and Control/ISR Pilots
- Fighter Pilots
- Tanker Pilots
- Spec Ops and Help Pilots
- Airlift Pilots

The ranked responses from both groups are offered in Table 12.4 and suggest that the fighter pilot specialty garners the highest unwritten prestige among the pilot community. In both groups, nearly 100 percent of responders believe that the fighter operational category has the greatest amount of unwritten prestige. It is further recognized that there is near complete agreement that the UAV community has the least amount of unwritten prestige. Although the past ten years since 2003 has shown an extensive increase in the relevance and necessity for UAVs, and although in this same time period the role and necessity for the fighter aircraft has diminished to only limited tactical strikes in support of ground operations, the overall prestige remains with the fighter community, and the UAV community receives the lowest assessment. The organizational consequence of having the greatest amount of prestige going to the operational specialty that has the least amount of operational capability in the current context is an interesting paradox. In a large sense, this directly supports Builder's 1994 work that suggests the primary focus of

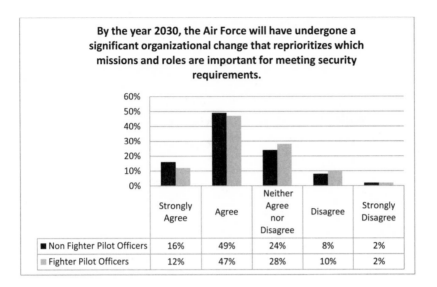

By the year 2030, the Air Force will have undergone a significant organizational change that reprioritizes which missions and roles are important for meeting security requirements.

	Strongly Agree	Agree	Neither Agree nor Disagree	Disagree	Strongly Disagree
■ Non Fighter Pilot Officers	16%	49%	24%	8%	2%
▧ Fighter Pilot Officers	12%	47%	28%	10%	2%

Figure 12.12

the USAF is on the airplanes they get to fly rather than on the capabilities needed to effectively support national military engagements.[7]

The final question considered on this survey relates to how the officer corps sees the future of the USAF organizationally. Officers were asked: By the year 2030, the Air Force will have undergone a significant organizational change that reprioritizes which missions and roles are important for meeting security requirements. This final question was intended to capture how officers perceived the overall organizational structure of the USAF today and how that perception might change by 2030. Although it is understood that each responder could only speculate, their opinions were based on their personal experiences in the USAF as well as their experiences in the two wars being waged, in Afghanistan and Iraq. The responses to this final question are offered in Figure 12.12 and suggest that a majority of officers in both the non–fighter pilot officers and the currently dominant fighter pilot community believe that the USAF will undergo significant organizational change. This response from such a large number of officers suggests they acknowledge a future need for change.

The synthesis of these survey results is an important indicator for how the internal culture of the USAF is changing. As was the case in both Periods One and Two, the dynamic saw those in charge at the beginning of the period being challenged over time by gradually emerging sub-groups that gained in both influence and capability. This survey, taken at what would be approximately halfway through the previous two periods,[8] suggests a similar timing of internal imbalance as was evidenced in prior period analysis.

13

FRAMING THE SURVEY PERSPECTIVES

FROM THE INFORMATION CAPTURED IN THE SURVEY, IT appears clear that there is disequilibrium between the non–fighter pilot officer's perspective and the fighter pilot officer's perspective. In summary, both groups of officers agree that the future will be characterized by an increase in unconventional war over conventional war, and both do not believe that the traditional air superiority and strategic strike perspectives of the fighter-operations community adequately inform and explain airpower operations in unconventional war. As a result, it appears the non–fighter pilot officers believe there are now more important considerations in terms of systems, procurement, and capabilities than the fighter-operations perspective offers. However, the fighter community clearly disagrees, responding to all questions that challenged or degraded the fighter perspective with responses supporting the fighter-operations status quo.

One of the more striking observations taken from the survey involved how each group perceived the future of UAVs relative to manned flight. The non–fighter pilot officers believe that UAVs will eventually replace fighters, while the fighter community does not agree. Furthermore, when the two groups were asked to prioritize systems for purchase, the non–fighter pilot community had UAVs in the top three and fighters last; the fighter pilot community had fighters as the top priority and UAVs last. Finally, the imbalance in perspective between the two groups is further cemented in the assessment of whether fighter pilots should hold the senior leadership positions when considering the current and future mission of the USAF. The non–fighter pilot officers overwhelmingly disagreed, while the fighter community overwhelmingly agreed. When these observations are considered in light of the last questions, which investigate the unwritten prestige of pilots and the further stratification of fighter pilots, the picture of where the USAF is in terms of culture becomes fairly clear: in transition.

It appears that the current culture of the USAF is showing signs of transition. The dominant fighter community, which enjoyed not only the fruits of victory in war throughout the 1990s and up to 2003 but also the knowledge that their mission was considered primary across the service, is being challenged by a growing number of non–fighter pilot officers, whose perspective differs considerably from that of the dominant group. The experiences of the past ten years, together with underlying and emerging asymmetric challenges that erupted as far back as 1992 in Somalia, have elevated a number of capabilities and new technologies to the top of the USAF list of responsibilities. The exponential increase in UAVs for ISR and even strike missions, the vast degree of space capabilities required by all services, the increase of special operations airpower working closely with ground forces, the increased requirement for humanitarian airlift in often-hostile regions, and the continuing need for theater-wide command, control, and dissemination of operational information have required the USAF to consider, as primary, alternative missions outside the traditional fighter-operations perspective. Moreover, the survey results suggest that within the large body of officers outside the fighter community (roughly 95 percent of USAF officers are not fighter pilots), their combat experience and lessons learned within the context of unconventional war have together provided them an opportunity for greater influence. However, as the survey equally shows, the fighter community is not "on board" with the majority of the USAF officer corps. The disequilibrium between the two groups and their diverse perspectives is evident, and theory suggests that this level of disequilibrium normally precedes organizational change. However, before beginning an effective consideration of what the organizational change might entail, further analysis as to why and how this disequilibrium exists is warranted.

Although there are numerous resources that attempt to assess the changing perspectives of the USAF, and many that have attempted to anticipate future challenges, the work by Carl Builder in 1994 stands out as the most explanatory and formidable work for analyzing the internal dynamics of the USAF. Builder's work is already heavily quoted and sourced throughout the current study, and drawing additional reference from Builder's 1994 *Icarus Syndrome* will prove invaluable to explaining the disequilibrium the survey has captured.

In an attempt to understand why the USAF is laden with internal tribes, factions, and a lack of a unifying identity, Carl Builder, working at the time for the RAND Corporation, was contracted by Gen Ford, Commandant of Air University's Air Command and Staff College, to investigate and write a report on the internal dynamics of the USAF officer corps.[1] However, Builder's work expanded beyond a traditional RAND report and was eventually published in 1994 as a book. Builder, tracing the history of the USAF in the development of airpower theory, determined that after gaining independence, the USAF transitioned from focusing on the ends that airpower made possible and instead began focusing solely on the means they preferred to employ. In his work, Builder suggests that the USAF loves the act of flying aircraft more than it cares about the end for which those aircraft are flown (to support our nation's wars). He characterizes this in the title of his book as the "Icarus Syndrome"; according to the Greek myth, Daedalus and his son Icarus used wings of feathers and wax to fly and escape from the island upon which they were imprisoned. Icarus, however, fell in love with flying so much that he lost sight of the mission of escape (the desired end state) and flew too close to the sun – melting the wax in his wings and falling to his death.[2] Builder suggests in this analogy that the USAF has become so committed to the "machines they fly" that they have lost sight of the reason those machines exist in the first place.

In order to fully develop and support this assertion, early in his argument Builder recounts:

> For the most part, the sellers of the air power theory were aviators, who were, understandably, always more interested in the means (the airplane) than the ends (war). They thought the leverages claimed for air power – speed and

vantage point – were uniquely embodied in the airplane; if one accepted the theory and its ends, the airplane was the only means for fulfillment of the ends. Therefore, they could afford to sell the theory in the terms of its serious ends rather than its more joyous means.[3]

Builder further supports this argument by asserting that the concept of "speed and vantage point" that only the airplane could offer was all the earlier pioneers needed to advance their demand for additional and more advanced airplanes – the end (advantage in war) was the justification for the means (airplanes). However, as Builder suggests,

> that concept worked out to the advantage of all involved so long as the airplane was the only means for fulfilling that concept. But when other means, such as unmanned aircraft, guided missiles, and spacecraft became available, it was the aviators who revealed, by deeds more than words, that their real affection was for their airplanes and not the concept of air power.[4]

Although Builder was referencing Periods One and Two with his observations, one can equally translate his analysis to the present period.

The air power theory advanced by the fighter-operations perspective, formally and organizationally codified in 1992, is that air superiority and strategic strikes aimed at targeting an enemy's vital centers of gravity will effectively and sufficiently reach the ends that our nation's political leaders desire. The leverage of speed and vantage point in this fighter-operations theory depended on and advanced by means of the only system capable of achieving the end results – fighter aircraft. As long as airpower was applied against a peer or near-peer competitor that had the required infrastructure, identifiable combatants, and a leadership hierarchy capable of being deterred, then the airpower concept formulated and advanced by the fighter-operations community would be successful.

Within this calculus, two advantages for the USAF would be realized: the nation would have the capability to meet its objectives in conventional war (ends), and the USAF would remain organized and dominated by the fighter community who "owned" the means to that end. However, as Builder points out in his argument, this concept only holds if the parameters it is built upon remain unchanged. When the conventional context changes to unconventional, and when within that context capabilities arise that can deliver airpower better than traditional fighters; when vantage point is dominated by space and ISR assets; and when

UAVs can provide both sustained surveillance and strategic strike, the dominance of the fighter-operations perspective is challenged.

In Builder's assessment as to how the airmen in the 1960s dealt with the emergence of missiles and space capabilities that threatened the uniqueness and necessity of the bomber aircraft, he offers that the space officers and missileers

> quickly recognized that the aviators who ran the Air Force were really more faithful to airplanes than they were to the concept of air power which could now be served by alternative means. The missile and space advocates, like the aviators before them, had found new means [speed and vantage point] to the old ends of air power [advantage in war], only to find that the institutional leadership was devoted to the old means more than the old ends. The new means would be accepted but clearly not favored within the institution.[5]

There is perhaps no clearer explanation for the disequilibrium observed in the survey the current work presents. The emerging operational capabilities of UAVs, space-based assets, ISR systems, and special operations are challenging the dominant fighter-operations perspective by advancing the concept of airpower by alternative means. As the survey responses from the fighter pilot group revealed, these new and emerging advances in support of airpower are "accepted but clearly not favored within the institution."

One final attribute of Builder's argument important to include in this analysis is his assessment of how the USAF evolved into tribes and "stovepipes," where operational specialties could have tacit and unwritten prestige that promoted friction through in-group and out-group dynamics. In his discussion of how the bomber pilots dealt with the missileers who were challenging their unique capabilities, Builder asserts,

> When the development of missiles reached the point where their efficacy could no longer be denied ... the Air Force leadership was finally compelled to include them. But the admission of missile and then space advocates into the Air Force was not as full citizens. The aviators dominated the institution; and while they tolerated others pursuing their own interests in different means or specialties, they demonstrated in many ways that aviators and airplanes were the mainstream of the Air Force. This attitude was the beginning of an institutional divisiveness that would be even more destructive than the split between the fighter and bomber pilots. It was destructive because the discrimination was not in favor of an altruistic mission – striking quickly and decisively at the heart of an enemy – but in favor of an elite class: the pilots.[6]

Forwarding a similar argument as explanation for the responses observed in the survey, we may suggest that the fighter community accepts
the advent of unconventional war and acknowledges the importance
of the emerging capabilities of various subgroups – but not as "full citizens." It appears, judging by the responses from the fighter pilot group,
that they are "tolerating others pursuing their own interests in different
means or specialties," but that they continue to believe that fighters and
fighter pilots "are the mainstream of the Air Force." The subsequent "institutional divisiveness" that this disequilibrium between non–fighter
pilot officers and fighter pilot officers creates is "destructive" because it
"favors an elite class: fighter pilots."

One explanation for the disparate opinions between these two
groups comes from Krepinevich: "The impetus for change is muted by
the realization that real change will likely alter the military's pecking
order. Subcultures of a military service that are viewed as peripheral may
become dominant, while the currently dominant subculture may have
to cede pride of place or even be marginalized."[7] In line with organizational change models and group psychology, Krepinevich's observation
suggests that the fighter community may well be dragging their feet in
terms of changing perspectives, anxious that the looming change may
further minimize their current hold on power and rearrange the pecking
order that put them on top in 1992.

In summary, putting this analysis into context, Builder was writing
in the early 1990s, and his observations were aimed at what he saw occurring in the years before he published his work (1994). The timing of
his observations falls within the first few years of Period Three analysis
and is captured in the previous chapters as a time when the emerging
asymmetric threat of unconventional war was developing just below
the surface. Bringing the analysis up to date, it appears that the context
Builder was describing and attempting to explain in 1994 has now further advanced by 2013. However, going beyond Builder's argument, this
work seeks to determine how and to what extent this current divisiveness (disequilibrium) might foster major USAF organizational change.
The survey analysis shows there is clearly an emerging and important
voice across the USAF that is advocating a different means for projecting airpower than that formally codified in 1992 and up through 2003

by the fighter community. Furthermore, it appears that at this point in Period Three, the dominant culture within the USAF can no longer be assumed to be the fighter-operations culture to the degree it was in 1992. As the previous chapters suggested, it appears that the USAF is in a time of transition, where no single culture dominates or overly influences the organizational structure. Moreover, from the survey results and the previous analysis, it appears likely that the current culture within the USAF is evolving, and that the dominant culture that emerges may well be an amalgamation of numerous operational specialties not necessarily in line with the traditional fighter-operations perspective. In order to further investigate the possibility that the USAF is in a "transitional time" predictably on the path to future organizational change, the next chapter examines in greater detail the operational characteristics of the senior USAF leadership in 2010.

14

CHANGING LEADERSHIP

THE OVERALL CONCLUSION FROM THE PREVIOUS SURVEY analysis is that the USAF is in a transitional time, when the fighter-operations community that dominated the USAF in 1992 is now experiencing internal challenges. Much of the previous analysis focused on the internal cultural dynamics revealed by responses to the survey questions, which examined officers' beliefs, perspectives, and opinions on what should be considered standard operating procedures, as well as the friction between the fighter-operations norms and the rest of the Air Force. In this transitional time, the USAF, as the previous chapter concluded, is experiencing the emergence of a new culture and the development of a new organizational structure. Before attempting to predict the organizational direction this transitional path may take, this chapter will first consider specific senior leadership observations (current as of summer 2010).

According to organizational modeling, leadership is an important variable in examining the organizational dynamics of any institution. Furthermore, as Periods One and Two studies showed, leadership often reflects the dominant culture, and considerable insight can be gained about an organization by examining the leadership trends, characteristics, and demographics of those in the highest positions. For the USAF, the four-star officer rank is the highest obtainable rank; those selected have the greatest amount of influence regarding the current and future directions of the USAF. Although previous work used a comparison of three- and four-star general officer changes in 1992, 2001, and 2010 to identify any trends, examination of four-star generals in particular offers additional insight. At the four-star level, the USAF has only nine to twelve officers who have been highly successful, have received the approval of DoD leadership, and have been vetted by the congressional and even the presidential oversight process. Given this process, the characteristics of those in the four-star billets should be some indication of what the U.S. government perceives as most important; of what the DoD has determined will provide the best war-fighting leadership; and of what operational specialties within the Air Force are receiving the highest level of representation and recognition. As modeling and the previous case studies suggest, observing who occupies the most senior and most influential leadership positions will provide considerable information that can be used not only to identify the presence of a transitional time, but also to help to assess what direction any identifiable transition may be taking.

Trends are best identified by comparing previous data with current data in order to determine specific changes. Comparing the operational specialties of the nine four-star generals in 1992 to the current four-star generals in 2010 (all in the same leadership positions) will capture important changes and insight. Table 14.1 presents the name, leadership position, and individual operational specialty of each four-star general at the start of the period in 1992. All of the highest ranking officers in the USAF were fighter pilots. Important to note is that even Space Command, not a pilot-specific operational area, was led by a fighter pilot. Indeed, Air Mobility Command, where fighter aircraft were not flown at all, was led by a fighter pilot. The fact that all four-star positions were dominated by the fighter pilot community suggests that organizationally the USAF was structured and wholly represented by the fighter-operations perspective. However, one other element revealed by these facts is vital to understanding why this particular line of analysis is important.

It was presented in a previous chapter that in 1992 and the years that followed, considerable discontent existed within the officer corps of the USAF. The brown papers that made national-level news are a good indicator that the officer corps was not in agreement. Builder's observations constructed and published in 1994 further support the existence

Table 14.1. Four-Star Air Force Leadership: 1992

General Officer	Leadership Position	Operational Specialty
Gen Merrill A. McPeak	Chief of Staff of the Air Force	Fighter Pilot
Gen Michael P. C. Carns	Vice Chief of Staff of the Air Force	Fighter Pilot
Gen John M. Loh	Commander Air Combat Command	Fighter Pilot
Gen Joseph W. Ashy	Commander Air Education and Training Command	Fighter Pilot
Gen Ronald W. Bates	Commander Air Force Material Command	Fighter Pilot
Gen C. Donald Kutyna	Commander Air Force Space Command	Fighter Pilot
Gen Hansford T. Johnson	Commander Air Mobility Command	Fighter Pilot
Gen Jimmie V. Adams	Commander Pacific Air Forces	Fighter Pilot
Gen Robert C. Oaks	Commander Air Forces Europe	Fighter Pilot

of divisiveness between the fighter community and the other subgroups within different operational specialties. However, the most important point to consider is that within the cultural and organizational struggle, only one group was consistently given the most senior leadership positions – fighter pilots. As long as only one group *exclusively* among the many operational subgroups achieved the highest leadership positions, then those operational perspectives that the "elite" group most affectionately favored would naturally receive the greatest amount of support. Importantly, the support was not necessarily resource support; rather, it was support for a very particular and primary USAF mission perspective – the fighter-operations perspective.

It was from this dominant perspective, held by all the four-stars in 1992, that the USAF would organize, train, and equip. The fighter-operations perspective that the four-star leadership supported had not only been successful in "their type of war," but also was the mechanism by which they had all been elevated to the rank of four-star general. The perspective and environment within which they had successfully risen, and which they were now in charge of preserving, was clear – air superiority, strategic strikes against predetermined vital centers, and targeting of identifiable fielded forces. Since there was little that the fighter-operations perspective had to offer in counterinsurgency or asymmetric conflicts, such as Somalia, Rwanda, or Bosnia in 1995, there was little motivation for the top leadership four-star generals to organize, train, or equip for these emerging threats.

Regardless of internal discontent from other subgroup operational specialties, as long as the fighter community dominated the four-star general officer positions, then any subgroup friction could be "managed" within the senior ranks. Only external pressures (political, emerging new conflicts, DoD leadership, etc.) could stand any chance of changing such a monopoly on leadership.

Advancing now to 2010, comparison of the same four-star positions will provide data as to any changes that might indicate that the USAF is transitioning away from the 1992 fighter-operations domination. Table 14.2 lists all the 2010 four-star general officers occupying the same duty positions as those previously presented for 1992. By the summer of 2010, only three of nine four-star generals were fighter pilots. The CSAF, for the very first time since 1986, is not a fighter pilot. Air Combat Command is led by a bomber pilot – not a fighter pilot. And the Commander of Air Forces Europe, historically a fighter-operations stronghold where the threat of a traditional war drove all war-plans and context, is now under the leadership of a mobility officer. Compared to the 1992 four-star data, there now appears a much broader representation in the highest USAF officer ranks, which suggests a diverse perspective, consideration for subgroup operational necessity, and, most importantly, an end to the exclusive fighter elite organizational support that had the potential to bias the way the USAF organizes, trains, and equips for current and future conflicts. Evidence for how this diverse leadership may be influencing the USAF can be determined, in part, by some of the language, guidance, and public support these officers provide.

Much of the "power of the office" within the four-star positions comes from what the leaders are saying, what they openly support, and what initiatives they encourage. However, perhaps the most important voice in terms of service-wide guidance, encouragement, and influence comes from the top four-star leader – the Chief of Staff of the Air Force.

Table 14.2. Four-Star Air Force Leadership: 2010

General Officer	Leadership Position	Operational Specialty
Gen Norton A. Schwartz	Chief of Staff of the Air Force	Special Ops Pilot
Gen Carrol H. Chandler	Vice Chief of Staff of the Air Force	Fighter Pilot
Gen William M. Fraser III	Commander Air Combat Command	Bomber Pilot
Gen Stephen R. Lorenz	Commander Air Education and Training Command	Airlift Pilot
Gen Donald J. Hoffman	Commander Air Force Material Command	Fighter Pilot
Gen C. Robert Kehler	Commander Air Force Space Command	Space Officer
Gen Raymond E. Johnson	Commander Air Mobility Command	Airlift Pilot
Gen Gary L. North	Commander Pacific Air Forces	Fighter Pilot
Gen Roger A. Brady	Commander Air Forces Europe	Airlift Pilot

The following is a partial presentation of what the top four-star officer in 2010, Gen Norton Schwartz, provided in terms of his senior and influential vision for the USAF.

In a 2008 brief titled "The CSAF's Perspective," Gen Schwartz intended to instill both vision and confidence in the direction the USAF is headed. He included the following bullets directed as top-level guidance to the entire USAF population:[1]

> CSAF Priorities:
>> Partner with the Joint and Coalition team to win today's fight:
>>> Aggressively adapt Air Force ways and means across the spectrum: C2, ISR, *non-traditional roles*
>>> Enhance support to Joint operations with *specific emphasis on air-ground integration and* ISR
>> Modernize our aging air and space inventories:
>>> We will build a balanced force for the future . . . no litmus test
>>> Achieve *balance between conventional and Irregular Warfare Capabilities*
>> Our Role in National Defense
>> USAF Responsibilities:
>>> Surveil the planet
>>> From air, space, and cyberspace
>>> Detect & analyze enemy activity, capability & intent

Global vigilance, Global Reach, Global Power . . . done your way
Thoughts for Consideration #1
   Ground forces have primacy in this fight
   Your role is to broaden and deepen understanding of air contributions to the
   Joint team
      Not limited to what we like doing, what we're good at, or where it fits

A close read of these selected points taken from the chief's brief (especially those emphasized in italics) suggest the chief's recognition that the
USAF can no longer only prepare for "what we like doing" or "what we're
good at." The chief, giving this guidance across all USAF commands and
to all operational specialties, was sending a significant message – the
USAF can no longer afford to focus only on the fighter-operations perspective and its unique/bounded way of war. It must expand.

Furthermore, the chief offered the following statements drawn from
a number of speeches and accessible through the official web site of the
Air Force:[2]

AFA Orlando Keynote (Thursday, February 26, 2009)

. . . Even if we devise the most compelling capabilities in any given domain or
form of warfare, that capability is of little benefit to us if we cannot effectively
command it for our purposes in the field, or integrate that capability with a host
of others to bring about our desired end-state. As we consider these strategic
issues together, I invite everyone to think about this area of vital importance.

      . . .

For the Air Force will be called upon in a variety of ways in the future to create a
variety of effects around the globe in response to a variety of challenges in diverse stra-
tegic contexts. But the one constant in every single one of these scenarios is the
need for command and control of these and other Joint capabilities. It doesn't
matter if we are talking humanitarian assistance, global mobility, aeromedical
evacuation, ISR, special operations, or major theater conflict contests for air,
space or cyberspace superiority. Scalable, reliable, and interoperable command
and control forms the foundation for success in each and every case. America's
Air Force is poised to leverage both the capabilities and cooperation necessary
to ensure we deliver world-class integrated domain control in any context.

      . . .

We must foster a culture of merit that fuels innovation with the very best ideas
regardless of their origin, or with whom the ideas originate. It is only through this
process of discovery and promotion that we will *poise ourselves to meet the chal-*
lenges of tomorrow. For *the future security environment will demand unprecedented*

thinking and cooperative action through collaboration with others. This is our challenge in our ongoing efforts to train and develop future leaders. *Future challenges will require Airmen who are comfortable with complexity, collaboration, continuous learning, courageous innovation and the ability to jettison obsolescent ideas.* We must never underestimate the need for Airmen who are ready and able to contribute to Joint, Interagency and Coalition successes. Achievements in conventional challenges are the work of brilliance, but *achievements in future challenges will be the work of collaborative genius.* This is the price of admission in the foreseeable future of our Nation's military instrument. Future leaders will have to develop and rely on collaborative genius in order to be fully successful members of the national security team.

American Legion 49th Annual Washington Conference (Tuesday, March 3, 2009)

. . . Let there be no doubt – we, in your Air Force, are "all in" and ready to "double down" in the face of adversity. Our priority is to partner with the Joint and Coalition team to win today's fight. And our Nation's Airmen are fully committed to helping do just that. We are taking every feasible initiative to serve as a trustworthy partner in delivering game-changing capabilities with precision and reliability. Whether it is *serving alongside ground forces* in convoys or in Joint Terminal Attack Controller roles, or *providing game-changing Intelligence, Surveillance and Reconnaissance capabilities with unmanned aerial vehicles,* or helping our wounded warriors with life-saving medical care and aeromedical evacuation, or providing rapid and precise strike capabilities in counterinsurgency or close air support roles, hear me loud and clear when I say that we are all in. This is our priority as an Air Force.

. . .

I could not be more proud of our Airmen, and you need to know that no Airman measures his or her worth by their proximity to the fight. Everyone counts, everyone contributes. *No job or specialty is more worthy than another* because it takes all of us playing our respective positions to be successful.

Air Force Enduring Contributions to National Defense (Thursday, May 21, 2009)

Enduring Air Force contributions that incorporate air, space and cyber capabilities applied across the spectrum of conflict:
The ability to conduct persistent global intelligence, surveillance and reconnaissance operations.
The ability to deliver both kinetic and non-kinetic effects at global distances, serving to dissuade, deter or defeat adversary efforts.
The ability to command and control U.S. and Coalition air, space and cyber assets to achieve Combatant Commander objectives.

And the ability to assess Joint effects across the globe, reinforcing ongoing friendly freedom of action in any domain.

... Let there be no doubt, America's Air Force is "All In" – ready to contribute in any way necessary to win today's fight – even as we *prepare for the challenges of tomorrow. For the ways and means with which we make our contributions are changing and will no doubt continue to do so.*

...

we consider together the *changing ways and means necessary* to continue our distinctive heritage as the world's finest Air Force and the world's finest Joint Force.

In an open letter regarding the importance of the emerging responsibilities of cyberspace operations and addressed to "All Airmen," the CSAF and the Secretary of the Air Force Michael Donley penned the following comments on August 20, 2009:[3]

Cyberspace pervades every other domain and transcends traditional boundaries. Without question, cyberspace is *vital to today's fight and to the future* U.S. military advantage over our adversaries. It is the intent of the United States Air Force to provide a full spectrum of cyberspace capabilities to Joint Force Commanders whenever and wherever needed.

These are important organizational steps, but they are just the beginning. To make significant progress we must also change the way we think about the cyberspace domain, and accordingly change our culture. Like air and space, we must think of *cyberspace as a mission-critical domain* where operations are characterized by rigor and discipline, and are executed with precision and reliability. We must recognize the unique demands of operating in the cyber domain. We must establish close and continuing relationships with our joint partners, industry, and academia. We must develop a personnel strategy with compelling cyber career and training pathways.

These excerpts reflect not only a clear acknowledgment of the changing importance of specific subgroups (in this case cyberspace), but also reflect a four-star-level initiative to "change our culture." The message is clear and reinforces the assertion that the USAF is in transition from the fighter-operations perspective to a new perspective that considers a larger and more diverse airpower mission.

This collection of CSAF and secretary statements could go on for many more pages; however, the overall message is the same in all of his guidance – the USAF will/must change in order to meet the current and future war-fighting requirements. In many of these presentations, the CSAF is accompanied by other four-star officers as well as the secretary of the Air Force. Leaders at the highest level of the USAF structure are demanding change in the traditional culture and appear to be openly responding to new operational considerations. This body of statements and CSAF correspondence further supports the assessment that the USAF is transitioning and that major organizational change is on the horizon. What this change will or should look like will, in many ways, be determined by how the future unfolds, who is selected for USAF senior leadership positions, and to what extent a new dominant culture within the USAF emerges and reifies its place in the organizational structure.

15

PREDICTING THE FUTURE

CONSIDERATION FOR HOW THE FUTURE MAY UNFOLD AND how conditions may affect the organizational structure of the USAF is important when understanding that much of the procurement of new systems, training of personnel with the appropriate skill sets, and investing in research and development all have significant lead times often measured in decades. For USAF leadership and planners, determining the appropriate organizational structure of the USAF in 2030 requires analysis of what path should be initiated today. As previously shown in the first two period case studies, organizational change within the USAF followed an evolution where external events, internal culture, and leadership changes together culminated into major organizational change. However, because future USAF organizational change will depend in part on the external events that occur in the future, and because future external events and internal pressures cannot be known, prediction for how Period Three might unfold out to 2030 can only be based on the trends and observations noted in the first nineteen years (1992–2011). By combining the current internal culture assessment drawn from the survey that showed clear disequilibrium among the officer corps, the current demographics of senior USAF leadership, and the observation of a growing trend toward unconventional war, a prediction of the future organizational structure of the USAF in 2030 is offered.

As described by Lebow and Lichbach, researchers within the social sciences should not fall into the trap of "prediction" in the traditional hard-sciences sense where given a controlled input a predictable outcome is certain.[1] Instead, predictive analysis developed within the context of social science acknowledges that unknowns are exactly that – unknown. For military planners, the uncertainties of the future are too numerous to anticipate with exact precision. As pointed out in recent analysis regarding future war,

> There are simply too many uncertainties regarding the course of future events to provide precise answers . . . Existing and potential enemies have the incentive and increasingly the means to present the U.S. military with challenges very different from and more formidable than those to which it is accustomed.[2]

However, notwithstanding the uncertainties, military planners, and in this case USAF planners, are still responsible to prepare for the future. In order to anticipate the future and hence prepare for possible responsibilities within the context of uncertainty, research guided by theory can develop "*if-then*" scenarios for how the future might unfold – in other words, if certain outlined assumptions hold, then predictable outcomes are likely to occur.[3] However, it is important to note that the work presented in this chapter does not attempt to follow a "recipe" where the three independent variables offered at various degrees are expected to result in a certain and determined outcome (a traditional hard-science perspective). Scenarios "do not predict the future; they do, however, highlight the kinds of challenges for which a military must prepare."[4] Therefore, when assessing the future, this work draws upon the explanatory power of the outlined organizational change models, draws upon the knowledge of how USAF organizational change progressed in the past (Periods One, Two, and part one of Period Three), considers current cultural and leadership trends, and only then offers a *possible* scenario for how the organizational structure of the USAF *might* develop given those considerations.

Within the specific focus of this work and in developing the organizational prediction that follows, the "drivers" of culture, leadership, and external events are used to "connect" and anticipate future USAF organizational change. This approach is widely accepted as researchers have at their disposal the guidance of previously assessed and *substantiated theory* in which to erect an appropriate methodology that effectively builds the "chain of logic" required to predict the future.[5] In this work, the importance of "forecasting" is that it offers USAF leadership and planners a possible glimpse into the future and provides organizational considerations helpful in the planning process required today.

To begin, objective analysis will first require acknowledgment of what *certainties* exist and an outline of the fundamental *assumptions*. In this way, a rational starting point can be developed from which various future contingencies can then be considered and context within that frame can be evaluated for its potential for major USAF organizational change. From analysis offered in the previous chapters, it appears that the USAF is in a period of transition from the fighter-operations organizational structure that hallmarked the service in 1992. However, within that observation is the understanding that several elements of the USAF will continue well into the future and will expand to various degrees. Furthermore, there are certainties that can be offered and considered within the building of an initial context that will help guide subsequent analysis. Krepinevich outlines the importance of recognizing certainties when predicting future context,

> If the future were entirely uncertain, [predictive] planning would be a waste of time. But certain things are predictable or at least highly likely. Scenario planners call these things "predetermined elements." While not quite "done deals," they are sufficiently well known that their probability of occurring is quite high....[6]

Therefore, in line with the need to recognize what is known, and given the previous analysis up to 2011, the following certainties and assumptions are considered "highly probable."

ASSUMPTIONS ABOUT THE FUTURE

- Conflict throughout the world will continue to various levels and degrees
- The U.S. will continue to have global interests that will require and even force military involvement
- The USAF will continue to be responsible for conventional capabilities in that future state-on-state war remains highly probable
    Air superiority
    Strategic strikes

Speed, access, and survivability
- The USAF now fully realizes its responsibility for providing unconventional war capabilities and future unconventional, asymmetric conflicts remain highly probable
  Intelligence, Surveillance, Reconnaissance (manned, unmanned, and space based)
  Space based launch detection
  Command and control
- Nuclear capabilities will remain an important national requirement
  Missiles (on and off alert status)
  Space based launch detection
  Command and control
- Combat airlift both strategic and tactical will be required to some degree in nearly all contexts
- Humanitarian airlift will continue to be required in both modern and rural settings
- Reliance on the global cyberspace digital networks will increase potential threats and the need for effective defense
- Enemies will continually adapt

Within each of the areas listed, there are capabilities that currently exist which will need to be appropriately maintained as well as emerging capabilities that will need to be developed. Within the future context, the USAF will be required to determine how best to organize, train, and equip for these responsibilities. As previously offered, effectively meeting the requirements for these areas in the future will require planners to begin initiatives today. In consideration of these certainties and assumptions, specific USAF roles and missions can be identified.

In line with the future certainties and assumptions, a "big-picture" list of what the USAF must continue to provide operationally is important to consider.

KNOWN FUTURE REQUIREMENTS

- Air to air fighter aircraft
- Air to ground strike aircraft

- Close air support aircraft
- Heavy bomber aircraft
- Special Operations aircraft and personnel
- Survivable tactical airlift
- Aerial refueling aircraft
- Precision guided munitions
- ISR capabilities
- Space based capabilities
- Nuclear missile technologies and maintenance
- Secure communications
- Cyber offence and defense
- Effective command and control

It is understood that within this list there exists numerous support, regulatory, administrative, and logistical responsibilities paramount to their ultimate success and every system within this list will need to be closely *integrated across all services.* Furthermore, as the events in Period Three have shown, the USAF of the future must significantly widen its aperture and be willing to expand its perspective of war regarding what it considers its "primary" mission. As the CSAF Gen Schwartz repeatedly pointed out, the USAF must be "all-in" and not consider any single one of these capabilities as secondary to what the USAF "prefers to do." By "all-in" the Chief was demanding that the USAF of today and the future be willing, able, and motivated to lead or support military engagements with any and all available resources without prejudice or primacy given to any particular capability. Moreover, note that within the capabilities listed, there is no assumption that any of the aircraft systems are necessarily manned or unmanned. In fact, as the post-2003 analysis has already shown, unmanned technologies are offering both cost effective alternatives to traditional manned aircraft and, in many cases, increased capability. It is further assumed, and supported already by the historical record, that technology may change the means of the capabilities listed but that the requirements of the capabilities will remain constant at least through 2030.

A final consideration prior to offering a prediction for USAF organizational change involves acknowledging that one of the most dynamic and influential variables considered in this work has been the external events that have pressured and shaped the organizational structure of the USAF. From the earliest engagements in World War I recorded in Period One analysis, to the unprecedented success of fighter operations in the 1991 Gulf war recorded at the end of Period Two, external events have either directed, re-directed, or preserved USAF operational perspectives and subsequent organizational structure. Unfortunately, when considering the future, the possible external events (anything outside of the USAF that can potentially put pressure on or challenge USAF capabilities) are infinite. Technological breakthroughs in ground-to-air systems could make no aircraft survivable. Biological or chemical war could so contaminate a region that access would be too costly. Extensive geological conditions (volcanic ash for example) could render traditional airborne operations impossible. Domestic U.S. fiscal realities might so decay that the DoD is unable to maintain readiness. Specific nuclear detonations, especially Electronic Magnetic Pulse, could render the advanced electronics required in nearly all USAF systems to be inoperable. These possible events, and many others, would all have significant effect on the operations of the USAF and all have the potential to drastically alter the current operational trends observed in Period Three up to this point. However, it is understood that within all future analysis, events can be created for which there would be little to no acceptable response. Given this understanding, it is of limited practical value to consider events that would render the USAF irrelevant. Instead, consideration for *what is most likely based on the current data and trends* will guide this assessment and ensure an appropriate level of rigor and objective analysis remains central to this study. With the confidence that the USAF is in an organizational transition based on the analysis offered in this and previous chapters, and the emergent requirement for unconventional war capabilities, a prediction for future USAF organizational structure can now be considered.

PREDICTING USAF ORGANIZATIONAL CHANGE

The prediction and scenario that follows regarding the future organizational changes within the USAF is based exclusively on what the data allows one to infer. Although it is tempting to insert subjective "what-ifs" or to develop a context where the USAF would be forced to redirect or reorganize along a completely unexpected path, the prediction that follows is based entirely on what the data and modeling suggests will likely occur. As mentioned prior, external or internal context could change and render the data-driven prediction irrelevant; however, such consideration would be speculative only, would lack discipline, and would fall outside of the rigor this work attempts to preserve. Therefore, taking into account how the previous case studies revealed an evolution along a traceable path to organizational change together with the observations accounted for in part one of Period Three and the current "state of the USAF" offered to this point, the prediction that follows is considered objective, based on rational data analysis, and supported by all the previous work up to this point.

Given the experiences of the post-2003 environment and clear emergence of the unconventional responsibilities, the USAF will continue down a predictable path away from the 1992 fighter-pilot dominated perspective. Furthermore, given the experiences in Afghanistan and Iraq, and assuming that more conventional and unconventional conflicts parallel these actions in the future, then the organizational changes to the USAF will likely center on and encompass a more holistic and synergistic perspective towards war. Rather than a single weapon system or sub-group (bomber operations or fighter operations for example), focus will shift to a "combined arms" perspective where context will determine the amalgamation of several different sub-groups all coordinating as primary capabilities. In this organizational structure the capability and holistic combination of sub-groups and their operational specialties across the USAF would be greater than the sum of their individual parts and are best described as *"synergistic-operations."*

The major organizational change that will occur in the next twenty years will result from a "maturing" of the USAF:

· The continuing and historical clamor for "independence"
   will subside and the USAF will focus on its role in the greater
   spectrum of warfare capabilities

- Fighter pilots will continue to have a significant voice; however, their voice will not be dominant among the sub-groups of the USAF
- The complexities of three-dimension warfare encompassing air, space and cyberspace domains will force senior officer selection to be based on proven strategic thinking abilities over purely operational specialty backgrounds
- The first non-pilot CSAF will be appointed based on strategic thinking capabilities and hallmarking the importance of all USAF capabilities and operational specialties
- Those aspiring to the highest grades (3 and 4 Star) will be required to be literate in a vast cross-section of operational specialties and will require significantly higher levels of strategic level education and training (true generalists)
- New officers will be "conditioned" by the dominant *synergistic-operations* perspective and by 2030 will eventually bring a holistic, breadth and depth to the USAF senior officer corps
- Air-to-Ground capabilities in direct support of ground operations will be organized, trained, and equipped as a primary and seamless USAF competency
- The USAF will further organize and equip ISR in order to provide the entire US military with required information across the entire battle space in all domains
- USAF Space capabilities will continue to emerge and require significant investment and increased command and control processes
- Cyber operations (offense and defense) will challenge the entire US system from commerce to military operations – requiring the USAF to dedicate a sustained capability across both traditional and non-traditional battle space

Although beyond the scope of this predictive analysis to determine, at least one new major command will be established which will encompass several of the lessons learned from the unconventional warfare environment. It may be an "Information Operations Command (IOC)" where the UAVS, ISR, various space capabilities, and Special Operations meld together.

Whatever the actual details of the organizational change, the overarching conclusion of this work is that the emergence of unconventional war alongside the continued need for conventional war capabilities justifies a major organizational change that removes the fighter-operations perspective from its place of dominance and replaces it with a wider spectrum of capability centered on holistic, *synergistic-operations*. The fighter-operations perspective will still exist in its fullest form; however, it will only be one of many capabilities and will no longer have primacy among all capabilities. This organizational structure based on synergistic-operations will direct attention away from the traditional focus which has historically been based on "means" and instead focus and organize around a *network of capabilities* directed at the "ends." This new organizational structure based on a synergistic-operations perspective will address and ameliorate Builder's 1994 critique regarding the USAF's myopic attention to aircraft over the more important focus needed on wartime objectives.[7] Within this context, ISR, Special Operations, air-to-ground, unmanned/ remotely manned systems, cyberspace operations, and spaced based capabilities will expand their organizational influence while the fighter-operations influence will decrease.

The emphasis on systems outside the traditional 1992 focus of the fighter-operations perspective will require procurement of aircraft specifically designed to support ground operations; systems whose capabilities are necessary although not necessarily decisive; and capabilities needed for successful operations in politically constrained or asymmetric environments. The net change will produce equilibrium internally among officers across specialties (as observed in the survey) and further equalize the requirement demanded of external exigencies (conventional and unconventional war).

By 2030 the emerging culture will be a *"synergistic-operations"* perspective adopted throughout the USAF and it will dominate the fighter-operations perspective which was formalized at the beginning of the period in 1992. The USAF will be restructured to organize, train and equip (as primary) across several capabilities and operational specialties. The idea of the USAF "maturing" suggests that this organizational change will not just change focus from one operational specialty to another as it did in the past; rather, this change will reflect the USAF coming of age and realizing that its primary mission should always be defined by the ends required rather than by the means. Although there will continue to be a "pecking order," as is the case in any large organization, those who reach the highest and most influential positions will be a reflection of the new and dominant synergistic-operations perspective.

Figure 15.1 presents the Period Three graphic with "Synergistic-Operations" as the title for the emerging and future dominant USAF perspective. As the years unfold and the synergistic-operations perspective increases across both new recruits and the older USAF leadership, the USAF culture will also change. Standard operating procedures, norms, values, and beliefs will all be formulated from a perspective that acknowledges a much wider and more capable operational dynamic than the fighter perspective alone. From the synergistic-operations perspective, future senior leaders (those who are the three and four star generals in fifteen to twenty years) will all have experienced and will support the need to organize the USAF in such a way as to enhance and support synergistic-operations. The responsibility to organize, train, and equip for future conflicts will be generated from a posture that understands the need to expand operations, network available capabilities, and focus on ends rather than on means – synergistic-operations.

As mentioned, there are obviously numerous unforeseen events that could drastically alter the current organizational trends observed and predicted in this work. However, planners within the USAF do not have a "crystal ball" and must therefore rely upon analysis based on theoretical guidance, past observations, and current trends. Offered within such an analytical framework is the prediction that the USAF will undergo a major organizational change by the year 2030 that elevates synergistic-operations to a dominant position. As the future unfolds and additional information becomes available, adjustments to this analysis is possible. However, at this point, the USAF would be wise to acknowledge the needed changes and begin to develop very specific organizational elements which will enhance and support synergistic-operations.

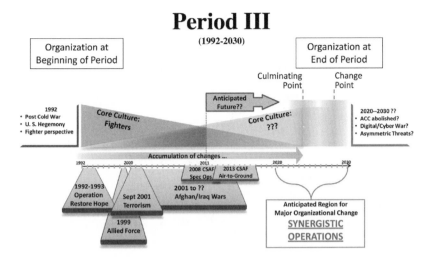

Period III
(1992-2030)

Figure 15.1

At this stage it important to acknowledge that the prediction for *synergistic-operations* to become the new dominant operational perspective and subsequently influence the USAF organizational structure is based on the guidance obtained from the validated organizational change models, the previous case studies, and analysis (qualitative and quantitative) regarding current and future trends. The prediction is based on what is available for analysis and takes great care to ensure subjectively, ethnocentricity, or bias is kept to a minimum. In other words, the data, as presented, forms the basis for the prediction of USAF organizational change. However, based on the analysis and the understanding that this work is additionally intended to provide senior USAF leadership with actionable considerations, the next and final chapter provides specific recommendations that reach beyond the data in order to offer USAF leadership practical and proactive considerations for how they might best anticipate and organizationally prepare the USAF for an uncertain future.

The most important thing that air power theorists can do today is to try to get their perceptions of the future right.

CARL BUILDER

16

SUMMARY AND RECOMMENDATIONS

DRAWING FROM ORGANIZATIONAL CHANGE MODELS, I HAVE used the independent variables of external responsibilities, internal culture, and leadership in this study to trace the changes observed in the period of time prior to major USAF organizational change. At the beginning of Period One, in 1907, the advent of airpower into military application was dominated by a *ground-operations* perspective. Originating in the U.S. Army, airpower developed in relation to how it might best be used to support traditional ground battles. However, recalling that "any factors outside the organization that modify or threaten the organization's ability to produce or market its goods or services serve as external forces for change,"[1] and that organizations "constantly receive inputs from their environment and must respond to changes in those inputs,"[2] this study took into account major external events during this time period. As Period One analysis showed, the external pressures of World War I and World War II offered airpower advocates an opportunity to display how airpower might be used both independently and decisively. Culminating with the dropping of the atomic bomb on Japan in 1947, the experiences from 1907 to 1947 developed the dominant airpower perspective of *bomber-operations*.

Equally influential, during the same period of time between 1907 and 1947, was that the internal culture and organizational leadership responsible for airpower operations grew further apart from the ground-operations perspective that dominated early in the period. Recalling that when organizations expand or decrease operations, new internal challenges often force the development of new positions, the elimination of old positions, and the possibility of redefined power relations among subgroups, analysis of the internal characteristics (culture and leadership) of airpower throughout the period revealed important insights. By 1947, airpower enjoyed its own organizational structure separate from the U.S. Army, had its own "airmen" leadership structure, and had organized to effectively promote and carry out independent operations.[3] Together, these observable and traceable changes helped to explain and even anticipate the major organizational change that occurred in September of 1947 when the USAF became a separate and independent military service.

Following the major organizational change in 1947 that brought independence to the USAF, the dominating perspective was centered on *bomber-operations*. As was the case in Period One, the beginning of Period Two was characterized by a dominant group within the organization of airpower, with the bomber community having the greatest organizational influence. Using the same investigative methods, Period Two analysis considered the major external events from 1947 to 1992, which included the Korean War, Vietnam War, fall of the Soviet Union, and Gulf War I. These external events brought pressure to the USAF bomber community, and eventually those pressures created disequilibrium between what the environment required of airpower and what the USAF was organized and centered upon accomplishing. The traditional bomber-centric perspective, characterized in large part by nuclear strikes against the Soviet Union, was challenged by the emerging requirement of limited war, in which nuclear operations were not a realistic consideration given the context of the particular wars. Tactical airpower, limited aims, and political considerations emerged as elements that could not be avoided. However, under the traditional *bomber-operations* perspective, the emerging elements were not appropriately informed. By the end of the period, *fighter-operations* had emerged as the dominant perspective, and the internal culture and organizational leadership within the USAF by 1992 reflected the shift. Subsequently, the major organizational change that occurred in 1992 was effectively represented and explained by the outlined organizational change modeling.

Period Three began the same as the previous periods, with the exception that the *fighter-operations* perspective was clearly dominant. The major organizational change in 1992 that abolished Strategic Air Command and its hold on USAF organizational prerogatives, and the establishment of Air Combat Command and its dominant fighter-operations perspective, set the stage for analysis of the time period from 1992 through 2012. The objective of the first part of Period Three analysis was to determine what trends and changes in the three variables of external responsibilities, internal culture, and leadership might be observed in order to develop a rational and logical prediction for how the future organizational structure of the USAF might develop (beyond 2012). It was determined that in the 1990s, an underlying and emerging new form of warfare was developing for which the USAF was not appropriately preparing. Drawing upon the events of Somalia, Bosnia, and Operation Allied Force as external exigencies, I argued that the USAF under the fighter-operations perspective was myopic and failed to consider, to any significant degree, the possibility of fighting a war where fighter-operations were not appropriate or even relevant. The lack of appreciation for possible unconventional, asymmetric, urban warfare and the unique responsibilities required of such context left the USAF unprepared to effectively engage in the post-2003 conflicts in Iraq and Afghanistan. Just as the previous Period One and Two case studies showed, in Period Three analysis, the external exigencies did not line up with the dominant organizational characteristics of the fighter-operations perspective. It was observed that the disequilibrium that built up through the 1990s and early 2000s and which currently exists in the USAF parallels the disequilibrium observed in the previous case studies that preceded major organizational change. Specifically, the dominant and most important capabilities required of the USAF do not come from the fighter-operations community; rather, those responsible for intelligence, surveillance, and reconnaissance, together with space-based capabilities, cyberspace operations, logistics, tactical airlift, and special operations are dominating current conflicts. The disequilibrium between the perspective that dominated the 1992 organizational change (fighter-operations) and the external requirements of war in the post-2003 environment was clearly outlined.

In order to effectively determine the current internal cultural perspectives of USAF officers and to further examine whether the external disequilibrium equally exists internally between the fighter-operations perspective and some new emerging perspective, I administered a survey across Air University. Using statistical software to aid in the analysis, responders were sorted into two groups: fighter pilots and everyone else. The survey results indicated that there is agreement among all officers that the future will likely be characterized by more unconventional war; however, traditional conventional engagements will continue to be a threat as well. The two groups differed considerably when responding to what systems should be given the greatest priority for the future, which officers should be placed in the most senior leadership positions, and what the overall priorities of the USAF should be. The fighter pilot community strongly supported the traditional fighter-operations perspective, called for procurement of fighter aircraft, and believed that fighter-pilots are most qualified for the senior level positions. The non–fighter pilot group (everyone else) believed that unmanned or remotely manned systems would dominate in the future, placed fighters lowest in priority for procurement, believed ISR was becoming (or has already become) a primary USAF mission and that leadership should be based on intellectual strategic ability rather than simply on an individual's operational specialty. The divisiveness among the two groups is stark, and the survey verified that the disequilibrium noted in the analysis of the external events equally exists with respect to internal culture among officers within these two groups.

Finally, the results of this study indicate that the leadership characteristics of the four-star general positions across the USAF have significantly changed since 1992. In the early years of Period Three, all four-star generals were fighter pilots, while as of 2010 only three of the nine four-stars had a fighter-pilot background. When the observation of the leadership changes was combined with the disequilibrium noted by the external and internal analysis, it was suggested that the USAF is on a path leading to another major organizational change. In light of further analysis and consideration of what the current combat environment is demanding – the guidance of the previous non–fighter pilot CSAF, Gen Norty Swartz, regarding UAVs, ISR, spaced-based capabilities, cyberspace responsibilities, and Special Operations – and the continued realization that unconventional war will continue well into the future, I offer the prediction that a *synergistic-operations* perspective will dominate the future organizational structure of the USAF, replacing the *fighter-operations* perspective that opened Period Three in 1992.

Framing the dominant characteristics of the fighter-oriented perspective led to the understanding that since 1992 the USAF has focused on three axioms it considers central: air superiority is paramount; targeting coveted enemy infrastructure is a primary capability; and the ability to effectively attrite numbers of fielded combatants is essential. Given these three axioms of airpower, it makes sense that the USAF would have the capabilities that it has today. In terms of combat operations, these axioms require air-to-air fighters, precision-guided munitions (carried by fighters), and air-to-ground munitions carried by fighters, bombers, and aircraft like the AC-130 Gunship. These systems and capabilities, although not representative of everything the USAF is capable of doing, do represent what is often considered the most important capability under the dominant fighter perspective. However, what if the context of the conflict is such that the enemy has neither capability nor intention of challenging the United States for air superiority? What use does the air-superiority fighter provide in that context? Furthermore, what if the enemy does not have any coveted infrastructure? In fact, what if the enemy actually prefers we destroy infrastructure in order to turn the will of the people against the United States? In that context, what use are precision-guided munitions beyond a few time-sensitive targets when a house or a car is identified as containing a specific belligerent? Finally, what if the enemy combatant is not identifiable against the background of the local population? How will air-to-ground capabilities target fielded forces if they are not "fielded"? Again, although there are cases where enemy combatants are identified through intelligence processes, these are often small numbers and, in nearly all cases, targeting the belligerents results in the collateral damage of innocents being killed due to the close proximity of the combatants with noncombatants. This often ends with a tactical victory in the elimination of a few belligerents, but a strategic loss in terms of the negative reaction the operation drives at home and abroad.

The point here is that if the context changes, then the dominant perspective that informs a particular organizational construct may not be appropriate for the new context. This was the case in Period One; the original ground perspective saw airpower purely as a support technology to the ground war, but as the context of war changed to a battle targeting the enemy industrial base, the bomber capability became dominant and eventually overpowered the original ground perspective. Moreover, when the bomber perspective in Period Two faced a limited, politically constrained conflict, it was the fighter perspective that slowly achieved dominance to meet the changing context of war. So too goes the current trend in warfare: the fighter perspective does not meet the needs of the emerging asymmetric nature of warfare, which means that an organizational change must be considered in order for the USAF to maintain the appropriate level of relevance and validity within the emerging new context.

It is paramount at this point to understand that organizational change away from what was the central and dominant perspective to a new perspective does not mean that the old operational requirements once dominating Air Force thinking disappear or are no longer needed. Even after the bomber perspective dominated airpower toward the end of Period One, there was still a significant need for air-to-ground support, ISR, and signaling that dominated airpower operations in the beginning of the period. At the end of Period Two, when the fighter perspective finally took the mantle of leadership away from the bomber community, bombers still provided important capability. So too in the organizational change this work recommends: fighters will remain vital and important to the overall mission; but the fighter perspective will no longer dominate the organizational construct.

The future will likely involve both irregular and regular warfare. In this regard, what must happen is a widening of the USAF aperture in terms of capability. The USAF cannot afford to prepare only for those engagements it prefers; rather, it must expand its spectrum to include the full variance of possibility. This is the fundamental driver behind the need for USAF organizational change: in order to meet this enlarged arena of required capability (regular and irregular war), the USAF can no longer center its dominant position on a specific system or capability. The USAF must consider all of its systems under a larger strategic vision of *synergistic operations* – operations capable of truly flexing across the entire spectrum of future warfare possibilities. The future USAF must be able to "travel" across the full spectrum of warfare. Currently, and in the past, Air Force capability was often not appropriate for the given context, forcing the USAF to stretch its capabilities. Airpower advocates often called this stretching the flexibility of airpower. However, what this work has shown is that airpower capability does not stretch as well as some might believe. In fact, the inability of airpower to effectively extend to new and emerging contexts was the underlying cause for the organizational change that occurred in Periods One and Two. Ground perspectives that dominated in the early years of Period One could not appropriately stretch to meet the needs of the emerged bomber force requirements. The Strategic Air Command, although phenomenally important in the early stages of Period Two, could not appropriately stretch to meet the emerging responsibilities carried by the fighter community. Today, the capabilities of the fighter community established in the early years of Period Three, although important and successful, are not able to stretch to meet the external responsibilities of irregular war, urban engagements, and the asymmetric context. As in the past, the USAF will need to change its organizational perspective in order to meet these emerging requirements. The USAF must be capable of "traveling" across the full spectrum of war with the planning and procurement understanding that "stretching" will not suffice.

As each organizational change brings the service into better balance with external responsibilities, internal culture, and leadership variables, the overall spectrum of capability increases. The dominant capabilities that ruled the day in years past do not go away – they simply are no longer dominant. Bombers and fighters will remain an important and formidable part of the USAF, but with the maturing of the service, they will no longer define the USAF. Instead, the future of the USAF will be defined and centered around a *synergistic-perspective* where multiple capabilities, operating simultaneously across a much wider spectrum of operations, will dominate the USAF perspective. Obviously, this transition will require organizational change across the service.

The process of changing the organizational structure of the USAF will likely parallel that reflected in the previous case studies of Periods One and Two: an evolutionary incrementalism will continue in which new recruits are taught and will perceive the emerging *synergistic-op-*

erations perspective as the norm. As Schein points out regarding how internal culture changes and change is eventually adopted within an organization, what characterizes such change is

> a pattern of shared basic assumptions that was learned by a group as it solved its problems of external adaptation and internal integration, that has worked well enough to be considered valid and, therefore, to be taught to new members as the correct way to perceive, think, and feel in relation to those problems.[4]

In this regard, the current study predicts that the synergistic-operations perspective will eventually become the norm. Furthermore, when the external events, internal culture, and internal leadership all support the new perspective as dominant, the USAF will be forced to undergo a major organizational change that structures itself in such a way that it can effectively organize, train, and equip within the new and influential perspective. When this change occurs, the required organizational structure will be so different and demand such diverse requirements from the 1992 fighter-operations organizational structure that Period Three will come to an end and the USAF will enter into a fourth period beyond 2030. Given the wider spectrum of operational capability under the synergistic-operations perspective encompassing nearly all of the important subgroups within a network of specialties, the USAF may find that its new organization is capable of sustaining its organizational structure, sustaining its identity, and establishing its foundational position well into the future. It will have finally "matured" as a separate service.

USAF ORGANIZATIONAL CONSIDERATIONS.

Where the USAF eventually ends up by 2030 and beyond will in large measure be determined by the decisions made by its leaders regarding which systems to procure, which missions to embrace (and which missions not to embrace), and to what extent those who "fly" aircraft are willing to step aside for the greater cause defined and framed outside of traditional manned flight. Builder suggests,

> If the Air Force mission is effectively redefined so as to be rationalized with history and future trends, less chauvinistic in its claims and demands, and embracing rather than discriminating among its contributors and practitioners, then the Air Force leadership has a fair chance of creating a vibrant, committed military institution.[5]

Although in the past the dominant operational perspective was centered on a specific system or aircraft type (bombers or fighters), the future will need to be centered on a capability not necessarily connected to a specific airplane type of mission (i.e., to be centered on synergistic-operations). This transition will be difficult in that the very nature of the Air Force has always been to focus on flying aircraft. However, as history has shown and as technology has advanced, the need for and appropriateness of manned flight as the primary USAF focus has diminished.

As a service, we have rightfully transitioned to thinking about controlling "domains" rather than the toys used to control them. Those in the USAF unable to separate themselves from their flying machines will eventually become relics and will be replaced by a new generation of "airmen" whose understanding regarding the depth and breadth of airpower goes well beyond aircraft and instead focuses on how best to advantage war-fighting domains (air, space, cyber). However, as Builder suggests,

> as the Air Force is compelled in the near future to reduce its force structure under the pressure of budget reductions, there will be a strong tendency to preserve those forces which have dominated the mission spectrum in the past rather than those which might dominate in the future. To be explicit, there will be a natural tendency to preserve the fighter and bomber forces at the expense of the supporting forces ... this tension between institutional proclivities and perceptions of the future illustrates the importance of the latter to the evolution of air power theory.[6]

In this regard, the greatest challenge that the USAF must overcome is its inability to focus on the ends rather than on the means. *When the USAF finally realizes that its greatest strength comes from its ability to take advantage of all elements within the airpower domain (air, space, and cyber) and not merely on a particular system, that is when the USAF will have obtained a level of maturity capable of sustaining its operations without fear of continual, periodic change.* This long-view transition will require the USAF to force itself out of "white scarf syndrome," where the means (flying aircraft) are more important than the ends of providing the nation with the greatest possible amount of airpower options. Unfortunately, if the USAF continues to rationalize its existence under the pretense of decisive operations, continually strives to prove its independence, and views its primary mission in terms of the aircraft it flies, then its future validity and relevance is questionable. However, if the USAF realigns under a more strategic, long-view perspective, then the future USAF will be undeniably important for national security and will remain unquestionably relevant. It will require significant leadership at the highest levels of the USAF to strategically communicate this new synergistic perspective, coordinate with the joint community, and influence the congressional process for appropriate funding of airpower. This will require phenomenal leadership at the CSAF and Secretary of the Air Force levels. This dynamic and call for a formidable plan going forward holds nothing less at stake than the future of the USAF.

Taking on the assumption that the USAF will widen its aperture and further advance its spectrum beyond just manned flight, there are a number of important initiatives that must begin if a relevant USAF is to be fully realized. The following is a list of considerations that USAF leadership should thoughtfully debate. Although this is not an exhaustive list, all these items need to be considered if the USAF is to effectively transition its organizational structure in support of a new *synergistic-operations* perspective:

- ISR should be advanced to organize, train, and equip for kinetic operations – intelligence surveillance, reconnaissance, attack (ISRA). Within this operational capability, connectivity with ground forces must be seamless, and the command chain should not be determined by the system (i.e., airmen in charge of air assets); rather, it should be determined by the needs of the end user. This will force a heightened amount of coordination and cooperation among those forces that require airpower capability. The axiom that an airman must be the final authority in all things regarding airpower will need to be contextually based and not always considered the default position. This will run contrary to much of the discussion that has developed regarding the need for an airmen to command airpower; however, although that requirement may well exist in many contextual settings, it must be considered that in some asymmetric environments, the use of airpower may need to be determined by the end user, who will likely not be an airman.
- Every appropriate unmanned/remotely manned capability should be fully researched, developed, and procured. In all

decisions of procurement, the required end-state and national objectives must determine the best capability to develop. Although there are many in the Air Force who find tremendous personal satisfaction in flying aircraft (especially fast and low), individual desires should not be a consideration when developing the future Air Force strategic posture. Although pilots have exuberated over the experience of flight since the airplane was first introduced, serious consideration for how the air domain can best be dominated within current and emerging global dynamics should determine Air Force future operations. This may well force a decrease in manned flight capability and increase remotely manned operations. If the strategic assessment is such that remotely manned systems can better meet national security requirements within emerging fiscal, political, and global considerations, then the Air Force must acknowledge and shape itself around that reality.

· Increased exercises among all the services where the USAF embraces a support role should be instituted and fully encouraged. Airmen must understand how airpower fits into the larger element of modern and future combat and not be limited to understanding only those conditions conducive to airpower decisiveness and independence. One perspective that helps explain this necessity is the consideration that the Army can do very little to support the mission of the USAF; however, the USAF can provide substantial support to the Army mission. This observation does not make either service more or less capable or important than the other – it simply acknowledges that the relationship is not symmetric and never has been. The USAF, and airpower in general, must focus less on what it independently brings to the fight, and focus more on how it empowers the U.S. military team.

· Although junior general officer promotions should be determined in part by specific operational specialty requirements (fighters command fighters, airlift commands airlift, space commands space, etc.), senior USAF leadership at the strategic war planning level (three and four stars) should be filled by officers based on their proven intellectual and strategic thinking abilities and not solely on their operational specialty. It may well be that the most appropriate CSAF in the future will come from outside the pilot community. This will require modification of the promotion system as well as new direction in how officers are trained and educated for the highest ranks. General officers should be exactly that: generalists in their strategic understanding of airpower. Rather than a single operational specialty path, those aspiring to these highest ranks within the USAF should be on a "spiral-up" path where they are able to gain experience across a wide range of air, space, and cyber capabilities.

· The USAF should take responsibility for ensuring future theaters have secure communications among all services, a network of intelligence developed within a dissemination process that meets the needs of all commanders across all services, and offensive and defensive cyber capabilities. The USAF should harness the responsibility for theater-wide command and control requirements – not as the service that necessarily commands, but as the service ensuring that effective command and control capabilities are available to theater commanders. As a highly technological force, the USAF must enable the U.S. military team using its capabilities in space and cyber to provide predictable and reliable theater command and control capability.

· When politically appropriate, the USAF should militarize space and encourage, organize, train, and equip any and all forms of space-based capabilities that support national objectives. Future space-based capability to identify, track, and target nearly all objects on earth will revolutionize surface warfare. Military space-based operations, as the ultimate high ground, will require significant expertise and technology in launch, orbit, cyber, command and control, and communications – a responsibility the USAF is already well postured to accept.

· The current squadron, group, and wing command structure should be reevaluated to determine if the command opportunities such a structure develops are in fact the best way of preparing officers for senior-level strategic positions. The track to general officer should not be limited to a preordained or rigid path where officers highly capable at the strategic planning level are not recognized and promoted due to a lack of opportunity within a limited organizational promotion structure.

· Critical thinking is perhaps the most important skill set that Air Force senior leaders must possess. Consideration of second- and third-order effects is an art that must be taught and practiced. Effective critical thinkers are not currently identified – when they are, they are often seen as disruptive thinkers who challenge the status quo. Rather than embrace them, the current USAF promotion system sidelines these officers. It is vital to the future of our service that this flawed system change. Proven combat skills together with advanced education should be the dominant considerations for any and all senior officer appointments. The importance of the warrior-scholar has never risen above the level of rhetoric. It must be formally tied as a primary consideration in promoting officers to the higher strategic ranks. It is often the case that an officer who serves as an executive officer or aide to a general is more likely to be promoted early to the next higher grade than another officer who has proven war-fighting or strategic thinking skills. The system in which officers are promoted based on a tacit "sponsored" relationship (an officer who is brought up early through the ranks due in part to a relationship to a general officer) does not serve the USAF or the nation well. Proven war-fighters, highly capable strategic thinkers, exceptionally educated and trained officers who perform in these areas above their peers should be the only ones consideration for promotion; for whom one works should not determine promotion status. Promotions within the USAF should never be personal; they should be practical.

All of the above considerations fall under the rubric of developing a synergistic-operations perspective. In this regard, the term "perspective" denotes not simply a way of employing operational systems; rather, it is a way of thinking expressed by how one sees the world and how, subsequently, one maximizes the capabilities of airpower and all of its domains (air, space, and cyber). Importantly, the major organizational change in Period Three that this work predicts will occur by 2030 will require the most significant change encountered in airpower since its military inception in 1907. The change that shifts perspective to synergistic-operations will realign the USAF behind a vision and subsequent mission that begins with first understanding and acknowledging the end-state called upon by our national leadership and then organizing a force capable of success within that context. The change will require a shift away from thinking in terms of dominant aircraft, primary systems, or independent or decisive operational specialties, and instead focus completely on requirements, equilibrium with external exigencies, and unbiased, objective security needs-analysis. In this way, synergistic-operations will apply equally well in both conventional and unconventional contexts.

Within this emerging design, airpower leaders must first recognize and then remain closely tied to the three enduring principles of airpower: speed, access, economy of risk. Since 1907, airpower has afforded these unique capabilities across the full spectrum of warfare. No other service provides these attributes across context, time, and space. The political tempo across an interconnected globe requires timely options (speed). Political, national security options range from instant humanitarian aid to instant retribution. Multinational relations, commitments, alliances, shared security requirements, and interdependencies require open avenues into any environment (access). Although clearly a continuing political debate with juridical considerations, the ability to hold any target at risk is uniquely an enduring airpower capability. Fiscal and social restraints require options that provide good stewardship of national treasure, both human and fiscal, without requiring long-term U.S. commitments (economy of risk). Airpower has always offered these principles, and the USAF must be both mindful and careful to ensure that their obligations to national security are hallmarked by these principles rather than by the operational dynamics of specific systems. If the USAF is able to effectively transition into an institution hallmarked by these enduring principles, then they will have finally matured as a service. Simply put, the credibility of airpower rests with its direct correlation to U.S. national security. As a service, the USAF provides airpower just as the Army provides land power and the Navy provides sea power. And, just as is true for our sister services, what we provide is in direct support of U.S. national security. The USAF further provides it in a unique and politically flexible way.[7]

Of final consideration is the important attribute of strategic communication. The USAF can no longer wander in the wilderness, suffering from an identity crisis largely centered on the adolescent perspective of independence. In fact, it is the realization of "dependence" that will propel the USAF in terms of credibility and relevance. The message for the service is that airpower is necessary in nearly all contexts across multiple global engagements from humanitarian to total war. All of these contexts require the attributes that airpower brings, and therefore nearly all engagements are *dependent* on airpower. The best advertisement for the USAF should not come from within; rather, it should come from U.S. national-level decision makers and sister services that require airpower's dominant capability in air, space, and cyber. Simply understood, there is no conceivable context where U.S. military operations could succeed without the prerequisite of airpower control. When discussing airpower in this sense, it does not consist of the three domains of air, space, and cyber; rather, it is a single domain of airpower that consists of air, space and cyber capabilities – the difference matters. Given airpower dominance (air, space, cyber), all services can provide their important and core capabilities synergistically. In other words, airpower is *necessary,* and most operations are dependent upon airpower's capabilities (air, space, cyber), but this fact does not mean that airpower is *sufficient.* This simply suggests the importance of describing national security operations within the profession of arms as *dependent on airpower* over the more fractured argument regarding the independence of airpower; this is about effective messaging. In terms of strategic communication, the idea of "dependence" rather than independence is significant and cannot be understated. It should and must define airpower's capability and ultimately its identity.

The USAF is an incredibly capable, innovative, and vitally important arm of U.S. national security. It has always been the requirement of airmen to be good stewards of the resources we are provided and the responsibilities we are given. However the future unfolds, and whatever challenges confront the United States, the USAF must put itself on a path that enables it to address the desired ends of national security rather than the means. This transition will require visionary leaders unbiased by their own system allegiances, and capable of thinking and planning strategically beyond the horizon. It is clear that in the near and distant future, airpower will remain an integral and paramount capability for U.S. national security. Within this reality, the USAF must make the appropriate organizational decisions today for how it should be postured tomorrow – the future relevance of the service depends on it.

NOTES

INTRODUCTION

1. Schein, "Organizational Culture: What It Is and How to Change It," 1990; Schein, *Organizational Culture and Leadership,* 2004.

2. Bennis, 1969; Burke, 2008; Hira and Hira, 2000.

3. Reitz, 1987, p. 562; Heffron, 1989, p. 183.

4. Brown, 2000.

5. Schein, *Organizational Culture and Leadership,* 2004; Bennis, 1969; Child and Kieser, *Development of Organizations Over Time,* 1981; Demers, 2007.

6. Worden, 1998, pp. 236–238.

1. THE BIRTH OF MILITARY AIRPOWER

Epigraph: Mitchell, 1925/1988, p. ix.

1. Hurley and Heimdahl, 1997, p. 10.

2. Hennessy, 1985, p. 15.

3. Frisbee, 1996.

4. Frisbee, 1996; Mets, 1999; Meilinger, 2001.

5. Trest, 1998; Sherry, 1987; Hennessy, 1985.

6. Hurley and Heimdahl, 1997, p. 11.

7. Ibid., p. 14.

8. Ibid., p. 15; emphasis added.

9. Ibid., p. 18.

10. Ibid., p. 21.

11. Ibid., p. 21.

12. Ibid., p. 22.

13. Ibid., p. 22.

14. Frisbee, 1996; Watson, 1997; Hennessy, 1985.

15. Hurley and Heimdahl, 1997, p. 26.

16. Ibid., p. 27.

17. Ibid., p. 27.

18. Ibid., p. 29.

19. Hennessy, 1985; Builder, 1994; Frisbee, 1996.

20. Hurley and Heimdahl, 1997, p. 32.

21. Ibid., p. 33.

2. WORLD WAR I AND THE INTERWAR YEARS

1. Mortensen, 1997, p. 36.

2. Hurley and Heimdahl, 1997; Mortensen, 1997.

3. Mortensen, 1997, p. 48.

4. Ibid., p. 39.

5. Hall and Nordoff, 1920, pp. 17–22.

6. Mortensen, 1997, p. 37.

7. Ibid., p. 37, emphasis added.

8. Ibid.; Morrow, 1993.

9. Ibid., p. 40.

10. Ibid., p. 50.

11. Maurer, 1978, p. vii.

12. Ibid., p. viii.

13. Ibid., pp. 60–61.

14. Ibid., pp. viii–ix.

15. Ibid., p. viii.

16. Ibid., pp. 16–51.

17. Hudson, 1968, p. 186.

18. Higham, 1994, p. 24.

19. Mortensen, 1997, p. 51.
20. Ibid., p. 51.
21. Ibid., p. 56.
22. Mitchell 1918 letter, Air Force Historical Research Agency, Maxwell AFB, 2009.
23. Shiner, 1997, p. 72.
24. Ibid., p. 74.
25. Ibid., pp. 67–78.
26. Ibid., pp. 76–77.
27. Ibid., p. 79.
28. Shiner, 1997; Hall and Nordoff, 1920; Hudson, 1968.
29. Douhet, 1921.
30. Shiner, 1997, pp. 91–96.
31. Ibid., p. 99; Frisbee, 1996; Westhoff, 2007.
32. Shiner, pp. 102–103.
33. Shiner, 1997, p. 105, emphasis added.
34. Ibid., p. 104.
35. Ibid., p. 106.
36. Ibid., p. 106.
37. Ibid., pp. 111–112.
38. Sherry, 1987, p. 50.
39. Shiner, 1997, p. 112.
40. Ibid., p. 120.
41. Ibid., p. 121.
42. Ibid., p. 120.
43. Ibid., p. 127.
44. Ibid., p. 128.
45. Shiner, 1997, pp. 132–133; Frisbee, 1996; Meilinger, 2001.
46. Ibid., p. 134.
47. Ibid., pp. 138–139.
48. Futrell, 1989, p. 64.
49. Shiner, 1997, pp. 141–142.
50. Futrell, 1989; Meilinger, 2001; Watts, 1984.
51. Shiner, 1997, p. 145.
52. Ibid., p. 146.
53. Ibid., pp. 150–152.
54. Ibid., p. 156.
55. Stephens, 1994, pp. 57–58.

3. WORLD WAR II
1. Tate, 1998, p. 2.
2. Sherry, 1987, pp. 48–49.
3. Faber, 1997, p. 212.
4. Nalty, 1997, p. 172.
5. Shiner, 1997, p. 162.
6. Nalty, 1997, p. 173.
7. Ibid., p. 179.
8. Ibid., pp. 179–180, emphasis added.
9. Ibid., p. 181.
10. Ibid., p. 187.
11. Ibid., p. 218.
12. Ibid., pp. 224–225.
13. Douhet, 1921.
14. Builder, 1994; Futrell R. F., 1989; Trest, 1998; Westhoff, 2007; Frisbee, 1996.
15. Nalty, 1997, p. 225.
16. Momyer, 1982, p. 40.
17. Ibid., p. 40.
18. Ibid., p. 40.
19. Ibid., pp. 43–45.
20. Hastings, 1979, p. 43, emphasis added.
21. Overy, 1994, p. 114.
22. Ibid., 1995, pp. 114–115.
23. Stephens, 1994, pp. 62–63.
24. Ibid., pp. 61–65.
25. Davis, 1993, p. 564.
26. Hastings, 1979, p. 351.
27. Pape, 1996, pp. 260–263.
28. Builder, 1994; Ford, 1992; Frisbee, 1996; Futrell R. F., 1989; Meilinger, 2001; Wolk, 1997; Tate, 1998; Davis, 1993.
29. Watson, 1997, p. 268.
30. Nalty, 1997, p. 321.
31. Ibid., p. 321.
32. Ibid., p. 322.
33. Ibid., p. 323.
34. Ibid., p. 325.
35. Ibid., p. 325.
36. Ibid.
37. Ibid.
38. Ibid., p. 326.
39. Nalty, 1997; Builder, 1994; Futrell R. F., 1989.
40. Wolk, 1997, p. 374.
41. Ibid., pp. 374–375.
42. Ibid., p. 391.
43. Ibid., p. 375.
44. Ibid., p. 395.

4. "COUNTING" THE CHANGES IN PERIOD ONE

1. Air Force Historical Research Agency, 2009.

2. *The Almanac of Airpower*, 1989, p. 54.

5. THE RISE OF BOMBER DOMINANCE: 1947–1965

Epigraph: Coram, 2002, p. 59.

1. Trest and Watson, 1998, pp. 399–400.

2. Ibid., p. 402, emphasis added.

3. Ibid., p. 403.

4. Worden, 1998, p. 31.

5. Ibid., p. 38.

6. Ibid., p. 29.

7. Ibid., p. 39.

8. Ibid., p. 29.

9. Boyne, 1997, p. 53.

10. Frisbee, 1996; Westhoff, 2007; Boyne, 1997.

11. Moody, 1996, p. 32.

12. Boyne, 1997, p. 53.

13. Worden, 1998, p. 39.

14. Ibid., p. 44.

15. Boyne, 1997; Worden, 1998.

16. Boyne, 1997.

17. Ibid., pp. 63–64.

18. Worden, 1998, p. 40.

19. Thompson, 1997, p. 6, emphasis added.

20. Thompson, 1997; Boyne, 1997.

21. Thompson, 1997, p. 11.

22. Ibid., p. 11.

23. Ibid., p. 16.

24. Momyer, 1982, pp. 57–59.

25. Futrell, 1983, p. 50.

26. Winnefeld and Johnson, 1991, p. 27.

27. Ibid., p. 27.

28. Futrell, 1983, pp. 704–708.

29. Thompson, 1997, pp. 17–19.

30. Boyne, 1997, p. 94.

31. Ibid., p. 94, emphasis added.

32. Worden, 1998, p. 42.

33. Ibid., p. 43.

34. Thompson, 1997, pp. 64–65.

35. Boyne, 1997, p. 96.

36. Ibid.

37. Moody, Neufeld, and Hall, 1997, p. 74, emphasis added.

38. Ibid., p. 75.

39. Boyne, 1997, p. 97.

40. Moody and Trest, 1997, p. 103.

41. Ibid., p. 103.

42. Worden, 1998, p. 43.

43. Ibid., p. 74.

44. Ibid., p. 77.

45. Ibid.

46. Ibid., p. 85.

47. Ibid.

48. Ibid., p. 86.

49. Ibid., p. 89.

50. Builder, 1994, p. 146, emphasis added.

51. Worden, 1998, p. 104.

52. Ibid., pp. 107–108.

6. BOMBER DECLINE: 1965–1992

1. Drew, 1997, p. 334.

2. Worden, 1998, p. 109.

3. Ibid., p. 110.

4. Ibid., p. 110.

5. Ibid., p. 114.

6. Ibid., p. 115.

7. Ibid., p. 144.

8. Ibid., p. 164.

9. At the end of the war, McConnell was replaced by a bomber pilot as CSAF, and the bomber pilot trend continued through three additional CSAF appointments up until 1986.

10. Worden, 1998, p. 173.

11. Ibid., p. 174.

12. Ibid., p. 176.

13. Trest, 1998, p. 200.

14. Builder, 1994, p. 187.

15. Worden, 1998, p. 192.

16. Ibid., p. 204.

17. Drew, 1997, p. 334.

18. Worden, 1998.

19. Trest, 1998, p. 227.

20. Col (ret) Steven Chiabotti, interview by author at SAASS, Maxwell AFB, October 2009.

21. Boyne, 1997, pp. 245–248.

22. Ibid., pp. 248–249.

23. Worden, 1998; Boyne, 1997; Frisbee, 1996; Pape, 1996.

24. Boyne, 1997, p. 250; Builder, 1994; Worden, 1998.

25. Worden, 1998, p. 190.

26. Ibid., p. 224.

27. Worden, 1998, p. 236.

28. Ibid., pp. 237–238.

29. Ibid., p. 238.

30. Y'Blood, 1997, p. 448.

31. Mann, 1995, p. 35.

32. Y'Blood, 1997, pp. 444–445.

33. Mann, 1995, pp. 44–45.

34. Col (ret) Rob Ehlers, interview by author, SAASS, Maxwell AFB, 2009.

7. THE CHANGING LEADERSHIP OF PERIOD TWO

1. Worden, 1998, p. 107, emphasis added.

2. Air Force Historical Research Agency, 2009.

3. Ford, 1992, p. 36.

4. Builder, 1994, p. 179.

5. Worden, 1998, p. 190.

6. Ibid., p. 235.

7. Ibid., p. 236.

8. Ibid.

9. Clark, 1993, p. 63.

10. Worden, 1998; Moody, 1996; Moody, Neufeld, and Hall, 1997.

8. FIGHTER PILOT DOMINANCE: 1992–1994

Epigraph: Clausewitz, p. 88.

1. Boyne, 1997, p. 315.

2. Ibid., p. 317.

3. Ibid., p. 318.

4. Anonymous, 1991, p. 3.

5. Evans, 1991, p. 19.

6. Anonymous, 1991, pp. 4–6.

7. Y'Blood, 1997, pp. 538–539.

8. Boyne, 1997, p. 319.

9. Ibid., p. 319.

10. Boyne, 1997, pp. 317–320.

11. Bussiere, 2001, p. v.

12. Smiley, 2007.

13. Boyne, 1997, p. 320.

14. Swan, 2004.

15. Rutherford, 2008.

16. Ibid., pp. 38–65.

17. Ibid., p. 167.

18. Cran, 2001.

19. Ibid., 2001, emphasis added.

20. Ibid., 2001.

21. Ibid., 2001.

9. FROM BOSNIA TO ALLIED FORCE: 1994–1999

1. Daalder, 2000, p. 5; Brune, 1998, p. 81.

2. Daalder, 2000, p. 6.

3. Brune, 1998.

4. Mason, 1994, p. 180.

5. Ibid., p. 174.

6. Brune, 1998.

7. Burg, 2004, pp. 54–55.

8. Mason, 1994, p. 181, emphasis added.

9. Larson, Lindstrom, Hura, Gardiner, Keffer, and Little, 2003.

10. Mason, 1994, pp. 182–186.

11. Larson, Lindstrom, Hura, Gardiner, Keffer, and Little, 2003, pp. 26–31.

12. Burg, 2004, pp. 53–54.

13. Mason, 1994, p. 190.

14. Ibid., p. 193.

15. Larson, Lindstrom, Hura, Gardiner, Keffer, and Little, 2003, pp. 22–48.

16. Mason, 1994, p. 195.

17. Burg, 2004, p. 164.

18. Finlan, 2004, pp. 83–86.

19. Barnett, 2004, p. 59, emphasis added.

20. Keegan, 1999.

21. Hinman, 2001.

22. Dudney, 1999.

23. Hinman, 2001, pp. 29–31.

24. Cohen and Shelton, 1999.

25. Short, 2002.

26. Barnett, 2004, p. 61.
27. Burg, 2004.
28. Cooper, 2003, p. 6.
29. Ibid., p. 16.
30. Ibid., p. 17.
31. Ibid., p. 18.
32. Clausewitz, 1984, p. 87.

10. SEPTEMBER 11, AFGHANISTAN, AND IRAQ: 2001–2011

1. McCaleb, 2001.
2. BBC, "US Strikes Continue in Daylight," 2001.
3. BBC, "Last Al-Qaeda Stronghold 'Falls,'" 2001.
4. BBC, Karzai takes power in Kabul, 2001.
5. Ibid.
6. Brunner, 2007.
7. Ibid.
8. CNN, 2003.
9. Biddle et al., 2003.
10. Ricks, 2006, p. 135.
11. Ibid.
12. Ibid.
13. Pape, 1996.
14. Gates, 2008.
15. Scales, 1999.
16. Barnett, 2004, p. 62.
17. Chizek, 2003.
18. Ibid., p. 2.
19. Ibid., p. 4.
20. Ibid., p. 13.
21. Ibid., p. 14.
22. Deptula, 2007.
23. Ibid.
24. Schwartz, 2009.
25. Schwartz, 2009, emphasis added.
26. Brook, 2009.
27. Deptula, 2007.

11. SIGNS OF CHANGE: 1992–2010

1. Builder, 1994, p. 210.
2. Ibid., p. 210, emphasis in original.
3. Ibid., p. 210.
4. Allison, 1971.
5. Clausewitz, 1984, p. 88.

12. ANTICIPATING USAF CHANGE

Epigraph: Builder, 1994, p. 285.
1. Bernstein, Lebow, Stein, and Weber, 2007, p. 236.
2. The survey was sent out electronically, and responses were automatically retrieved and organized using the Air Force licensed software *Inquisite*. The survey work was preapproved by the Washington State University Institutional Review Board as well as Air University leadership. The Likert-scale was used for the first seventeen questions and a multiple choice, rank order option was used for the final three questions. In all cases, the survey was sent to internal, individual student email accounts (an email system contained and closed within Air University), and responses are not identifiable to any specific individual.
3. Brown, 2000.
4. Schein, 2004; Bennis, 1969; Child and Kieser, 1981; Demers, 2007.
5. Schein, 2004.
6. Schwartz, 2009.
7. Builder, 1994.
8. Period One lasted from 1907 to 1947 – 40 years. Period Two lasted from 1947 to 1992 – 45 years. This survey conducted in Period Three, at the 18-year point, represents what might be considered "halfway" through Period Three.

13. FRAMING THE SURVEY PERSPECTIVES

1. Builder, 1994, pp. xvi–xviii.
2. Ibid., p. 97.
3. Ibid., p. 31.
4. Ibid., p. 32.
5. Ibid., p. 34.
6. Ibid., p. 166.
7. Krepinevich, 2009, p. 18.

14. CHANGING LEADERSHIP

1. Schwartz, 2008, emphasis added.
2. Schwartz, 2009, emphasis added.
3. Schwartz, 2009, emphasis added.

15. PREDICTING THE FUTURE

1. Lebow & Lichbach, 2007.

2. Krepinevich, 2009, pp. 10–11.

3. Lebow & Lichbach, 2007, pp. 10, 236.

4. Krepinevich, 2009, p. 21.

5. Bernstein, Lebow, Stein, & Weber, 2007, p. 237.

6. Krepinevich, 2009, pp. 14–15.

7. Builder, 1994.

16. SUMMARY AND RECOMMENDATIONS

Epigraph: Builder, 1994, p. 289.

1. Reitz, 1987, p. 562.

2. Heffron, 1989, p. 183.

3. Ashkanasy, Wilderom, and Peterson, 2000; Burke, 2008; Demers, 2007.

4. Schein, 2004, p. 17.

5. Builder, 1994, p. 282.

6. Ibid., p. 256.

7. Some of this discussion on "guiding principles" came from work accomplished at the School of Advanced Air and Space Studies in April of 2013. Answering a call by the Chief of Staff of the Air Force to provide airpower's guiding principles, a team of seven SAASS students from Class XXII, three SAASS professors, and the author participated in developing a response. Some of the information from that work is presented, in part, in this paragraph.

BIBLIOGRAPHY

Aberbach, Joel D., and Bert A. Rockman. "Conducting and Coding Elite Interviews." *PS: Political Science and Politics* 35, no. 4 (2002): 673–676.

Ahmed, Amel, and Rudra Sil. "Is Multi-Method Research Really Better?" *Newsletter of the American Political Science Association* 7, no. 2 (Fall 2009): 2–6.

Air Force Historical Research Agency. Historical Archives Building, Maxwell AFB, Montgomery, Alabama, October–December 2009.

Almanac of Airpower. New York: ARCO, 1989.

Allison, Graham T. *Essence of Decision: Explaining the Cuban Missile Crisis.* Harvard University: Harper Collins Publishers, 1971.

Anonymous. "TAC-umsizing the Air Force: The Emerging Vision of the Future." "Brown paper" received by author through unofficial channels. August 1991.

Ashkanasy, Neal M., Celeste P. M. Wilderom, and Mark F. Peterson. *Handbook of Organizational Culture and Climate.* Thousand Oaks: Sage, 2000.

Bakke, E. Wight. "Concept of the Social Organization." In *Modern Organization Theory,* edited by Mason Haire. New York: John Wiley and Sons, 1965.

Barnett, Thomas P. M. *The Pentagon's New Map: War and Peace in the Twenty-First Century.* New York: G. P. Putnam's Sons, 2004.

BBC. *Karazi Takes Power in Kabul.* December 22, 2001. http://news.bbc .co.uk/2/hi/south_asia/1724641.stm (accessed April 13, 2010).

———. *Last Al-Qaeda Stronghold "Falls."* December 16, 2001. http://news.bbc .co.uk/2/hi/south_asia/1714095.stm (accessed April 13, 2010).

———. *US Strikes Continue in Daylight.* October 10, 2001. http://news.bbc .co.uk/2/hi/south_asia/1589334.stm (accessed April 13, 2010).

Bennis, J. K. *Organizational Development: Its Nature, Origins, and Prospects.* Reading, MA: Addison-Wesley, 1969.

Bernstein, Steven, Richard Ned Lebow, Janice Gross Stein, and Steven Weber. "Social Science as Case-Based Diagnostics." In *Theory and Evidence in Comparative Politics and International Relations,* edited by Richard Ned Lebow and Mark Irving Lichbach. New York: Palgrave Macmillan, 2007.

Biddle, Stephen, et al. *Iraq and the Future of Warfare: Implications for Army and Defense Policy.* Leavenworth: U.S. Army War College, 2003.

Booker, David Lyons. *Cultural Conditioning and Ideology in Public Organizations: The Case of the Air Force.* Dissertation,

Tuscaloosa: University of Alabama,
1995.

Boyne, Walter J. *A History of the U.S. Air
Force: 1947–1997*. New York: St. Martin's
Press, 1997.

Brook, Tom V. "Fleet of Spy Planes Gives
U.S. 'an Edge' in Afghan Mission." *USA
Today*, June 13, 2009.

Brown, Rupert. *Group Processes*. Malden:
Blackwell, 2000.

Brune, Lester H. *The United States and
Post-Cold War Interventions: Bush and
Clinton in Somalia, Haiti, and Bosnia,
1992–1998*. Claremont, CA: Regina
Books, 1998.

Brunner, Borgna. *Iraq Timeline*. 2007.
http://www.infoplease.com/spot/
iraqtimeline2.html (accessed April 13,
2010).

Builder, Carl H. *The Icarus Syndrome: The
Role of Air Power Theory in the Evolu-
tion and Fate of the U.S. Air Force*. New
Brunswick: Transaction, 1994.

Burg, Steven L. "Intervention in Internal
Conflict: The Case of Bosnia." In *Mili-
tary Intervention: Cases in Context for the
Twenty-First Century*, edited by William
J. Lahneman. New York: Rowan and
Littlefield, 2004.

Burke, W. Warner. *Organization Change:
Theory and Practice*. London: Sage,
2008.

Burns, T., and G. M. Stalker. *The Management of Innovation*. London: Tavistock,
1961.

Burns, Tony. "Aristotle." In *Political Think-
ers: From Socrates to Present*, edited by
David Boucher and Paul Kelly. Oxford:
Oxford University Press, 2003.

Bussiere, Thomas. *General Merrill A. Mc-
Peak and Organizational Leadership*.
Maxwell Air Force Base: Air University,
2001.

Cahn, Steven M. *Classics of Political and
Moral Philosophy*. Oxford: Oxford University Press, 2002.

Child, J. "Organization, Structure, Environment, and Performance: The Role
of Strategic Choice." *Sociology* 6, no. 1
(1972): 1–22.

Child, J., and A. Kieser. *Handbook of Organizational Design: Adapting Organizations to Their Environments*, edited by
W. Starbuck and P. Nystrom. Oxford:
Oxford University Press, 1981.

Chizek, Judy G. *Military Transformation:
Intelligence, Surveillance and Reconnais-
sance*. Washington, DC: Foreign Affairs,
Defense, and Trade Division, 2003.

Clark, Thomas William. *Organizational
Change in the United States Air Force*.
Dissertation, Fairfax: George Mason
University, 1993.

Clausewitz, Carl von. *On War*. Edited
and translated by Michael Howard and
Peter Paret. Princeton, N.J.: Princeton
University Press, 1984.

Clemens, Elisabeth S., and James M.
Cook. "Politics and Institutionalism:
Explaining Durability and Change."
Annual Review of Sociology 25 (1999):
441–466.

CNN. *Bush Calls End to "Major Combat."*
May 2, 2003. http://www.cnn
.com/2003/WORLD/meast/05/01/sprj
.irq.main/ (accessed April 16, 2010).

Cohen, William S., and Henry H. Shelton.
"Kosovo after Action Review." Presented before the Senate Armed Services
Committee, October 14, 1999. http://
www.au.af.mil/au/awc/awcgate/
kosovoaa/jointstmt.htm.

Cooper, Scott. "Air Power and the Co-
ercive Use of Force." In *Immaculate
Warfare*, edited by Stephen D. Wrage.
Wesport: Praeger, 2003.

Coram, Robert. *Boyd*. New York: Back Bay
Books/Little Brown, 2002.

Cortell, Andrew P., and Susan Petersen.
"Altered States: Explaining Domestic
Institutional Change." *British Journal of
Political Science* 29, no. 1 (1999): 177–203.

Cran, William. "Ambush in Mogadishu." *Frontline*, PBS. November 1, 2001. http://www.pbs.org/wgbh/pages/frontline/shows/ambush/etc/script .html (accessed March 2010).

Daalder, Ivo H. *Getting to Dayton: The Making of America's Bosnia Policy.* Washington, DC: Brookings Institution Press, 2000.

Dacin, M. Tina, Jerry Goodstein, and W. Richard Scott. "Institutional Theory and Institutional Change: Introduction to the Special Research Forum." *Academy of Management Journal* 15, no. 1 (2002).

Davis, Richard. *Carl A. Spaatz and the Air War in Europe.* Washington, DC: U.S. Government Printing Office, 1993.

Demers, Christiane. *Organizational Change Theories: A Synthesis.* London: Sage Publications, 2007.

Deptula, David. "Transformation and Air Force Intelligence, Surveillance and Reconnaissance." *Air Force Defense Strategy Seminar,* Washington, DC, 2007.

Donaldson, L. *For Positivist Organization Theory: Proving the Hard Core.* London: Sage, 1996.

Douhet, Giulio. *Command of the Air.* Washington, DC: United States Government Printing Office, 1921. (Reprinted in numerous sources.)

Drew, Dennis. "Air Theory, Air Force, and Low Intensity Conflict: A Short Journey to Confusion." In *The Paths of Heaven: The Evolution of Airpower Theory,* edited by Col Phillip S. Meilinger. Maxwell Air Force Base: Air University Press, 1997.

Dudney, Robert S. "Verbatim." *Air Force Magazine,* December 1999: 58.

Evans, David. "Report Lampoons Air Force's 'Manly Men' – Fighter Jocks." October 4, 1991: 19.

Faber, Peter R. "Interwar US Army Aviation and the Air Corps Tactical School: Incubators of American Airpower." In *The Paths of Heaven: The Evolution of Airpower Theory,* edited by Col Phillip S. Meilinger. Maxwell Air Force Base, Alabama: Air University Press, 1997.

Feynman, Richard. *The Value of Science.* Perseus Books Group, 1999.

Field, Edsel R. *Managing Change: Strategies for Air Force Organization.* End-of-course thesis, Air University, Maxwell Air Force Base: Air War College (internal only), 1974.

Finlan, Alastair. *The Collapse of Yugoslavia: 1991–1999.* London: Osprey, 2004.

Ford, James M. *Air Force Culture and Conventional Strategic Airpower.* Thesis, Maxwell Air Force Base: School of Advanced Air and Space Studies, 1992.

Franzese, Robert J. "Multi-causality, Context-Conditionality and Endogeneity." In *The Oxford Handbook of Comparative Politics,* edited by Boix and Stokes. Oxford: Oxford University Press, 2007.

Frisbee, John L. *Makers of the United States Air Force.* Washington, DC: Office of Air Force History, 1996.

Futrell, Robert F. *The United States Air Force in Korea.* Washington, DC: Office of Air Force History, 1983.

———. *Ideas, Concepts, Doctrine: Basic Thinking in the United States Air Force, 1907–1960.* Maxwell Air Force Base: Air University Press, 1989.

George, Alexander L., and Andrew Bennett. *Case Studies and Theory Development in the Social Sciences.* Cambridge: MIT Press, 2005.

Gerring, John. "What Is a Case Study and What Is It Good for?" *American Political Science Review* 98, no. 2 (May 2004): 341–353.

Greenwood, Royston, and C. R. Hinings. "Understanding Radical Organizational Change: Bringing Together the Old and the New Institutionalism." *Academy of Management Review* 21, no. 4 (1996): 1022–1054.

Greif, Avner, and David D. Laitin. "A Theory of Endogenous Institutional Change." *American Political Science Review* 98, no. 4 (2004): 633–652.

Hall, James Norman, and Charles Bernard Nordoff. *The Lafayette Flying Corps.* Port Washington, NY: Kennikat, 1920.

Hastings, Max. *Bomber Command.* New York: Dial Press, 1979.

Heffron, Florence. *Organization Theory and Public Organizations.* Englewood Cliffs: Prentice Hall, 1989.

Hemeon, Howard, Hollace Lyon, Ann Martens, and Thomas Walker. *An Investigation of the Relationships between U.S. Air Force Leadership and Organizational Psychological Types as a Means for Addressing Change.* Thesis, Maxwell Air Force Base: Air Command and Staff College, 1995.

Hennessy, Juliette A. *The United States Army Air Arm, April 1861 to April 1917.* Washington, DC: Office of Air Force History, 1985.

Higham, Robin. "Air Power in World War I, 1914–1918." In Stephens, ed., *The War in the Air.*

Hinman, Ellwood. "Context and Theory: Lessons from Operation Allied Force." *Air Power History* 48, no. 2 (Summer 2001): 26.

Hira, Anil, and Ron Hira. "The New Institutionalism: Contradictory Notions of Change." *American Journal of Economics and Sociology* 59, no. 2 (2000): 267–282.

Huddy, L. "Group Identity and Political Cohesion." In *The Oxford Handbook of Political Psychology,* edited by by Leonie Huddy, Robert Jervis, and David O. Sears. New York: Oxford University Press, 2003.

Hudson, James J. *Hostile Skies: A Combat History of the American Air Service in World War I.* Syracuse: Syracuse University Press, 1968.

Hurley, Alfred F., and William C. Heimdahl. "The Roots of U.S. Military

Aviation." In Nalty, ed., *Winged Shield, Winged Sword,* vol. 1, 1997.

Kanter, Rosabeth Moss, Barry A. Stein, and Todd D. Jick. *The Challenge of Institutional Change: How Companies Experience It and Leaders Guide It.* New York: Free Press, 1992.

Keegan, John. "Please, Mr. Blair, Never Take Such a Risk Again." *London Daily Telegraph,* June 6, 1999.

Khandwalla, P. N. "Viable and Effective Design Firms." *Academy of Management Journal* 16, no. 3 (1973): 481–495.

King, Gary. "Publication, Publication." *Political Science and Politics,* 2006: 119–125.

King, Gary, Robert O. Keohane, and Sidney Verba. *Designing Social Inquiry: Scientific Inference in Qualitative Research.* Princeton: Princeton University Press, 1994.

Kohn, Richard H. "The Early Retirement of Gen Ronald R. Fogleman, Chief of Staff, United States Air Force." *Aerospace Power Journal,* Spring 2001: 6–23.

Krepinevich, Andrew F. *7 Deadly Scenarios: A Military Futurist Explores War in the 21st Century.* New York: Bantam Books, 2009.

Larson, Eric, Gustav Lindstrom, Myron Hura, Ken Gardiner, Jim Keffer, and Bill Little. *Interoperability of the U.S. and NATO Allied Air Forces: Supporting Data and Case Studies.* Santa Monica: RAND Corporation, 2003.

Lawrence, P. R., and J. W. Lorsch. *Organization and Environment: Managing Differentiation and Integration.* Homewood: Richard D. Irwin, 1969.

Lebow, Richard Ned, and Mark Irving Lichbach. *Theory and Evidence in Comparative Politics and International Relations.* New York: Palgrave, 2007.

Lustick, Ian S. "History, Historiography, and Political Science: Multiple Historical Records and the Problem of Selection Bias." *American Political Science*

Review 90, no. 3 (September 1996): 605–618.

Maanen, John Van. *Qualitative Studies of Organizations*. Thousand Oaks: Sage, 1998.

Mahoney, James, and Gary Goertz. "A Tale of Two Cultures: Contrasting Quantitative and Qualitative Research." *Political Analysis* 14 (June 2006): 227–249.

Mann, Edward C. *Thunder and Lightning: Desert Storm and the Airpower Debates*. Maxwell Air Force Base: Air University Press, 1995.

Mason, Tony. *Air Power: A Centennial Appraisal*. London: Brassey's, 1994.

Maurer, M. *The U.S. Air Service in World War I*. Vol. 2. Washington, DC: Office of Air Force History, 1978.

McCaleb, Ian Christopher. "Defense Officials: Air Operations to Last 'Several Days.'" CNN, October 7, 2001. http://archives.cnn.com/2001/US/10/07/ret.attack.pentagon/ (accessed April 13, 2010).

Meilinger, Col Phillip S. *Airmen and Air Theory: A Review of the Sources*. Maxwell Air Force Base: Air University Press, 2001.

Mets, David R. *The Air Campaign: John Warden and the Classical Airpower Theorists*. Maxwell Air Force Base: Air University Press, 1999.

Meyerson, D., and J. Martin. "Cultural Change: An Integration of Three Different Views." *Journal of Management Studies* 24, no. 6 (1987): 623–647.

Mitchell, William "Billy." *Winged Defense*. New York: G. P. Putnam's Sons, 1925. Repr. New York: Dover 1988.

Momyer, William W. *Airpower in Three Wars (WWII, Korea, Vietnam)*. Washington, DC: U.S. Government Printing Office, 1982.

Moody, Walton S. *Building a Strategic Air Force*. Washington, DC: Air Force History and Museums Program, 1996.

Moody, Walton S., and Warren A. Trest. "The Air Force as an Institution." In Nalty, ed., *Winged Shield, Winged Sword*, vol. 2, 1997.

Moody, Walton S., Jacob Neufeld, and R. Cargill Hall. "The Emergence of the Strategic Air Command." In Nalty, ed., *Winged Shield, Winged Sword*, vol. 2, 1997.

Morrow, John H. *The Great War in the Air: Military Aviation from 1909–1921*. Washington, DC: Smithsonian, 1993.

Mortensen, Daniel R. "The Air Service in the Great War." In Nalty, ed., *Winged Shield, Winged Sword*, vol. 1, 1997.

Nalty, Bernard C., ed. *Winged Shield, Winged Sword: A History of the United States Air Force*. 2 vols. Washington D.C.: Air Force History and Museums Program, 1997.

Neuman, W. Lawrence. *Basics of Social Research: Qualitative and Quantitative Approaches*. Boston: Pearson Education, 2007.

Overy, Richard. *Why the Allies Won*. New York: Norton, 1995.

———. "World War II: The Bombing of Germany." In Stephens, ed., *The War in the Air*.

Pape, Robert A. *Bombing to Win: Airpower and Coercion in War*. Ithaca, New York: Cornell University Press, 1996.

Peters, B. Guy. *Institutional Theory in Political Science*. New York: Continuum, 2005.

Pugh, D., D. Hickson, C. Hinings, and C. Turner. "The Context of Organizational Structures." In *Organizational Growth and Development*, edited by W. Starbuck. Harmondsworth, UK: Penguin Books, 1971.

Ragin, Charles C. *Constructing Social Research*. Thousand Oaks: Pine Forge Press, 1994.

Reicher, Stephen, and Nick Hopkins. "Psychology and the End of History: A Critique and a Proposal for the Psychology of Social Categorization." *Political Psychology,* 2001: 383–407.

Reitz, H. Joseph. *Behavior in Organizations.* Homewood: Irwin, 1987.

Ricks, Thomas E. *Fiasco: The American Military Adventure in Iraq.* New York: Penguin Press, 2006.

Rutherford, Kenneth R. *Humanitarianism Under Fire: The US and UN Intervention in Somalia.* Sterling, VA: Kumarian Press, 2008.

Sartori, Giovanni. "Concept Misformation in Comparative Politics." *American Political Science Review* 64, no. 4 (1970): 1033–1053.

Scales, Robert H. "Adaptive Enemies: Dealing with the Strategic Threat after 2010." *Strategic Review* 27, no. 1 (Winter 1999): 5–14.

Schein, Edgar H. *Organizational Culture and Leadership.* San Francisco: Jossey-Bass, 2004.

———. "Organizational Culture: What It Is and How to Change It." In *Human Resource Management in International Firms,* edited by P. Evans, Y. Doz, and A. Laurent. New York: St. Martin's Press, 1990.

Schwartz, Norty [Norton A]. "The Future of Unmanned Systems." Speech given to mutiple audiences, 2009.

Scott, W. Richard. *Institutions and Organizations.* Los Angeles: Sage, 2008.

Sherry, Michael S. *The Rise of American Airpower.* New Haven: Yale University Press, 1987.

Shiner, John F. "From Air Service to Air Corps: The Era of Billy Mitchell." In Nalty, ed., *Winged Shield, Winged Sword: A History of the United States Air Force,* vol. 1.

Short, Lt Gen Michael, interview by Major Jeffrey Smith. Washington, DC, (2002).

Smiley, George. "Shades of Tony McPeak." *In From the Cold.* Online blog. December 19, 2007. http://formerspook .blogspot.com/2007/12/shades-of-tony-mcpeak.html (accessed March 12, 2010).

Stephen, W., and C. L. Renfro. "The Role of Threat in Intergroup Relations." In *From Prejudice to Intergroup Emotions,* edited by D. Mackie and E. Smith. New York: Psychology Press, 2003.

Stephens, Alan. "The True Believers: Air Power Between the Wars." In Stephens, ed., *The War in the Air.*

Stephens, Alan, ed. *The War in the Air.* Fairbairn, Australia: Air Power Studies Center, 1994.

Strauss, Leo, and Joseph Cropsey. *History of Political Philosophy.* Chicago: University of Chicago Press, 1987.

Swan, Mark. "Air Force to Switch to New Uniforms." *Military Photos.* May 21, 2004. http://www.militaryphotos.net/forums/showthread.php?13130-Air-Force-To-Switch-To-New-Uniforms (accessed March 13, 2010).

Tate, James P. *The Army and Its Air Corps: Army Policy toward Aviation.* Maxwell Air Force Base: Air University Press, 1998.

Thomas, William Clark. *Organizational Change in the United States Air Force.* Dissertation, Fairfax, VA: George Mason University, 2002.

Thompson, J. D. *Organizations in Action.* New York: McGraw-Hill, 1967.

Thompson, Wayne. "The Air War over Korea." In Nalty, ed., *Winged Shield, Winged Sword,* vol. 2, 1997.

Trest, Warren A. *Air Force Roles and Missions: A History.* Washington, DC: Air Force History and Museums Program, 1998.

Trest, Warren A., and George M. Watson. "Framing Air Force Missions." In Nalty, ed., *Winged Shield, Winged Sword,* vol. 1, 1997.

Vermillion, Lynne E. *Understanding the Air Force Culture.* Thesis, Maxwell Air Force Base: Air War College, 1996.

Watson, George M. Jr. "Building Air Pow-
    er." In Nalty, ed., *Winged Shield, Winged
    Sword*, vol.1, 1997.
Watts, Lt Col Barry D. *The Foundations
    of U.S. Air Force Doctrine: The Problem
    of Friction in War*. Maxwell Air Force
    Base: Air University Press, 1984.
Westhoff, Col Charles M. *Military Airpow-
    er: A Revised Digest of Airpower Opinions
    and Thoughts*. Maxwell Air Force Base:
    Air University Press, 2007.
Winnefeld, James A., and Dana J. Johnson.
    *Command and Control of Joint Air Op-
    erations*. Santa Monica: RAND, 1991.

Wolk, Herman S. "The Quest for Inde-
    pendence." In Nalty, ed., *Winged Shield,
    Winged Sword*, vol. 1, 1997.
Worden, Mike. *Rise of the Fighter Gener-
    als: The Problem of Air Force Leadership
    1945–1982*. Maxwell Air Force Base: Air
    University Press, 1998.
Y'Blood, William T. "From the Deserts to
    the Mountains." In Nalty, ed., *Winged
    Shield, Winged Sword*, vol. 2, 1997.
Yzerbyt, V., M. Dumont, E. Gordijn, and
    D. Wigbolds. "Intergroup Emotions and
    Self-Categorization." In *From Prejudice
    to Intergroup Emotions*, edited by D.
    Mackie and E. Smith. New York: Psy-
    chology Press, 2003.

INDEX

Numbers in *italic* text indicate pages with tables and figures.

Adams, Jimmie V., *194*

Afghanistan: battlefield information and data, importance of, 147–148; combat operations to destroy terrorist operations in, 133–134; dominance of fighter-culture in operations, 134, 135, 137–138; humanitarian relief operations, 134; insurgency warfare and counterinsurgency in, 142–144, 155–156, 159, 215; ISR operations in, 144; victory declaration in, 134–135

Air Combat Command (ACC): activation of, 91, 92, 107, 109, 154, 215; leadership of, *194, 195, 196*

Air Corps, U.S. Army: Army authority over, 28; authority over and oversight of aviation, 32–33, 37, 39; autonomy of under Marshall, 38; bomber doctrine and strategy development for, 28–30; budgets and funding, 28, 34–35; coastal defense operations, 31; creation of, 27–28, 37; legislation to establish, 27–28; relationship between Army and, 31–32; resources for, 28

Air Corps Act (1926), 27–28, 30

Air Corps Tactical School (ACTS), 28–30, 37

Air Defense Command (ADC), 59

Air Force, U.S. (USAF): affection for flying over mission, 182–183, 187–188, 209,

221; bomber-culture organizational structure, 59–62, 68–74; budgets and funding, 69, 72, 84; Carter administration relationship with, 82–83; coordination control agreement with Navy, 66; core values of, xii; downsizing of, 84; establishment as independent service, 5, 12, 48–49, 54–55, *55*, 214; history of, xii; leadership evolution, 52–53; officer corps, report on internal dynamics of, 187–188; organization and preparations to fight types of war preferred by, 115–117, 123–126, 128–132, 197; organizational change and reprioritized roles and missions, 124–126, 154–159, 183, *183*, 185–191, 196–200, 205, 217–219, 220–228; organizational changes to, 2–6, 53, 54–55, *55*, 91–92, 105; program cuts and operational and national security, 4; Reagan administration relationship with, 83–84; rebuilding phase, 82; relevance and value of, 1–2, 220–228; uniforms, 112–113. *See also* future of the Air Force

Air Mobility Command, 193

Air University, 162–164, *163*, 187, 233n2

aircraft: advances in, 30–31, 32; affection for over mission, 182–183, 187–188, 209, 221; bomber aircraft, procurement of, 34–35, 38; bomber aircraft, vulnerability of, 40, 43; development of, 20–21; fighter aircraft, development of improved, 82, 83, 98; fighter aircraft,

Army Air Service, U.S.: Battle of St. Mihiel, 22–23; combat arm, recognition as, 25; contributions of, appreciation for, 22–25, 26; force strength and capabilities for WWI, 21, 23; leadership of, 24, 25–26; loyalty of airmen to Army, 26; non-flyers in leadership positions, 24, 25–26; organizational structure of, 25–26; WWI use of airpower, 21–24

Army aviation: authority over and oversight of, responsibilities for, 24–25, 32–33, 37, 39; autonomy of and aviation as independent service, 16, 24–25, 26–27, 30, 32, 33, 54–55, 55; bomber culture of, 30, 33–34, 35, 50, 54–55, 55, 57; expansion of, 38; lying about capabilities of, accusation about, 27, 33; organizational change for autonomy of, 35, 36, 38–39, 42, 44, 48–49, 214; organizational system to manage, 22, 23, 213–214; personnel in, increase in, 53–54; romanticized image of airmen, 23; Secretary of War leadership of, 22

Army Signal Corps, U.S.: Aeronautical Division, 12–13, 50–52; aviation funding for, 13; leadership of, 20; organization of air operations in, 16

Arnold, Henry "Hap": airpower training, development of, 13–14; Army Air Forces command, 39; assessment of airpower WWII role, 45, 46; WWII bombing campaign, 41

Ashy, Joseph W., 194

asymmetric and unconventional warfare: air superiority and, 217; battlefield information and data, importance of, 147–148; capabilities for, responsibility for providing, 204; challenge to fighter-operations perspective, 116–117, 188–191, 215; fighter-operations perspective and, 154–159, 164, 166–171, 166, 167, 169, 170, 171, 189–190, 216; increase in, 185, 186; Military Operations Other Than War (MOOTW), 155; peacekeeping operations, 118–126, 128–129; perspective and preparations to fight, 115–117, 123–126, 128–132, 155–159, 215; prestige of pilots

and unwritten cultural hierarchies, 164, 166, 179–183, 180, 181, 182, 189–190; reprioritized roles and missions to fight, 154–159, 196–200, 205, 217–219, 220–228; synergistic-operations perspective and capabilities for, 207–211. See also insurgency warfare and counterinsurgency (COIN) operations

B-1 bombers, 83, 84
B-2 stealth bombers, 134
B-17 Flying Fortress, 34–35, 43
B-25 bombers, 40
B-29 bombers, 65, 68
B-52 bombers, 78, 83, 89, 134
Bates, Ronald W., 194
bomber perspective and operations: accuracy of strikes, 40–41, 43, 44; air war against Germany, plans for, 39; area bombing doctrine, 43, 44; assessment of WWII role, 45–47, 48–49; bomber aircraft, procurement of, 34–35, 38; challenge to bomber-operations culture and the Vietnam War, 75–80, 81–82, 95–98, 115–116, 122, 143, 214; decisive warfighting capabilities of, 26–27, 28–30, 33–35, 44–49, 55, 60; decline of, 6, 57, 81–87, 107–108, 214; demoralizing the enemy through, 26–27, 41, 44; doctrine and strategy development for, 28–30, 33–36, 37; emergence and dominance of bomber-operations perspective, 5, 213–214; fighter escorts for bombers, 43, 44, 62; fighter operations expansion and, 6, 57; Korean War strategy, 62–68, 94, 213; organizational structure of USAF based on, 59–62, 68–74; precision bombing doctrine, 29; reprioritized roles and missions, 217–219; strategic bombing strategy, 33–36, 37, 38, 39, 40–41, 47, 59–62; strategic bombing strategy and Vietnam War, 78–80, 85–86; success of, 44; targeting enemy positions and resources with, 19–20, 29, 39–41, 43–44; vulnerability of bomber aircraft, 40, 43; WWII bombing campaign, 39–44,

COLONEL JEFFREY J. SMITH, US Air Force, is the Commandant
and Dean of the School of Advance Air and Space Studies,
Maxwell Air Force Base, Alabama. He is an Air Force pilot
with over 2,300 flying hours and has served in numerous
command and staff positions. Colonel Smith holds a PhD
in political science from Washington State University.